A CENTURY OF SERVICE

A HISTORY OF THE
WORLD ALLIANCE
OF REFORMED CHURCHES
1875–1975

MARCEL PRADERVAND

WILLIAM B. EERDMANS PUBLISHING COMPANY
Grand Rapids, Michigan

© World Alliance of Reformed Churches 1975

First published in 1975 by
THE SAINT ANDREW PRESS
121 George Street, Edinburgh
on behalf of the
World Alliance of Reformed Churches
(Presbyterian and Congregational)

Published in the USA by
William B. Eerdmans Publishing Company

Library of Congress Cataloging in Publication Data

Pradervand, Marcel.
    A century of service.

    Includes bibliographical references and index.
    1.   World Alliance of Reformed Churches (Presbyterian
and Congregational)   I. Title.
BX8905.W63P7   1976   262', 05   75-32554
ISBN 0-8028-3466-3

Printed and bound in Great Britain

Contents

Foreword

The history of the ecumenical movement during the past century is a fabric with many strands. Missionary activity, with its increasing awareness of the immensity of need and the paucity of resources, stands out brightest. It supplied the motivation for co-operation in witness, comity, and for the creation of permanent conciliar structures to deal with relations among the churches. Another strand clearly discernible is the dawning of a new self-consciousness on the part of certain traditions, that by the latter half of the nineteenth century were represented by churches scattered around the globe. Their genesis was, for the most part, in Western Europe, but emigration had by this time penetrated the Americas, Africa, Asia, Australia, and New Zealand, and vigorous younger bodies were coming to life in the wake of the missionary enterprise.

Presbyterian and Reformed churchmen in the British Isles and in North America, grasped by a new vision of unity, began to call for a new organization of their world family, succeeded in meeting in London in the summer of 1875, proposed a constitution and adopted the name 'The Alliance of Reformed Churches throughout the World holding the Presbyterian System' for their projected instrument, and laid plans for a General Council that was held in Edinburgh in July, 1877. Thus was born the oldest organized world family of Protestant churches, an organization that now includes one hundred and forty-two ecclesiastical bodies in its membership, a total constituency of more than fifty-five million souls.

Dr Marcel Pradervand, who served brilliantly as General Secretary of the Alliance for more than two decades, has written the first complete history of the organized life of this world family. He has traced not only the historical events in the course of the past century but has also captured the spirit of an organization which was designed to serve the Church of Jesus Christ and which has been content to remain small in programme and staff and to resist the temptation to bureaucracy. As one reads the early chapters, it becomes apparent that the Alliance was instrumental in the sequence of events that culminated in the formation of a World Council of Churches in 1948. The World Council's first General Secretary is quoted as having said that 'without the Alliance, there would have been no World Council,' and the present General Secretary has spoken recently of the World Council as 'the child of the Reformed Alliance.' Early in the history of the World Council the Executive Committee of the Alliance defined the organization's role in an ecumenical age: 'It is the true nature of Presbyterianism never to be merely an end in itself, but to serve the Church Universal of Jesus Christ, the Church which is His Body.' It is interesting that when in 1961 the churches of East Asia vigorously protested the actions of world confessional bodies, the Reformed Alliance was excluded from their list of offenders. Apparently the Alliance had succeeded in maintaining its ecumenical stance while supporting in fellowship its member churches.

A new World Alliance of Reformed Churches (Presbyterian and Congregational) came into existence in a Uniting General Council held in Nairobi, Kenya, in August, 1970, and the history of the second parent body, the International Congregational Council, has also been told by the author in this volume. A few months after the Nairobi Council Dr Pradervand retired. His career spans one of the most eventful periods in the life of the Alliance. Elected General Secretary shortly after the Sixteenth General Council, which met in Geneva in 1948, he led the churches through the period of post-war reconstruction, displayed remarkable statesmanship in the midst of the tensions caused by the Cold War, and travelled incessantly to visit and support the churches in the Third World, churches that had only recently been missions and which make up now some two-thirds of the membership of the Alliance.

The new Alliance, as it faces a second century, shows no signs of suffering from an identity crisis, nor is there any evidence of its taking a backward step ecumenically and resolving itself into an ecclesiastical holding company. It represents the strength of a tradition and the reality of a worldwide family that is a part of the whole people of God. It continues to conceive its programme primarily in terms of theological endeavour and of co-operation and witness through which fellowship is maintained. The Second Vatican Council opened the door for a new era of dialogue, and the Alliance is now in theological discussion and consultation with Roman Catholics, Orthodox, Lutherans, and Baptists. It seeks in this way to be open to what the Spirit is saying to the churches through each tradition and to be faithful to its Reformed character.

Here is a volume that should be read by everyone who seeks a deeper understanding of how God has been at work in our midst, drawing churches out of isolation and into fellowship with each other. Our memory informs our hope. The reading of Dr Pradervand's volume will rekindle our memory of a century of service to Jesus Christ by one world family of churches and will give us direction as we seek to be more faithful in the quest for the unity in Christ that will one day involve all mankind.

JAMES I. McCORD

Preface

Although no history of the Alliance has as yet been written two attempts to do so have already been made.

In 1922 the Western Section of the Alliance thought that in view of the fiftieth anniversary of the Alliance it would be appropriate to write the history of the organization. A committee was appointed but a year later it reported that this task could not be undertaken.

In 1957 I was able to persuade Rev. Niall D. Watson to start writing the history of the Alliance. Mr Watson, who was then minister of the Scottish congregation in Geneva, worked on a part-time basis for the Alliance and was Associate Editor of *The Reformed and Presbyterian World*. Mr Watson wrote two chapters but pressure of work prevented him from continuing the lengthy research work which was necessary.

After a visit to the U.S.A. and Canada early in 1971, Rev. Edmond Perret, the new General Secretary of the Alliance, asked me if I would consider undertaking this task. I gladly accepted to do so as history has always interested me. In August of the same year the Executive Committee endorsed Dr Perret's suggestion.

My gratitude goes to Dr Edmond Perret for having taken the initiative of this book. However, I would not have undertaken this task without the assistance of my dear wife who is English-speaking whilst my mother tongue is French, and I am grateful to her for all the help she has given me.

My gratitude also goes to Rev. David Lewis, a former colleague in the Alliance and now a staff member of the World Council of Churches, who read the manuscript and suggested a number of changes.

The research work would have been impossible had not Miss Paulette Piguet, Associate Secretary of the Alliance, always kept the archives in such good order and given me constant access to them during these three years. For this I wish to thank her very warmly.

Last but not least I wish to thank Mrs Christa Rothenbühler, my faithful secretary for several years at the Alliance's General Secretariat, who typed the final manuscript.

The book is now ready. I hope it will help readers to see that in spite of its very modest organization the World Alliance of Reformed Churches has in the course of the first century of its existence accomplished many a useful task.

SOLI DEO GLORIA

MARCEL PRADERVAND

MEETINGS OF THE GENERAL COUNCIL
OF THE WORLD ALLIANCE OF REFORMED CHURCHES
1877–1977

1.	1877	Edinburgh, Scotland
2.	1880	Philadelphia, U.S.A.
3.	1884	Belfast, Northern Ireland
4.	1888	London, England
5.	1892	Toronto, Canada
6.	1896	Glasgow, Scotland
7.	1899	Washington, D.C., U.S.A.
8.	1904	Liverpool, England
9.	1909	New York, U.S.A.
10.	1913	Aberdeen, Scotland
11.	1921	Pittsburgh, U.S.A.
12.	1925	Cardiff, Wales
13.	1929	Boston, U.S.A.
14.	1933	Belfast, Northern Ireland
15.	1937	Montreal, Canada
16.	1948	Geneva, Switzerland
17.	1954	Princeton, U.S.A.
18.	1959	São Paulo, Brazil
19.	1964	Frankfurt, Germany
20.	1970	Nairobi, Kenya
		(Union with International Congregational Council)
21.	1977	St Andrew's, Scotland (Centennial Consultation)

PRESIDENTS
OF THE WORLD ALLIANCE OF REFORMED CHURCHES
1888 to date

1.	1888–1892	Rev. Prof. W. G. Blaikie, D.D., Edinburgh
2.	1892–1896	Rev. Prof. T. W. Chambers, D.D., New York
3.	1896	Rev. William Henry Roberts, D.D., Cincinnati
4.	1896–1899	Rev. J. Marshall Lang, D.D., Glasgow
5.	1899–1904	Rev. Prin. W. Caven, D.D., Toronto
6.	1904–1909	Rev. Prin. J. O. Dykes, D.D., Cambridge
7.	1909–1913	Rev. David J. Burrell, D.D., New York
8.	1913–1921	Rev. W. Park, D.D., Belfast
9.	1921–1925	Rev. Pres. John McNaugher, D.D., Pittsburgh
10.	1925–1926	Rev. J. N. Ogilvie, D.D., Edinburgh
11.	1926–1929	Rev. C. M. d'Aubigne, D.D., Paris
12.	1929–1933	Rev. Pres. George W. Richards, D.D., Lancaster
13.	1933–1937	Rev. Prin. William A. Curtis, D.D., Edinburgh
14.	1937–1940	Rev. Robert Laird, D.D., Toronto
15.	1940–1948	Rev. George H. Donald, D.D., Montreal
16.	1948–1954	Rev. Edward J. Hagan, D.D., Edinburgh
17.	1954–1959	Rev. Pres. John A. Mackay, D.D., Princeton
18.	1959–1964	Rev. Pres. Ralph Waldo Lloyd, D.D., Maryville
19.	1964–1970	Rev. Prof. Wilhelm Niesel, D.D., Schöller
20.	1970–	Mr William P. Thompson, J.D., New York

GENERAL SECRETARIES
OF THE WORLD ALLIANCE OF REFORMED CHURCHES
1888 to date

1.	1888–1913	Rev. George D. Matthews, D.D. (Office in London)
2.	1913–1918	Rev. R. Dykes Shaw, D.D. (Office in Edinburgh)
3.	1918–1927	Rev. J. R. Fleming, D.D. (Office in Edinburgh)
4.	1927–1948	Rev. W. H. Hamilton, D.D. (Office in Edinburgh)
5.	1949–1970	Rev. Marcel Pradervand, D.D. (Office in Geneva)
6.	1970–	Rev. Edmond Perret, D.D. (Office in Geneva)

Note: In 1875, Rev. Dr Pres. James McCosh of Princeton University served as Chairman of the Constituting Conference, in the calling of which he had been so prominent. Each of the first four General Councils elected officers for its own sessions only. The first permanent President was not elected until 1888, in which year also the office of full-time General Secretary was created by the 4th General Council.

PART I
1875–1948

CHAPTER ONE

The Reformed Churches in the Middle of the Nineteenth Century

The Reformers of the sixteenth century had no intention of founding new Churches; their aim was simply to work for the renewal of the whole Christian Church. The result was quite different from what they had expected, and soon there were Lutheran and Reformed Churches on the Continent of Europe, while the Church of England became independent of the Roman See.

Nevertheless the Reformers, and especially Calvin, had the vision of a reconstituted Christian unity. In a letter written in 1552, in answer to an invitation from Archbishop Cranmer to attend a conference in London which was intended to promote unity of doctrine, Calvin wrote: 'One of the greatest events of the time is that the Churches are so widely separated from each other that there is not even a temporal or human intercourse carried on between them; we may well therefore be silent as to a holy communion of the members of Christ, which is in everybody's mouth, but no sign of which exists in the heart. The body of Christ is torn asunder, because the members are separated. So far as I am concerned, if I can be of any use, I will readily pass over ten seas to affect the object in view. If the welfare of England alone were concerned, I should regard it as a sufficient reason to act thus. But at present, when our purpose is to unite the sentiments of all good and learned men, and so, according to the rule of Scripture, to bring the separate Churches into one, neither labour nor trouble of any kind ought to be spared.'[1]

The idea was embodied in the Second Book of Discipline of the Church of Scotland (1580), and given a definite form in a section reading: 'But there is a more general kind of Assembly, which is of all nations and estates within the Kirk, representing the

Universal Kirk of Christ, which may be called properly the General Assembly or General Council of the whole Kirk of God.'²

Alas, the vision of the authors of the Second Book of Discipline failed to become a reality, and the divisions between the Churches of the Reformed family, not to mention the divisions between Lutherans, Reformed, Anglicans, Baptists and others, became more numerous in the course of the next hundred and fifty years.

What was the situation of the Reformed Churches in the middle of the nineteenth century? A quick look at these Churches may help us to understand the services rendered by the—still to be born—World Alliance of Reformed Churches.

On the Continent of Europe, the cradle of the Calvinist Reformation, the situation was anything but hopeful.

France had endured the wars of religion, and the Revocation of the Edict of Nantes (1685) sent into exile tens of thousands of Protestants. The Reformed Church was almost crushed; still, a small and faithful minority survived. In the nineteenth century, doctrinal disputes brought new difficulties. The 1848 General Assembly of the Reformed Church of France having refused to adopt a Confession of Faith, a schism took place, and in 1849 the Union of Evangelical Free Churches of France was formed.

In the Netherlands, one of the two continental countries where the Reformed Church held a majority position (the other being Switzerland), the Reformed Church had also experienced doctrinal disputes. In 1834, as a result of a dispute over the articles of Dordrecht, a first schism took place and a Free Reformed Church was formed. A large schism was still to take place in 1886. In 1892, the two Church communities which grew out of these movements united to form the Reformed Churches in the Netherlands ('Gereformeerde Kerken in Nederland').

In Switzerland, there was no national Church. Switzerland was a Confederation of 22 cantons, each of which was responsible for Church matters. The Reformed Churches were therefore cantonal Churches, with few contacts between them. Moreover, the doctrinal disputes which had broken the unity of the Reformed Churches of France and of the Netherlands were to have similar results in Switzerland, at least in the French-speaking part of the country. An Evangelical Free Church was founded in Geneva in 1849; in the neighbouring canton of Vaud (Lausanne) a Free Church had been formed in 1845 and in Neuchâtel, a split was to take place in the National Church as late as 1873, with the creation of an 'Evangelical Church Independent of the State'.

In the Austro-Hungarian Empire, there was the largest Reformed Church of the Continent, the Reformed Church of Hungary. The Church had been battered under the Counter-Reformation, and it was not until 1790 that civil rights were restored to Protestants. The Reformed Church had faced further reprisals after the War of Independence against Austria in 1848–49. But the Church remained vigorous and united.

The other Churches of the Empire, in Austria, were but small minorities which had been struggling for centuries for their survival. The Reformed Church of Bohemia and of Moravia, as well as the Lutheran Church, had been granted a measure of religious liberty in 1781, by a Royal Patent of Toleration, and they made full use of their freedom to proclaim the Gospel. The small Reformed Church of Austria had suffered a similar fate and was grateful for the measure of liberty recovered in 1781.

In the Russian Empire, there were small Reformed Churches in what are now the People's Republic of Poland and the Lithuanian S.S.R. (USSR); their situation was difficult. Apart from the indigenous Reformed Churches, there was a large Reformed congregation in St Petersburg (now Leningrad).

In Germany, the land of the Reformation, Reformed Christians had always been in a minority. Moreover, in 1817, the Reformed Church in the Kingdom of Prussia had become part of the United Church of Prussia; other United Churches followed in other parts of Germany, and only two small Reformed Churches kept their identity. It was not until 1884 that Reformed Churches and congregations formed themselves into the 'Reformierter Bund', an organization which has since then taken an increasingly large place in the life of our German Reformed brethren.

In nearby Belgium, a State which had become independent in 1830 after seceding from the Netherlands, the small Belgian Christian Missionary Church (now the Reformed Church of Belgium) was formed in 1837; it soon became a vigorous Church, interested in the evangelization of the French part of the Kingdom. The 'Union of the Protestant Churches of Belgium' (now the Protestant Church of Belgium) was formed in 1839 and soon afterwards was recognized by the State.

In Italy, the Waldensian Church experienced centuries of

difficulties and persecution. In 1848, it was granted an Edict
which ensured the civil rights of the Church. Immediately the
Waldensians began evangelizing; there were many new converts
added to the Church, but in 1854, some of these new members
broke away from the Church and formed the Free Church of
Italy. It was not until 1885 that the reunion of the two Churches
was completed.

In Spain, it was not until 1868 that the First Protestant Church
was established in Madrid, though, in spite of great difficulties,
Bible work had been courageously started by Borrow in 1835. In
Portugal there was no Reformed group in the middle of the
nineteenth century.

In Greece, Evangelical work started in 1828, but it was not
until 1858 that the first Church was organized.

*   *   *

We can be grateful for the fact that the Geneva Reformation did
not remain a continental affair but spread to Scotland thanks to
the remarkable witness of John Knox. There is no doubt that it is
through Scotland that the Reformed Churches spread throughout
the world and became a real world family.

However, if there was more life in the Scottish Church of the
middle of the nineteenth century than was the case in some of the
continental Churches, the situation, as regards unity, was anything
but bright. The Church history of Scotland in the eighteenth and
nineteenth centuries is a sad story of divisions and schisms. It is
not our intention to give here a complete list of these schisms.
Let us however mention a few. In 1733, the Associate Presbytery,
a Secession Church, was formed; soon, in 1743, some members
of that Synod withdrew to form the Reformed Presbytery, which
was to become the Reformed Presbyterian Church in 1811.
Meanwhile, the Seceder group broke into two in 1747 as the
General Associate Synod and the Associate Synod.

In 1761 the Presbytery of Relief was formed; in 1773 it became
the Relief Church of Scotland.

In 1843 the great Disruption, led by Thomas Chalmers,
resulted in the foundation of the Free Church of Scotland.

Fortunately the various moves in Scotland did not all result in
schisms; in 1820 a United Secession Church was formed by
certain segments of secession bodies, while others formed the

Associate Synod of Original Seceders in 1827. More important was the formation of the United Presbyterian Church in 1847, as a result of the union of the Relief Church with the United Secession Church. In 1876, the majority of Reformed Presbyterians joined the Free Church of Scotland.

In Ireland, the Scottish controversies had their counterpart in Ulster. However, in 1840, the Secession Church joined with the Synod of Ulster (the main Presbyterian body in Northern Ireland) and became the Presbyterian Church in Ireland.

In England, the Presbyterian Church was formed in 1836; in 1876, the United Presbyterian Church, which had grown there from secession movements in Scotland, joined with the Presbyterian Church in England, and became the Presbyterian Church of England.

Wales had a different history; the Presbyterian Church grew out of the evangelical revival of the eighteenth century. In 1811, the Presbyterians organized two Synods, or Associations (South Wales and North Wales). These were to become part of a General Assembly in 1864.

✻   ✻   ✻

Scottish influence was also to be felt across the Atlantic. In Canada, Scottish settlers began to arrive after the Treaty of Paris of 1763. The settlement of Scots in Nova Scotia brought many Presbyterians there. In 1817 the Synod of Nova Scotia was created, in connection with the Church of Scotland, and in 1835 a similar Synod was formed in New Brunswick. Secession groups did not remain inactive, and in 1826 they formed the United Presbytery of Canada. The great Disruption of 1843 in Scotland had its effects in Canada too, and in 1845 there were seven separate Presbyterian bodies in Canada! Happily, the needs of a developing country brought a spirit of co-operation between the different groups, and in 1875 they were all united in the Presbyterian Church of Canada.

The United States of America also felt the influence of Scottish Church struggles. However, the first Church of the Reformed family established in the U.S.A. in 1628 did not come from Scotland but from the Netherlands. It was a congregation of what is now the Reformed Church in America; its setting was Manhattan Island, then a Dutch settlement. The Reformed

Church in America proudly claims to be the oldest Church with a continuous history in the U.S.A.

The Scottish settlers organized their first Presbytery in Philadelphia in 1706, and in 1716 a Synod was formed. In 1741 the first schism appeared, but it was healed in 1758 and the Church took the name of the Synod of New York and Philadelphia.

In the nineteenth century there were further divisions. In 1810 the Cumberland Presbyterian Church was formed out of a purely American situation, i.e. frontier conditions. This Church, which attached great importance to evangelism and repudiated pre-destination, spread rapidly. The main body of this Church was to be re-united with the Presbyterian Church in the U.S.A. in 1906.

In 1801 the Presbyterians had accepted a plan of union with the Congregationalists. They did not merge but federated their home mission work on the frontier. However the plan was abrogated in 1837. The Assembly illegally expelled the federated Churches. Almost half the Church refused to recognize these acts; they joined the expelled group and declared themselves to be the genuine Presbyterian Church, taking the name of 'The Presbyterian Church, U.S.A.' and adding 'New School'. The other group became known as 'The Presbyterian Church, U.S.A., Old School'.

The dispute over slavery and the Civil War brought new problems. In 1861, the Old School passed a resolution which committed the Church to the northern view, with the result that the southern section of the Church seceded to form 'The Presbyterian Church in the Confederate States of America' (now the Presbyterian Church in the U.S.).

If the Civil War created divisions it also helped to end some schisms; in 1864, the United Synod of the South (largely New School) united with the Confederate Presbyterians of the South, and in 1870 the Old and New Schools were re-united in the Presbyterian Church in the U.S.A.

Around 1750, Covenanters, principally from Ireland, began arriving in America under the name of Reformed Presbyterians. In 1774 they formed their first Presbytery. Seceder Presbyterians had already organized a Presbytery in 1758. Both groups were located mainly in Pennsylvania. In 1782 the Reformed Presbyterians united with some of the Seceder (associate) Presbyterians.

It was not until 1852 that other secession groups joined them and together formed 'The United Presbyterian Church of North America' (now part of the United Presbyterian Church in the U.S.A.).

In the nineteenth century the Scots migrated in large numbers and founded Churches which were closely connected with the Church in their homeland.

In Australia, the first church body organized by Church of Scotland ministers was founded in 1826. As was to be expected the stormy years in Scotland had their counterpart in Australia. Happily, conditions were different, the country was expanding and a certain measure of unity became necessary. In 1865 the Presbyterian Church of New South Wales was formed by the union of different groups and in 1870 the Presbyterian Church of Victoria followed suit. Other States did likewise, but it was not until 1886 that a federal union of these Churches took place and one has to wait until 1901 to see the foundation of 'The Presbyterian Church of Australia' with its General Assembly.

In the middle of the nineteenth century there was no Presbyterian Church in New Zealand. The first Presbytery, the Presbytery of Otago in the South Island, was formed by Free Church ministers, while in the North Island the Presbytery of Auckland was formed in 1856. Both Churches grew rapidly and in 1901 the Presbyterian Church of New Zealand was formed.

*   *   *

As we have seen in the case of the United States of America, the Scots were not the only Reformed people to emigrate. The Dutch were a seafaring nation and their settlements were numerous although later they were to surrender some of them to Britain.

South Africa occupies a prominent place amidst the countries where they settled. As early as 1652 the Dutch Reformed Church was brought to that part of the world by the first Dutch settlers. The Church kept its connection with the Reformed Church in the Netherlands for over 150 years. However, the British annexation of the Cape of Good Hope put an end to these ties and in 1824, the first independent Synod of the Reformed Church of the Cape took place; other Synods were to follow, but they all came into existence after the middle of the nineteenth century.

In Ceylon, the first Dutch Reformed congregation was started in 1642 in Galle, in the south of Ceylon. During the period of the Dutch occupation, the Reformed Church flourished, but with the passing of Ceylon into the hands of the British, the situation changed. A small Dutch Reformed Church, however, continued its work there.

In the Dutch East Indies, now Indonesia, the Dutch settled at the beginning of the seventeenth century, after having ousted the Portuguese. With the victory of the Netherlands East India Company over the Portuguese, most of the Roman Catholic congregations became Reformed. The Reformed Church became a 'Company Church' (see *Indonesia: Church and Society*, by Frank L. Cooley, Friendship Press, New York, 1968, p. 40). An event of unusual importance for the spread of Christianity was the first translation of the Bible into the Malay language in 1733.

At the end of the Napoleonic wars the East Indies, which had for a time been under British rule, returned to the Dutch. The Reformed Church became subject to the control of the colonial government. What is now the Protestant Church in Indonesia ('Gereja Protestan Indonesia'), with its four sections in Molucca, Timor, Minahasa and Western Indonesia, grew rapidly and became a real force in the country. After 1830 mission work was allowed in the Dutch East Indies; it was mainly Reformed and, as a consequence, Reformed Churches were created in other parts of the East Indies. In the middle of the nineteenth century Reformed Christianity was therefore well established in what is now Indonesia.

It is an error to classify the Churches of Indonesia amongst the 'Younger Churches' as is often done—we have to remember that these Churches were established before the 'Older Churches' of Australia and New Zealand.

*   *   *

If one tries to sum up the situation of the Reformed Churches in the middle of the nineteenth century, it is clear that unity was not their most treasured possession. In his remarkable book, *A Church History of Scotland* (Oxford University Press, 1960) Professor J. H. S. Burleigh, writing on 'Dissension' can say: 'It is no accident that all these movements took place in lands where Calvinist Churches had been established since the Reformation. Lutheranism knew nothing of *Freikirchentum* and the idea of setting up a Free Church of England hardly occurred to the Anglo-Catholic Tractarians.'[3]

This is true; but there is another side to it. We have to remember that division is not the greatest sin of the Church; unfaithfulness is the greatest sin. And there is no doubt that some of the divisions which took place in our Reformed Churches in the eighteenth and nineteenth centuries were due to genuine evangelical revivals. Some of the Churches which came into existence as a result of these revivals showed a great evangelistic zeal, and it is amongst these Churches that the first missionary awakening was born. It is also worth remembering that if most of the Churches of the European Continent still had to discover their missionary responsibilities, Missionary Societies, which were the fruit of the evangelical revival, were beginning to take the great Commission seriously; and they were supported by members of the Reformed Churches, both National and Free.

As a result of this expanding missionary work, in Africa, Latin America and Asia, Native Reformed congregations were being created everywhere; Presbyteries were formed. But there were as yet no Independent National Churches. The 'Younger Churches' as we call them, were not in a position to have an influence on the association of the Reformed Churches in the World Alliance of Reformed Churches.

Everything was not dark in the Reformed Churches in the middle of the nineteenth century. But they had no vision of their common heritage; they did not yet realize that they belonged to a vast world family, and that they were all part of the Church Catholic.

REFERENCES
1. *Proceedings 1st General Council*, p. 1.
2. Idem.
3. Op. cit., p. 353.

CHAPTER TWO

The Coming Together. The Preliminary Discussions

Today we often speak of our modern world and of the speed of communications. We tend to believe that former centuries never had the feeling of being 'modern' or to have achieved real progress. The contrary is true, at least of the nineteenth century. Our forefathers saw a new world opening up before them with the discovery of the steam engine. Sea communications, which had been slow and hazardous, became relatively fast and safe, and people began travelling from one continent to another as never before.

If the Churches as a whole were still very 'national' and had little interest in the Christians of other countries, a growing number of people began to realize that Christianity was universal, and the desire to get to know Christians of other lands and to work in close co-operation with them became more urgent.

In 1846 the Evangelical Alliance was formed. It was to have a direct influence on the formation of the World Alliance of Reformed Churches; soon afterwards the Young Men's Christian Associations were born and other similar organizations were to follow.

On the denominational level, let us mention the first Lambeth Conference of Anglican Bishops, which took place in 1867.

Some Presbyterians felt that the time had come for them to organize as a fraternal world family. No one can claim the monopoly of having first thought about this. However, the idea was in the air, and several people began expressing their views on this subject. Among the earliest to do so was Professor Macgregor of New College, Edinburgh (Free Church of Scotland). Writing on 'Our Presbyterian Empire' in *The Presbyterian* of Edinburgh,

May 1868, he mentioned the desirability of 'holding a Council of Presbyterians who hold by the Presbyterian Standards, once in five, ten or twenty years, alternately at Edinburgh, London and New York, at which all the Churches might confer for ecumenical purposes, while each Church, for local purposes, would always retain her own autonomy, and hold herself perfectly free to accept the decisions of the Council in the exercise of her own independent judgment under Christ'.[1]

Similar views had been expressed from time to time by Rev. Dr James McCosh, a minister of the Free Church of Scotland, who had become Professor in Queen's College, Belfast, and later President of the College of New Jersey (now University of Princeton).

In Philadelphia in 1870, at the General Assembly of the Presbyterian Church in the United States of America marking the reunion of the 'Old School' and of the 'New School' (see p. 8), Dr McCosh voiced in a sermon his desire to see a Pan-Presbyterian Council. In 1872, he repeated the suggestion in a lecture on 'Presbyterianism in Foreign Lands' published in Philadelphia in *The Tercentenary Book*. It is worth quoting a few sentences of this lecture, as they show the kind of organization Dr McCosh had in view: 'It has long been a favourite idea of mine that all the Presbyterian Churches might be brought together at a Pan-Presbyterian Council, at which each of them might be represented. . . . Of course there must be a doctrinal basis. But this should not consist in a new creed or confession. Let each Church retain its own standards, and be admitted into the Union only on condition that these embrace the cardinal truths of salvation . . . There must also be certain principles of Church order presupposed . . . The Grand Council should have authority to see that their fundamental principles of doctrine and of government are carried out in each of the Churches, and might cut off those that deliberately departed from them in act or in profession. But beyond this it need have no other disciplinary power. Without interfering at all with the free action of the Churches, it might distribute judiciously the evangelistic work in the great field, which is the world; allocating a sphere to each, discouraging the plantation of two Churches where one might serve and the establishment of two missions at one place, while hundreds of other places have none. In this way the resources of the Church would be kept from being wasted, while her energies would be concentrated on great enterprises.'[2]

Among those who had heard Dr McCosh's sermon at the 1870 General Assembly was another Scot, Rev. Dr William G. Blaikie, Professor at New College, Edinburgh (Free Church of Scotland), who was to play an outstanding role in the life of the Alliance in its beginnings.

Dr Blaikie became an enthusiastic supporter of Dr McCosh's ideas; he spoke about this plan on several occasions during his visit to the U.S.A. and Canada. After returning home, he wrote an article in *The Presbyterian* (November 1871), under the title 'A Confederation of English-speaking Presbyterians—a Proposal'. The proposal was then limited to English-speaking Presbyterians, because of the language problem, but soon Dr Blaikie became convinced that such a Confederation should embrace Churches of other parts of the world. Seven objects were specified as worthy of being considered by such an alliance:

'1. To foster the idea of a large brotherhood, or ecclesiastical family, with the stimulating influence which that thought conveyed.

'2. To give to the various Churches more of "the communion of the saints", more real fellowship in each other's gifts and grace.

'3. To communicate to each other the results of experience in practical work.

'4. To show how the elements of true conservatism and legimate freedom and progress might be adjusted to each other.

'5. To divide the foreign and other fields of labour among the various Churches.

'6. To give opportunities for united prayer.

'7. To cultivate Christian friendship, bringing congenial souls into closer contact with each other, and deepening their interest in each other's work.'

The writer happily added 'that the due result of such an alliance would not be an increase in sectarianism, because Christian brotherhood, as it enlarged its fellowship, enlarged itself; and possibly the final result might be a federal gathering of all the Evangelical Churches, whether Presbyterian or not'.[3]

In 1872, another minister of the Free Church of Scotland, Rev. J. Moir Porteous, in a book entitled *The Government of the Kingdom of Christ*, suggested a consultative Assembly, composed of the representatives of all the Presbyterian Churches of the world. 'Would it not be a grand moral spectacle,' he wrote, 'were representative associate presbyters from all the Presbyterian Churches of the world to meet in the name and by the authority of the King and Head of the Church, to consult and determine as to the best means of removing obstacles to, and promoting the establishment of His Kingdom in every part of the world?'[4]

The year 1873 was to see more definite action on both sides of the Atlantic. In February 1873 Dr Knox of Belfast gave notice of an overture to the General Assembly of the Irish Presbyterian Church; the overture was approved and a Committee appointed to correspond with other Churches. Here is the text of this overture:

'Whereas there is a substantial unity in faith, discipline and worship among the Presbyterian Churches in this and other lands; whereas it is important to exhibit this unity to other Churches and the world; whereas a desire has been expressed in many lands for closer union, among all branches of the great and widely scattered family of Presbyterian Churches; it is overtured to the General Assembly favourably to consider this subject, and open up correspondence with other Churches, holding the Westminster Confession of Faith, with the view of bringing about an Ecumenical Council of such Churches, to consider subjects of common interest to all, and especially to promote harmony of action in the mission fields at home and abroad.'[5]

In May of the same year, Dr Nicolls of St Louis proposed an overture, in almost identical terms, to the General Assembly of the Presbyterian Church in the U.S.A., meeting in Baltimore. This overture was also approved.

The Assembly 'resolved that a Committee, consisting of the Moderator, the Stated Clerk, and President James McCosh, be appointed to correspond with sister Churches holding by the Westminster Standards'.[6]

In the autumn of 1873, when the Evangelical Alliance met in New York, an important meeting of ministers and laymen was held there, under the auspices of the Committee of the General Assembly of the Presbyterian Church in the U.S.A. About 150 persons attended, and the following resolutions were adopted unanimously:

'1. That, *Whereas*, the General Assembly of the Presbyterian Church in the U.S.A. and the General Assembly of the Presbyterian Church in Ireland, at their last meetings, passed resolutions in favour of an ecumenical council of Presbyterian Churches, we, providentially brought together at this time, and belonging to various branches of the Presbyterian family, cordially sympathize with these movements towards a General Council of the Presbyterian Churches in various lands.

'2. That a Committee be appointed to correspond with individuals and with organized bodies in order to ascertain the feelings of Presbyterians in regard to such a federal council, and to take such measures as may in their judgment promote this object.

'3. That this Committee be authorized to co-operate, as far as possible, with the General Assembly of the Presbyterian Church in Ireland and with the Committee of the General Assembly of the Presbyterian Church in the U.S.A.'[7]

The Committee thus formed consisted of the representatives of ten Presbyterian and Reformed Churches, the chairman being Rev. Dr James McCosh. The Secretary of the Committee, Rev. G. D. Mathews, was later to become the most important person in the life of the Alliance in the next decades. He was born in Ireland in 1828. After studying at the United Presbyterian Divinity Hall in Edinburgh, he was ordained to the ministry of the United Presbyterian Church and was for fourteen years minister of a United Presbyterian congregation in Scotland before being called to the pastorate of Westminster Presbyterian Church in New York, a pastorate he held for ten years; in 1878, he was to be called to the pastorate of Chalmers Presbyterian Church in Quebec. In 1888, he was to become the first General Secretary of the Alliance (after having been its American Secretary since the inception of the Alliance), a post he held until his death in 1913.

With such outstanding members as Dr McCosh and Rev. G. D. Mathews, the Committee immediately set to work. It issued a fraternal address to Presbyterian Churches. Should they approve of the suggestions, they were asked to express their approval in a formal way, to appoint a Committee to correspond with similar Committees from other bodies, and to make arrangements for carrying the scheme into effect.

The benefits of the proposed movement were stated in the address of this Committee:

'1st. It would exhibit before the world the substantial unity, quite consistent with minor diversities, of the one great family of Presbyterian Churches.

'2nd. It would greatly tend to hold up and strengthen weak and struggling Churches, by showing that they are members of a large body. The Protestant Churches of the Continent of Europe, for example, feel a great need of sympathy and support from Churches more favourably situated.

'3rd. It would enable Churches, which are not enclined to organic union, to manifest their belief in the unity of the Church, and to fraternize with those whom they love, while they still hold to their distinctive testimony.

'4th. Each Presbyterian Church would become acquainted with the constitution and work of sister Churches, and their interest in each other would be proportionally increased. Some might be led in this way to see in other Churches excellences which they would choose to adopt.

'5th. The Churches may thus be led to combine in behalf of the truth, and against prevalent errors . . .

'6th. Without interfering with the free action of the Churches, this Council might distribute judiciously the evangelical work in the great field "which is the world"; allocating a sphere to each, discouraging the planting of two congregations where one might serve, or the establishment of two missions at one place, while hundreds of other places have none. In this way the resources of the Church would be husbanded, and her energies concentrated on great enterprises.

'7th. It would demonstrate to the Christian world these great facts in the working of the Presbyterian system: That, by its reasonable polity, it consists with every form of civil government; that, by the simplicity of its usages, it is adapted to all the varying conditions of the Church upon the earth; and that, by its equal distance from licence and arrogance it is best prepared to recognize the kingship of all believers.

'8th. It would manifest the proportions and power of the Presbyterian Churches, and thus offer effectual resistance to the exclusive pretentions of Prelacy and Ritualism in all their forms.

'9th. From such a Council, hallowed and quickened by the Redeemer's presence, there might proceed, as from a heart, new impulses of spiritual life, bringing every member of the Church into closer fellowship with his Divine Master, into deeper affection for his brethren for his Master's sake, and into more consecration of all his powers to the Master's work.'[8]

This is a remarkable document. We can already see in it the concern for a *world strategy* though the title is of course absent. There is a concern for the minority Churches, weak and struggling; there is the desire to co-operate with other Churches of the Reformed family, wherever this proves possible, in order to increase the efficiency of the Reformed witness; and there is a strong desire for a missionary strategy. There is no doubt that our forefathers were—with all their limitations—real visionaries. And it is worth noting that they were already concerned with the renewal of the Churches and wanted the Alliance to be an instrument of this renewal.

In 1874, the problem was discussed in various General Assemblies and Synods, and Committees were appointed to correspond with similar committees of other Churches.

The Committee did not rely on correspondence only. In the summer of 1874, Dr McCosh, chairman of the New York Committee, visited Great Britain and conferred with members of the Committees appointed by the Churches in Scotland, England and Ireland. A meeting took place in Dr Blaikie's house, in Edinburgh.

As a result of Dr McCosh's visit to Great Britain, two preliminary meetings took place, one in Edinburgh on 13 November, the other in New York on 3 December 1874. Both meetings approved the convening of a preliminary conference of British, American, Continental and Colonial delegates in London, in the summer of 1875, to form a constitution for the proposed Council, and to determine the time and place of the first General Council.

Dr McCosh and Dr Blaikie were the leaders of the movement. Not only did they play a prominent role in the meetings held in Edinburgh and New York in the autumn of 1874 (though neither of them chaired the meetings), but they kept up an almost continual correspondence on the subject of the proposed organization. Some of these letters are preserved in the Alliance archives in Geneva[9] and they make very interesting reading. We have already seen that the founders of the Alliance had no desire to form a power block; they wanted the Reformed Churches to unite their efforts in order to better serve their Lord and Saviour. This is made clear in the correspondence between Dr McCosh and Dr Blaikie. In a letter dated 21 January 1875, Dr McCosh writes: 'You would notice that in our resolution adopted in New York we endeavoured to give the whole movement an evangelistic missionary character, rather than an ecclesiastical one. I attach great importance to this . . . May the Great Head watch over our movement.'[10] The same note is struck in a letter of 27 April 1875. And in a letter of 17 June 1875, Dr McCosh writes: 'The Americans have had three ends especially in view:

'(1) We wish to make the movement evangelistic rather than ecclesiastic. We are afraid lest your Scottish ecclesiasticism breaks us up.

'(2) The Council is to have no power to order the Churches. Our power is the moral, persuasive.

'(3) We must avoid being a mere talking body.'[11]

At the meetings of the General Assemblies and Synods in May 1875 the subject of the proposed Alliance of Reformed Churches continued to be regarded in a favourable light, and in most cases delegates were appointed to attend the Conference in London. The Presbyterian Church in the U.S. (Southern Church) decided to join in and appointed delegates to the London meeting.

In his 'Introductory Narrative' Dr Blaikie insists on the limitations put on the proposed General Council by the Churches which approved of it. He writes: '. . . in approving of the proposal of a General Council, it was understood among all, and expressly stated by some, that the General Council was not to be an authoritative body, that it was to have no jurisdiction even over the Churches represented in it, and that it was to exercise only a moral influence upon them. It may appear as if this reservation destroyed the chief ground on which such a Council had a claim to exist in the Presbyterian system. If that system demands a General Council to complete it, ought not that Council to possess the same sort of authority or jurisdiction as the other Assemblies or Synods of the several Churches? Logically, this may be correct; but the case is one in which the conclusions of logic require to be modified by practical considerations. An authoritative Council, ruling and controlling all the Churches represented in it, is an obvious impossibility in present circumstances. The varieties of language and race, the distance of Churches from one another, the diversity of historical traditions among them, the ignorance prevailing of one another's ways, would make a supreme authoritative Assembly an impossibility, at least for the present. The question to be considered was, whether an Assembly with only moral influence was not possible and worth the having, and whether it would not accomplish many of the ends for which the other might be theoretically proper.'[12]

It was providential that the founders of the Alliance saw this and were satisfied with an Assembly which was not a General Council in the strict Presbyterian sense of the term. Had they tried to have an authoritative General Council, the World Alliance of Reformed Churches would soon have ceased to exist. It is because they were satisfied with less than what was theoretically possible that the Alliance was to become a great world family of Reformed Churches.

REFERENCES

1. *Proceedings 1st General Council,* p. 2.
2. Op. cit., p. 2.
3. Op. cit., p. 3.
4. Op. cit., p. 3.
5. Op. cit., p. 3.
6. Op. cit., p. 378.
7. Op. cit., p. 4.
8. Op. cit., p. 4.
9. WARC Archives, Geneva, WPA–HA1.
10. Idem.
11. Idem.
12. *Proceedings 1st General Council,* p. 7.

CHAPTER THREE

The London Conference of 1875 and the First General Council

The story told in the preceding chapter of the efforts which were made to create a World Alliance of Reformed Churches may have given the impression that those who took an active part in the formation of the Alliance were concerned only with Great Britain and North America. Happily this was not the case. Both Dr McCosh and Dr Blaikie were eager that the Churches of Australia and New Zealand should also join the Alliance. Dr Blaikie wrote to these Churches, explaining the aims of the proposed organization. Contacts were also taken with missionaries working in different parts of the world. Last, but not least, the Churches of the European Continent were contacted.

It is true that for a long time the Alliance was to be mainly an Anglo-Saxon organization, with English as the only official language. It was only at the beginning of the twentieth century that Continental Conferences were organized. If the concern for the Continent was one of the first preoccupations of the early leaders of the Alliance, it was almost a paternalistic concern for Churches which were weak and struggling. This may be due to the fact that most of these men came from the great Scottish Disruption; and they were therefore suspicious of Churches related to the State. However, it would be wrong to think that our forefathers did not try to associate the European Churches with the Alliance. If they failed with most of the larger State Churches, it was the fault of the Churches themselves. Their thinking was entirely on a parochial level; being dependent on the State they could not take initiatives on the international level.

In the last chapter, we indicated that both the Edinburgh and the New York meetings of November–December 1874 were in favour of holding a Conference in London in the summer of 1875, with a view to officially forming the Alliance and adopting a Constitution.

This historic Conference opened in London on 21 July 1875. Admirable arrangements had been made by the Committee on Union of the Presbyterian Church of England. On the evening of 20 July a meeting of welcome was held in Regent Square Church, presided over by Rev. Dr Oswald Dykes, who, after devotional exercises, addressed the delegates and welcomed them to London. Among the replies made, two came from delegates of the Continent of Europe, the others from American and Scottish delegates.

The Conference met in the English Presbyterian College, in London, on 21 July. Rev. Dr J. McCosh, President of the College of New Jersey, Princeton, N.J., was appointed President of the Conference, while Professor Blaikie of Edinburgh and Rev. G. D. Mathews of New York were appointed clerks of the Conference.

A total of 101 delegates, representing 22 Churches, had been appointed to the London Conference, but only 64 were present; they represented 21 Churches. Unfortunately, the delegates of the United Presbyterian Church of America were unable to travel to London.

It is interesting to list the Churches represented at the first meeting. They were:

> The Presbyterian Church in the U.S.A.
> The Presbyterian Church in the U.S.
> The Synod of the Reformed Presbyterian Church
> The Reformed (Dutch) Church in America
> The Presbyterian Church in Canada
> The Presbyterian Church in England
> The Presbyterian Church in Wales (Calvinist Methodist)
> The Reformed Presbyterian Church of Scotland
> The Church of Scotland
> The Free Church of Scotland
> The United Presbyterian Church of Scotland
> The Presbyterian Church in Ireland
> The Reformed Church of France
> The Union of Evangelical Churches of France
> The Belgian Christian Missionary Church

The Free Evangelical Church of the Canton de Vaud,
   Switzerland
The Evangelical Church of Neuchâtel, Switzerland
The Waldensian Church of Italy
The Reformed Church of East Friesland, Germany
The Free Evangelical Church of Germany
The Evangelical Church of Spain.

The Conference spent most of two days in arranging a
constitution for the proposed Alliance. A short Constitution with
only four articles was adopted to be presented in draft form to the
first General Council of the Alliance. It was preceded by a
Preamble of which we quote a part, as it shows a real ecumenical
spirit:
   'In forming this Alliance, the Presbyterian Churches do not
mean to change their fraternal relations with other Churches, but
will be ready, as heretofore, to join with them in Christian
fellowship, and in advancing the cause of the Redeemer, on the
general principle maintained and taught in the Reformed Confessions that the Church of God on earth, though composed of
many members, is one body in the communion of the Holy
Ghost, of which body Christ is the Supreme Head, and the
Scriptures alone are the infallible law.'[1]
   The name of the new organization was adopted: 'The Alliance
of the Reformed Churches throughout the World holding the
Presbyterian System.'[2]
   Conditions for membership were clearly indicated in article II
of the proposed Constitution: 'Any Church organized on
Presbyterian principles which holds the supreme authority of the
Scriptures of the Old and New Testaments in matters of faith and
morals, and whose creed is in harmony with the consensus of the
Reformed Confessions, shall be eligible for admission into the
Alliance.'[3]
   Among the objects of the Council, indicated in article III, 4, we
note: '. . . it shall seek the welfare of Churches, especially such as
are weak or persecuted; . . . it shall entertain all subjects directly
connected with the work of Evangelisation, such as the relation
of the Christian Church to the Evangelisation of the world, the
distribution of mission work, the combination of Church
energies, especially in relation to great cities and destitute

districts, the training of ministers, the use of the Press . . .'[4]

This last word is interesting. Though one did not speak at the time of *mass media*, it shows that the founders of the Alliance were already conscious of the role of the Press and anxious to use it as fully as possible.

An invitation from the Scottish Churches to meet in Edinburgh was accepted, and it was decided that the first General Council should open on 4 July 1876 and that the maximum number of delegates should be 300, a very remarkable figure when one remembers that travel was slower and more difficult than today.

A General Committee, consisting of all the delegates to the London Conference, was appointed. The Committee divided into Local Committees for the different Churches. The Scottish Local Committee was appointed to take the initiative in making arrangements, in correspondence with other committees. Dr Blaikie was named Convener of the Scottish Committee, as well as of the General Committee.

*   *   *

It had been agreed in London that the first General Council should meet on 4 July 1876. However the arrangements for the meeting, with which the Scottish Committee were proceeding, underwent a sudden and somewhat unexpected interruption. After their return to the U.S.A. the American Committee sent a strong and urgent request that the meeting be delayed for a year, as the great Centennial Celebration of American Independence was also on 4 July 1876. This meant that the American delegation could not be in Edinburgh for the First General Council at the same time. The Scottish Committee was understandingly embarrassed, but ultimately they agreed to defer the meeting for a year.

Unfortunately, the communication from America was not received in time to stop the departure of several delegates from Australia and New Zealand. In order to show all due respect to these, the Scottish Committee held two meetings in Edinburgh, on 31 May 1876, at which the brethren had an opportunity of expressing their views and of receiving a welcome from their friends in Scotland. Though these delegates had time to spend in Scotland, they could not stay a whole year and had to return to their countries before the First General Council.

If the deferring of the Council was unfortunate from this point of view, it was providential as far as the European Continent was concerned. At the London Conference, the representation from the Continental Churches had been very poor. None of the great National Churches of Hungary, the Netherlands or Switzerland had sent representatives to London. So, in the autumn of 1876, Dr Blaikie set out on an extended tour of the continent, in the course of which he visited the Reformed Churches in Germany, Bohemia, Hungary, Italy, Switzerland, France and the Netherlands. Reporting on his mission, Dr Blaikie had an interesting paragraph on his contacts with Lutherans: 'Our mission formally was only to the "Reformed" Churches technically so-called. But often, especially in Germany, Hungary, and France, we were asked whether we excluded the Lutherans. It was represented to us that the government of the Lutheran Church was substantially Presbyterian, and we had good cause to know that in some Lutheran Churches, that of Wurtemberg especially, there is no small measure of evangelical life and unction. Our reply was that the Council itself must decide that question, but we encouraged the visit of Lutherans who were in sympathy with our movement generally, that they might become acquainted with it more fully, and that thus the question might be ripened.'[5] This clearly shows that the founders of the Alliance had no narrow 'Reformed' spirit and that they were anxious to bring together all Evangelical Christians.

In the course of his visit to the Continent, Dr Blaikie had to realize that several of the National Churches had no Creed and that it would be impossible for them to be officially represented at the Council. This problem was to become acute in the ensuing years, when the question of the submission to the Westminster Confession was raised with regard to the Cumberland Presbyterian Church. At this point however, Dr Blaikie simply suggested 'that at the ensuing meeting considerable encouragement should be afforded for the attendance of "associates" not formally delegated as yet by their Churches'.[6]

Early in 1875 Rev. Dr Philip Schaff, of Union Theological Seminary in New York, undertook a similar journey to Europe and to the Middle East; he spoke of the coming Council in France, Germany, Switzerland, as well as in Greece, Turkey, Egypt and Syria, inviting representatives to attend the Edinburgh Council.

A call to prayer on behalf of the Council was issued by the Convener: '. . . While trusting that many will remember it from time to time at prayer-meetings and on the Lord's Day, we would respectfully suggest that on the two preceding Sabbaths, 24th June and 1st July, it should be especially kept in view.'[7]

*   *   *

On Tuesday, 3 July 1877, the delegates to the First General Council met in the morning for worship in the High Kirk of Edinburgh (St Giles) and heard a sermon preached by Rev. Dr Robert Flint, Professor of Divinity in the University of Edinburgh. His text was John 17: 20–21: 'Neither pray I for these alone, but for them also which shall believe in me through their word. That they all may be one, as Thou, Father, art in me, and I in Thee, that they also may be one in us, that the world may believe that Thou hast sent me.' The sermon was an earnest plea for unity of spirit and purpose and counsel in advancing the kingdom of Christ in the world.

At 2.30 in the afternoon, the Council met in the Assembly Hall of the Free Church of Scotland (now the building where the General Assembly of the Church of Scotland meets). The Alliance had not, as at present, a President, to hold office from one Council to another. The steering Committee arranged for a number of delegates to take the chair in turn at the sessions of the Council. In this way the honour of chairing the first session fell to Rev. Dr Howard Crosby, of New York, a delegate of the Presbyterian Church in the U.S.A. Rev. George D. Mathews, also of New York, was appointed Clerk to the Council.

The report of the General Committee was presented by Rev. Dr Blaikie, Convener. He immediately dealt with the question of membership: 'It was agreed at London,' he said, 'that the Churches represented there should be held to be members of the Alliance, and that applications from other Churches, made through the Committee, should be decided on by the Council. The Committee report that, in addition to the 22 Churches represented at London, the following had more or less expressed a desire to be connected with the Alliance:[8]

The Reformed Church of Hungary
The Reformed Church of Bohemia and Moravia

The Reformed Church in Holland (Classis of Amsterdam and
  Oostermeer)
The Christian Reformed Church in the Netherlands
The National Church of the Canton de Vaud, Switzerland
The Reformed Church in Russia
The Free Italian Church
The Reformed Presbyterian Church of Ireland
The Reformed Presbyterian Church of Scotland
The Church of the Original Secession in Scotland
The Associate Reformed Synod of the South (USA)
The General Synod of the Reformed Presbyterian Church
  (USA)
The Welsh Calvinist Church (USA)
The German Reformed Church (USA)
The Dutch Reformed Church, Cape Colony
The Dutch Reformed Church, Orange Free State
The Dutch Reformed Church, Natal
The Presbytery of Natal
The Christian Reformed Church in South Africa
The Presbyterian Church of Victoria
The Presbyterian Church of New South Wales
The Presbyterian Church of Eastern Australia
The Presbyterian Church of Queensland
The Presbyterian Church of New Zealand
The Presbyterian Church of Otago (New Zealand)
The Presbytery of Ceylon
The Missionary Synod of the New Hebrides.'

Not all of these 27 Churches were represented at Edinburgh,
but as they had all 'more or less' expressed the wish to be
connected with the Alliance, they were all admitted, bringing the
Alliance membership to 49 Churches.

One could point out that some of the 'Churches' mentioned
were hardly Churches in the strict sense of the word. It is
doubtful, for instance, if a 'Classis' of the Nederlands Hervormde
Kerk had the right to become a member of the Alliance, this right
belonging solely to the Church as a whole.

However, there is no doubt that the Council at Edinburgh was
a very representative meeting, bringing together for the first time
representatives of British, American, Canadian, Australian and

New Zealand Churches, as well as delegates from the Dutch Reformed Churches of South Africa and the Reformed Churches of the European Continent, not to mention the first missionary Synods. Just as important was the fact that by bringing together representatives of the separated Churches of one country (there were for instance five Scottish Churches represented) the Alliance was bound to play a role in healing the divisions between these Churches.

If the first day ended with a Public Reception given by the Lord Provost of Edinburgh—a reception which was attended by a distinguished company of between five and six thousand people —the Council was first and foremost a working Assembly.

There was no theme for the Edinburgh meeting, but most subjects of importance to the Churches were discussed for one week in morning, afternoon and evening sessions.

One of the first problems to be discussed was the question of the 'Consensus of Reformed Confessions'. This subject, which was to occupy the minds of the Alliance leaders for several years, almost created a deadly crisis in the life of the young Alliance. The subject was introduced by Professor Philip Schaff, of New York. He reminded the Council that the Constitution adopted in London in 1875 'lays down as the doctrinal basis of the Alliance "the Consensus of the Reformed Confessions". But it did not define this Consensus, nor is there any recognized formula of the kind'.[9] Dr Schaff proposed 'a new ecumenical confession, which would be a testimony to the living faith of the Church, and a bond of union among the different branches of the Reformed Churches'.[10] At the same time, Dr Schaff must have been aware of the possible dangers of such a confession, for he added: 'It ought to be truly evangelical—catholic in spirit. A Confession which would intensify Presbyterianism and loosen the ties which unite us to other branches of Christ's kingdom I would regard as a calamity.'[11] Dr Schaff was also aware of the limitations of any Creed, and in concluding his lecture, he said: 'A creed is a response of man to the questions of God; but God's Word is better than the best human creed. A creed is a confession of faith, but faith is better than the confession of it, and without faith the best confession is but "as sounding brass or a tinkling cymbal".'[12]

These were wise words, but the Council decided all the same to appoint a committee, with Dr Schaff as chairman, to enquire into the matter, and report to the next Council. The Committee was to work in three sections: one for the United Kingdom and the Colonies, one for the United States and one for the Continent of Europe.

The Council devoted a whole day to Foreign Missions, a proof of the important role which the Alliance was to play in this field; an evening was devoted to the Continent of Europe, with speakers from several Continental Churches.

It is important to note the First General Council's attitude to Foreign Missions. Their immediate preoccupation was to develop practical co-operation between the Churches of the Reformed family in the Mission field. But it was made clear that such a co-operation should not be at the expense of co-operation with non-Presbyterian Churches. The words of a Scottish delegate, Rev. Dr J. C. Herdman, are worth quoting: 'We do not crave increased Presbyterian co-operation at the expense of that which is wider and more catholic. We are above all things *Christian*: "Presbyterian" only at a secondary rate; and I hope we shall be agreed to seek no closer bonds among ourselves in the foreign field, which would tend to separate us from others whom we acknowledge (and ought to love) as equally loyal to the Crucified-Risen Redeemer.'[13]

In the same session the same note was struck by Dr Thomson of Beirut when he said: 'We are far more than Presbyterians . . . Our Christian sympathies cannot be shut up within any merely ecclesiastical hedges . . . but we gladly . . . bid God-speed to all fellow-labourers in any part of the world.'[14]

It is good to read such declarations. They clearly show that the Presbyterian leaders of a century ago were no narrow confessionalists, but had the vision of the Church of Christ, Catholic. Their spirit was truly ecumenical, even if the word was not commonly used at that time.

But the members of the First Council were not only concerned with co-operation in the Foreign Mission fields. They had the desire to work as rapidly as possible toward the creation of Indigenous Churches.

Today, when the place of the foreign missionary is questioned by many of the 'Younger Churches', it is interesting to note that similar ideas were already expressed at the First Council. Dr Kalopothakes, of the Greek Evangelical Church, said: 'The very training of a foreign missionary, his customs and habits of living, are a wall between him and the natives. Can a foreign missionary sit down and eat off the same plate, and sleep in the same bed with a native? . . . as a general rule he neither could, nor would . . . the mission work can be done by the natives at less cost.'[15] Dr Thomas Smith of Edinburgh, who spoke after him, could only agree; he went even further and said: '. . . we ought to conduct our missionary operations with the view of making the native Churches, as soon as possible, independent of foreign aid . . . He considered it right that as soon as possible native Churches should be allowed to stand by themselves.'[16]

It is refreshing to hear such words. Alas, the older Churches were not ready to listen to these prophets; but there is no doubt that they helped our Churches to shape by and by, what is now the common policy of most Christian Churches. And it is good to remember that these pronouncements were made in 1877!

These were not isolated utterances. They reflected the mood of the Council. In the same session, Dr David Inglis, of Brooklyn, said: '. . . it was not their part to seek to build up in heathen countries Scotch, English, Irish or American denominations . . . but a great Church, to be thoroughly scriptural, and at the same time taking its special development from the circumstances of the country in which it was placed.'[17]

As for Rev. Dr Marquis, of Baltimore, he said: 'We may control the missionary . . . But as to the Church which grows from the work—let us consent that it shall be self-governing, free to frame its own enactments without any responsibility to us other than the responsibility of gratitude and love.'[18] Does this not sound amazingly contemporary?

The Council adopted a Resolution on Foreign Missions; it noted that 'it is of increasing importance that there should be the utmost attainable co-operation amongst the Churches of the Alliance.'[19] A Foreign Missions Committee was elected, and this Committee was given specific tasks with a view to developing this co-operation.

With regard to the Continent of Europe, we have already noted that a whole evening was devoted to the Churches of the Continent. Among the speakers on that evening was Dr Wagemann of Berlin, a Lutheran who had been invited to the Council. He spoke of the ecclesiastical state of Eastern Prussia.

After hearing reports from representatives of small and struggling Churches, Churches often deprived of true religious freedom, a Scottish delegate, Mr David Maclagan, expressed the feelings of most English-speaking delegates. He had 'a feeling of deep humiliation at the utterly inadequate work which their Churches at home were doing for the cause of Christ on the Continent. In fact, it seemed quite mysterious why their Churches, which had the missionary spirit in some degree, should not have, to a much larger extent, put their strength in this direction.'[20]

The Council passed a resolution expressing their joy at the presence of so many representatives from the Continent and decided to appoint a Committee 'On the Continent of Europe' 'for the purpose of considering the interests of the Continental Churches'.[21] This was not to remain an academic phrase, as the next chapters of this book will show. There is no doubt that the contact established at Edinburgh between Continental and Anglo-Saxon churchmen, the first in several centuries, was to have practical results of great importance.

Before ending its work, the Council passed several other resolutions and appointed several committees, especially a 'Committee on Business and Arrangements for next meeting of Council'.[22] It was agreed that the Second General Council should meet, D.V., in Philadelphia, on 21 September 1880.

The closing address of the Council was fittingly given by Rev. Dr Oswald Dykes, of London, who had presided over the meeting of welcome at the 1875 London Conference and had then addressed the delegates.

Let us quote some passages of this address, as it shows a real ecumenical spirit: 'A week ago we met, representing the whole of our great branch of Christ's Catholic Church, for the first time . . . to bow down in worship at the feet of God. And God's servant told us how our Alliance, if it is to be an instance of genuine Christian unity, and not of that which is mechanical or secular, must repose upon the basis, not of ecclesiastical polity alone, but of Christian life and Christian love. The spiritual oneness of Christians through their common oneness with Christ, their sole Head, is, we are reminded, the spirit of unity which is essential and priceless; without which no measure of ecclesiastical co-operation or even unification, could avail us much. Since that day we have been occupied to some extent with matters which were of necessity denominational, but much more with such as are of universal concern to Christian men. If we gave one day to Presbyterian questions, we have given the rest to wider ones . . . it would be fatal that we should treat them in a denominational spirit. Even a Council like this—wide as it may seem—is too narrow by far to represent that portion of Christendom which is actually and entirely at one on such great practical ends as have been discussed among us. Therefore it is still too narrow to satisfy the aspirations . . . of some of us; too narrow to fulfil that splendid hope, for the sake of which Calvin would have crossed many seas.'[23]

Dr Dyke was concerned not only with the problem of unity. He was also concerned with true spiritual life, and what he said to the delegates meeting in Edinburgh in 1877 may well be heard by all those who now attend a multitude of conferences and assemblies:

'A deeper spiritual life, a personal life of consecration to holy and noble aims, a life more habitually fed on God . . . this is what the Churches exist for; what the Lord of the Church died for! Our meetings could take no nobler aim . . . but it is an aim which is not to be attained by meetings merely, nor by alliances, nor even by Churches. There is an ecclesiasticism which kills instead of feeding the inner life. There is even an absorption in Christian work . . . which starves and does not nourish devotion . . . It is elsewhere that this sacred flame from heaven is to be kept alive and fanned. In the secret closet, at the foot of our Lord's cross . . . Brethren, let us pray for one another . . . And the blessing we shall ask for one another will be, before and above all other blessings, this, that we all may be one in the love and fellowship of our Divine Lord.'[24]

And so the Council came to an end, after a prayer and the benediction.

REFERENCES

1. *Proceedings 1st General Council*, p. 9.
2. Idem, p. 9.
3. Idem, p. 9.
4. Idem, p. 9.
5. Idem, p. 11.
6. Idem, p. 12.

7. Idem, p. 13.
8. Idem, p. 18.
9. Idem, p. 36.
10. Idem, p. 37.
11. Idem, p. 37.
12. Idem, p. 38.
13. Idem, p. 154.
14. Idem, p. 157.
15. Idem, p. 167.
16. Idem, p. 167.
17. Idem, p. 173.
18. Idem, p. 181.
19. Idem, p. 275.
20. Idem, p. 238.
21. Idem, p. 276.
22. Idem, p. 278.
23. Idem, p. 272.
24. Idem, p. 273.

CHAPTER FOUR

The Early Years

The First General Council had now come to an end. Committees had been appointed, including a Committee to prepare for the next Council. But there was no President of the Alliance and no Executive to direct the activities of the young organization. How was the work to be carried out? Was there not the danger that most delegates, having returned home, would soon forget the great experiences of Edinburgh and that the Alliance, which was born in prayer, joy and thanksgiving, would soon die for lack of leadership?

This could have happened. But by the providence of God, some men were ready to give their lives to the great cause for which they had already worked incessantly in the years preceding the First General Council. One of them deserves special mention, Rev. Dr William Garden Blaikie. Since returning home from the U.S.A. and after hearing Dr McCosh's speech at the General Assembly of the Presbyterian Church in the U.S.A. in 1870, he became the champion of the Alliance's cause among the British and Continental Churches.

It was he who was to start the first Alliance venture, *The Catholic Presbyterian*, of which the first issue appeared in January 1879. This was no small achievement, for the new publication was to appear monthly, each issue having 80 pages. When one thinks that Dr Blaikie started this work practically alone, one cannot but have a deep admiration for this great Scotsman, who had a full-time job as Professor at New College, and who in addition to that kept up a voluminous correspondence with Churches and individuals concerning the great cause which was so dear to his heart.

The title of the publication is interesting; it shows that from the beginning the leaders of the Alliance had an ecumenical spirit. In the first Editorial Dr Blaikie wrote: 'What of the relations of "Catholic Presbyterianism" to other sections of the Church, animated by the same evangelical spirit, and aiming at the same great ends? Catholic Presbyterianism cannot be a very exclusive Presbyterianism. Certainly our Presbyterian Alliance repudiates any such exclusivism . . . For our part . . . we regard other evangelical communions as part of the one Church Catholic.'[1]

The Catholic Presbyterian makes very interesting reading, and only limitations of space prevent us from quoting it as fully as it deserves. The articles appearing in the new monthly show the wide interest of the leaders of the Alliance and their burning desire to find a Christian solution to all problems.

In the field of what we now call Inter-Church Aid, the first volume raises the problem of regular help to the Waldensian Church of Italy, whose pastors' salaries were terribly insufficient. The problem of the labouring classes is also raised, and the author of the article points out that 'the prosperity of each is the prosperity of all'.[2] Had such a principle been taken seriously by Christians of last century, might not the class struggle have been avoided?

Naturally, the problem of religious freedom is often mentioned, as many of the small Churches of the Reformed family were then suffering from a lack of freedom or even from persecution. Austria, Spain and Turkey are mentioned in the first volumes; other countries were to follow.

We have already seen in the previous chapter that the problems of Mission were prominent in the minds of the leaders of the Alliance and that many of them were well in advance of their Churches generally. This appears clearly in *The Catholic Presbyterian*. In the second volume an article on the Church in heathen countries reads: 'The Churches established by our missionaries in foreign lands have, in many cases, a character as distinctly foreign to the country as the missionary himself. . . .

'To the naturalisation of the Church in any country, three things seem to be essential:

'I. The standards of doctrine and polity must be adapted as closely as possible to the actual, specific conditions of society in each country.

'II. All Churches, at one in their fundamental articles of doctrine and polity . . . should be organically united.

'III. Finally, in due time and order, there must be entire ecclesiastical severance from the parent Churches in Europe and in America.'[3]

These lines clearly show that some of our forefathers were not 'paternalistic' and that they had the vision of what was to come. Had these prophets been heeded the missionary movement would have known a smoother development and many of the conflicts between "Younger" and "Older" Churches could have been avoided.

The placing of ecumenical personnel from one Church at the disposal of another is now a common practice. But already in 1880, an article appearing in the Alliance monthly reads as follows: 'For some years, one or two American Presbyterian Churches have had men offering to go as missionaries, but the Churches have had no means to send them out. If the writer mistakes not, some sister Churches have had money, but not men. When such is the case, why should there not be some arrangement by which men of one Church could go under the auspices of a sister Church? . . . Is not the Master for whom we labour the same? And are we not to build up one Native Church in the end?'[4]

The early leaders of the Alliance were not interested in religious freedom for Reformed Christians alone; already in June 1880 an article appeared on Armenia and the fate of the Armenians, who were beginning to suffer terrible persecution at the hands of the Ottoman Empire.

*   *   *

1880 was also the year of the Second General Council and we shall now leave *The Catholic Presbyterian* to have a look at the great gathering in Philadelphia.

The Council started in the evening of 22 September with a reception by the Governor of Pennsylvania and the Mayor of Philadelphia; work began the next day and was to last until 3 October.

As in Edinburgh, it was a great gathering. The Committee on Credentials reported the presence of 220 Principals and 80 Associates. But if the British Isles were well represented and if American and Canadian delegates were numerous, the Continent of Europe had but five representatives; as for the rest of the world, two came from South Africa, one from Ceylon, one from

the New Hebrides and four from Australia. This can hardly be
called a 'world meeting' as we understand it today. However in
spite of these limitations, there is no doubt that the Philadelphia
Council was from the beginning concerned with problems of the
Church Catholic and that far-off lands were constantly present in
the minds of the delegates.

Once more, the spirit was not narrowly Presbyterian, but truly
Catholic. In his opening sermon, Rev. William Paxton of New
York said: 'We are not Catholics, but Catholic. We are not *the*
Catholic Church, but a part of the great Universal Church of
Jesus Christ.'[5]

In one of the first sessions, Rev. Dr R. D. Hitchcock, also of
New York, said: '. . . at last, in God's own time, far down the
horizon, we shall have, not only union, but unity, the real unity,
for which our Lord prayed, and the ages wait.'[6]

As in Edinburgh, the problem of the Consensus of the Reformed Confessions, or of a new Reformed Creed, came before
the Council. The 1877 Council had appointed a Committee on
Creeds and Confessions, with Dr Philip Schaff, of Union Theological Seminary, New York, as Chairman. The Committee
presented a voluminous and well documented report of over 150
pages on the Confessions of the Alliance member Churches[7] but
did not say anything about a Consensus which could be accepted
by all Churches. The Council therefore appointed a new Committee 'to consider the desirableness of defining the consensus of
the Reformed Confessions as required by our Constitution, and
to report to the next meeting of the Council'.[8] This Committee,
which met during the Philadelphia Council, decided to work in
three sections: British, Continental and American.

The absence of such a Consensus makes it hard to understand
why the Cumberland Presbyterian Church, a Church which had
been organized in 1810 as a result of a religious revival in
Kentucky and had departed from the Westminster Confession,
was not admitted. The application of the Church was refused as
there was not 'sufficient evidence that the Cumberland Church
now accepts the doctrinal basis of the Alliance'.[9] This question
was to be raised again at the next General Council; and the solution
then found put an end to the doctrinal examination of the
Churches applying for membership. But there is no doubt that
the decision of the Philadelphia Council could have had serious

consequences, since, as was to be pointed out at the Third
General Council, many of the Continental Reformed Churches
had no Confession of Faith and could not then become members
of the world family of Reformed Churches. The fact that the
Continental Churches were practically absent from the Philadelphia
Council explains why the decision met with little opposition.

As in 1877, the Second Council gave a great deal of time and
attention to missionary problems. The report of the European
section of the Committee on Foreign Missions notes that 'by none
has co-operation been more earnestly advocated than by the
missionaries themselves . . . Is each Church to aim at the transference to the mission field of its entire system, both in creed and
polity? . . . To do so would indefinitely postpone that unity of
the native Church which is generally admitted to be the most
desirable'.[10] And Rev. Dr J. Leighton Wilson said: 'What we
propose . . . is, that all the mission Churches gathered in the same
field by the representatives of the different branches of the
Presbyterian Church be encouraged to form one ecclesiastical
body; and that we carefully guard against the mistake of trying to
introduce into India, China, Africa, all the peculiarities which
characterize the different branches of the Presbyterian Church in
the home field.' And further: '. . . as soon as the Presbytery is
formed . . . the ecclesiastical powers of the evangelist, so far as
those Churches and that Presbytery are concerned, are brought to
an end. He may give advice and counsel afterwards . . . but he can
exercise no further jurisdiction over them.'[11]

The needs of the European Continent were also in the minds
of the delegates. We have already noted (see p. 35) that in its
first volume *The Catholic Presbyterian* raised the problem of what
we now call Inter-Church Aid with regard to the Waldensian
Church of Italy. At the Philadelphia Council, Dr Blaikie, reporting
in the name of the Committee on the Continent of Europe, was
able to go further. He indicated that £12,000 Sterling (U.S.
$60,000) were needed in order to raise the salaries of the
Waldensian pastors permanently (at the time of the Council they
were receiving £60 a year).

Dr Blaikie was able to announce that half of the necessary sum
had already been raised in Scotland before the Council; it was
hoped to raise another £3,000 in England, Ireland, and the
Colonies, while the U.S.A. was to provide the balance. One

marvels at the generosity of the Scottish Churches which had already raised £6,000. At that time it was a tremendous sum and it was raised without any publicity by Churches and Christian people who were conscious of their responsibilities to their weaker brethren.

It is interesting to note that the Council was also conscious of their Christian responsibility in the solution of the social problems. In a paper prepared by Dr Blaikie and presented before the Council, the author said: 'I lay the foundation of this paper on the principle that the Gospel is not only salvation for the individual, but regeneration for society; it was not soul, but society likewise that was shattered by the fall and any remedy, equal to the disorder, needed to make provision for the restoration of both.' He added: '. . . no plans for the benefit of work-people will come to much if they do not spring from a spirit of love, from a lively sense of Christian brotherhood.'[12] And Chief Justice C. D. Drake, of Washington, speaking of the needs of the working classes, mentioned 'security in their industry and in their gains', 'some solid foundation for hope of bettering their wordly condition' as well as 'a stated and regularly recurring day of rest from labor'.[13] Today these seem very mild demands, but we have to remember that they were made nearly a century ago, at a time when labour was exploited, the working man or woman having practically no legal protection. It is good to know that in an age when most Christians were totally unconcerned with their social responsibilities the men working together in the Alliance knew that they had something to say and something to do in this field.

Our forefathers were concerned with all these problems. But they did not forget that their Churches were made up of sinners and that they all needed renewal. The delegates to the Council were reminded of the essential by one of the speakers, Rev. Dr Edwin F. Hatfield, of New York. 'The one great need of the Church is the outpouring of the Spirit upon all people. The one great need of this Presbyterian Council . . . is such a baptism of the Holy Ghost as came upon the first Christian Council, at Jerusalem, on the first Pentecost . . . Most memorable in the annals of the Church would this Council be, if, thus baptized anew with the Holy Ghost, its members should return to their respective homes, so burdened with the heavenly gift, as to kindle, among the particular Churches of their several com-

munions, a burning desire and an intense zeal for the revival of
God's work among them . . .'[14]

The work of the Second General Council had now come to an
end. The sessions had been chaired in turn by delegates from
various Churches, but no President or Executive was elected to
supervise the business of the Alliance until the next General
Council. As in 1877, committees were appointed, which were
going to do excellent work in several fields, especially in those of
foreign missions and of the European Continent. A letter had been
sent by the Council to the member Churches, in which its
ecumenical spirit was clearly expressed: 'Presbyterianism has been
to us during our conference less than the consciousness of
Christendom. Christendom is one.'[15]

*   *   *

To know what the Alliance was doing and what were her main
interests during this period we have to turn again to *The Catholic
Presbyterian* which Dr Blaikie continued to edit practically unaided
until the end of 1883. The Second General Council had made an
appeal for support of the Alliance monthly; but like so many
appeals made later on, the result was very meagre.

In the last issue of 1880, the monthly indicated a positive result
of the work of the Alliance and especially of the Philadelphia
Council: 'Not the least satisfaction to American Presbyterians was
the sign of the healing of unhappy divisions at home . . . a tide
towards unity has began to rise, and it will sweep away whatever
may resist.'[16] This was perhaps too optimistic an utterance; but it
is certain that the Alliance was already felt as a positive influence
in the healing of the numerous divisions existing among
Presbyterians.

Racial problems did not yet seem to be in the forefront. But
The Catholic Presbyterian, in its June 1881 issue, had an article
raising the problem of the U.S.A. Indians and protesting against
the treatment inflicted on them. 'We are trodden down and
trampled on without mercy. We cry to God the Father of all
mercies for help . . . Brothers, why not try to save us?' writes an
Indian Presbyterian.[17]

The ecumenical spirit of the Alliance appears constantly. In
1881 there was an 'Oecumenical Wesleyan Conference' meeting in
London. The two clerks of the Council, Dr Blaikie and Dr

Mathews wrote a letter to this Conference which was reproduced in the monthly. 'Permit us . . . to give expression to the desire which we know animates many of our brethren, that the oecumenical confederations may one day have a wider scope, and may lead ultimately to closer relations among Christian Churches that, however separated otherwise, are near each other in their faith, their spirit, and their aims.'[18]

We often think of the nineteenth century as a period of peace. This was not really the case. The British–Boer antagonism had started and the Transvaal is mentioned on several occasions. In 1882 there were troubles in Egypt. But the reaction of Dr Blaikie to these troubles would certainly not be ours today. He wrote: '. . . it does not seem possible to obtain permanent tranquillity without the aid of such power as that of Great Britain.'[19] However before smiling condescendingly, let us ask ourselves what people of the end of the twenty-first century will think of our own judgments. Presbyterian leaders of the nineteenth century were men of their time, and if sometimes their attitudes seem strange to us, we cannot forget that in many respects they were ahead of their times and of their Churches.

As was seen at the Second General Council, the question of a Consensus of Reformed Confessions was in the minds of many. In 1882, Dr H. Calderwood, referring to this problem, wrote: 'If a concise consensus of reformed creeds could be attained, and could command universal approval in the Council, a great advance would be made . . . The attempt is, however, a delicate and critical one; and before it is openly entered upon, it is requisite to consider whether all Presbyterian Churches do at present occupy positions so closely analogous, as to warrant the hope of general concurrence in any concise statement of the substance of the Church's faith.'[20] Wise words indeed, which were to be taken seriously at the Third General Council.

So far, we have only spoken of Presbyterian 'men'. And indeed the Alliance was started by men and was a man's business. One has to wait until 1883 to find an article by a woman in *The Catholic Presbyterian*. But we doubt if what the author, Annie C. F. Cunningham, had to say on Women's Work in the American Church, would meet with the approval of women of today, not to speak of ardent feminists.—'Presbyterian women in the United States are, as a rule, firm in the belief that silence is woman's part in meetings where there is a mixture of sexes. Further, they believe that it is God's Word which imposes this silence and decides the question for them. But women are not excluded from Church work.'[21]

It is on a note more in tune with the feelings of our time that we would like to end our perusal of Volume X of *The Catholic Presbyterian*, the last volume of this remarkable monthly. In spite of the warm oral support given to his venture by the Philadelphia Council, Dr Blaikie had been left to edit the review single-handed and financial support for the paper was lacking. And so it is that this volume ended with a note to subscribers, saying that 'owing to the continued inadequacy of the circulation, it is necessary to stop the issue of the Journal'.[22] A regrettable, if inevitable decision.

1883 was the year of the four-hundredth anniversary of the birth of Luther, and Dr Blaikie had an excellent article on the celebrations related to the life of the Reformer. 'We hope this commemoration will help to foster a friendlier spirit than has often prevailed between the Lutheran and Reformed branches of the Protestant Church . . . The originators of the First Presbyterian Council at Edinburgh invited, *as* associates, several eminent divines of the German Evangelical Church . . . and we are sure their spirit thoroughly harmonised with that of the Council . . .'[23]

And the American Clerk of the Council, Dr G. D. Mathews, expressed his ecumenical feelings when, writing on Presbyterian and Methodist Union, he could say: 'Now, Presbyterians are Calvinists—Calvinists of many shapes and types—while Methodists are Armenian confessedly; but Armenian, as a rule, of a distinctly evangelical type. Fifty years hence there may be some "Plan of Union" existing between the two denominations, by which they may be more helpful to each other than at present; but at present they have this at least, but most notably, in common, a clear apprehension of the spiritual nature of true religion.'[24]

*   *   *

It was fitting that one of the earliest Councils of the Alliance should take place in Belfast, for the Irish Presbyterian Church had been the first, early in 1873, to accept an overture with a view to the formation of the organization. And so, when the 250 delegates walked into St Enoch's Presbyterian Church, Belfast, on Tuesday, 24 June 1884, they were welcomed by an enthusiastic congregation; the church, seating 3,000, was crowded.

The representation of the European Continent was happily better than at Philadelphia; but with eighteen delegates and four speakers, it was still pitifully small and did not make it possible for the Reformed Churches of the Continent to take a full part in the affairs of the Council. From Africa, there were only two missionaries. Australia had nine delegates, while two missionaries came from the New Hebrides and one from the Middle East. It is all the more remarkable that the concern of the Council was far wider than the constituency it represented.

In the Introduction to the *Proceedings of the Third General Council*, we read: 'Among the discussions, two were conspicuous: one bearing on the question, Whether it were desirable to attempt to frame a *Consensus* of the Reformed Creeds, that would indicate the great points of agreement among them; the other, Whether the application made by the Cumberland Presbyterian Church of the United States for admission into the Alliance, ought to be accepted or refused.

'Both were points of difficulty and delicacy, in reference to which difference of opinion was very naturally to be looked for. On many grounds it might have been desirable to define somewhat specifically the points of belief which all Churches of the Alliance must be regarded as maintaining. On the other hand, it was strongly felt that such an attempt might give rise to endless discussions, in which the time of the Alliance would be wasted, without any satisfactory conclusions being reached. As the definition of the Consensus could not be said to be a necessity, it was deemed best to let things remain for the present as they are. The temper of the Council was so reasonable and fair that at last all came to acquiesce in this conclusion. The case of the Cumberland Church involved the question of whether the Council was to make itself responsible for the *consistency* of every Church that sought admission to its fellowship. The question was discussed with great ability and admirable temper; the decision of the Council in favour of admitting the applicants, but without making itself accountable for their particular views, was carried by a great majority.'[25]

Two practical problems of importance were discussed at

length at the Belfast Council: (1) Co-operation in Foreign Missions and (2) Promotion of the Welfare of the Evangelical Church on the Continent of Europe.

On the subject of Foreign Missions, the American and the British Committees were both able to report that most of the Presbyterian Churches were ready for closer co-operation with each other.

Once more strong words were expressed on the need of the Native Church to be master of its own destiny: 'Native Churches have the same inalienable rights as have the Home Churches, to maintain their own absolute unity, their relations with each other, and their ecclesiastical autonomy, as well as their own languages, dresses, habits and other characteristics.'[26] And in a report on the 'Great Council formed at Amoy', the Belfast Council had prophetic words to say: 'It is a living example of the way to Organic Union, in which it may be God's will that the Churches in Mission lands will lead those of Christian countries that have so long failed of this grand result . . .'[27]

Once more the Council insisted on the need for the Native Church to become independent as early as possible: 'It is a prime duty of the missionary to train the native Churches to govern and support themselves, to stand and walk alone . . . Let the native presbyters be left to God and to the Word of His grace . . . The end will be reached: a strong, self-supporting, self-propagating native Church . . .'[28]

As for the role the Mission should play in the Church, it is good to read these words: 'The Mission is not an organ of the Church, but the Church is an organ of the Mission . . .'[29]

The Committee on Work on the European Continent was able to report that about £13,500 had been raised for the Waldensian Church—£1,500 over the original target. The Council approved the proposal to raise a further sum of £5,000 to help the Churches of Bohemia and Moravia with their building programme; this shows clearly that Inter-Church Aid was taken seriously by the young Alliance, even if this appellation does not appear in the reports of the Council.

At the end of the Council, the Committees on Foreign Missions and on Work on the Continent of Europe were continued, and a new Committee 'on Woman's Work' was appointed. But its membership consisted exclusively of men!

The end of the Council was also marked by a farewell to the man who, with Dr Blaikie, was the pioneer of the Alliance, President Dr J. McCosh, of Princeton, N.J. Principal Cairns, voicing the feelings of the Council, warmly thanked Dr McCosh: 'A Scotchman by birth, an Irishman in spirit and in work, and an American by adoption.'[30] The Council rose to give an ovation to this great man.

There is no doubt that, though many of the delegates were grateful for the existence of the Alliance and ready to appreciate its achievements, the majority realized that the organization needed something more in order to become an effective instrument in the service of the Reformed Churches. For those reasons the Council had appointed a 'Committee on the Better Organization of the Alliance' with Dr Blaikie as chairman. On the last day of the Council, Dr Blaikie reported that the Committee made the following proposals:

1. The appointment of an Executive Commission 'whose functions shall be, during the intervals between the meetings of the Council, to promote the objects of the Alliance'.[31] The Commission was to consist of no fewer than fifty members, and be divided into two sections, a European Section and an American Section, each having power to fill vacancies in its own number.

2. The appointment of a secretary for the Alliance. On this point, Dr Blaikie was very outspoken: 'Considering the magnitude of this Alliance, you cannot expect to do everything effectually without an efficient secretary . . . I, for my part, am quite willing— as I have done—to render all the services I can to this movement as a labour of love . . . At the same time, it is for a Council to consider whether, in making better and more permanent arrangements for the carrying out of the work, you should be dependent on services of that kind. Until you have a secretary, you lay upon the clerks an unreasonable amount of work.'[32]

In spite of these wise words, the Council only accepted the appointment of an Executive Commission, 'with power to appoint a Secretary'. But one has to wait until the Fourth General Council, in 1888, before seeing a Secretary appointed. Until then, the burden of the work was to continue to fall on the shoulders of a few devoted men, and especially on Dr Blaikie.

In his valedictory address, Principal John Cairns, of Edinburgh, expressed the ecumenical feelings of the Council when he said: 'After such great Lutheran celebrations as those in Wittenberg . . . in which all took part at home in some form or other, we must tend to more visible co-operation even with the Church of Luther . . .'[33] Ninety years later, the Leuenberg Agreement between Lutheran and Reformed Churches in Europe is at last showing that this is possible.

REFERENCES

1. *The Catholic Presbyterian*, vol. I, p. 6.
2. Idem, vol. I, p. 413.
3. Idem, vol. II, p. 347.
4. Idem, vol. III, p. 377.
5. *Proceedings 2nd General Council*, p. 31.
6. Idem, p. 71.
7. Idem, pp. 965–1123.
8. Idem, p. 394.
9. Idem, p. 24.
10. Idem, pp. 607–608.
11. Idem, pp. 619 and 623.
12. Idem, pp. 180–184.
13. Idem, pp. 190–191.
14. Idem, p. 823.
15. Idem, p. 890.
16. *The Catholic Presbyterian*, vol. IV, p. 454.
17. *The Catholic Presbyterian*, vol. V, p. 255.
18. Idem, vol. VI, p. 303.
19. Idem, vol. VIII, p. 57.
20. Idem, vol. VIII, p. 203.
21. Idem, vol. IX, p. 362.
22. Idem, vol. X, p. 476.
23. Idem, vol. X, p. 219.
24. Idem, vol. X, p. 302.
25. *Proceedings 3rd General Council*, p. IV.
26. Idem, p. 163.
27. Idem, p. 165.
28. Idem, p. 172.
29. Idem, p. 178.
30. Idem, p. 471.
31. Idem, p. 527.
32. Idem, pp. 525–526.
33. Idem, p. 541.

CHAPTER FIVE

The End of a Century

The Third General Council had come to an end. The Alliance was still without a General Secretary, in spite of the wish expressed at the Council by Dr Blaikie. There was no President to supervise the work, but an Executive Commission—in two sections—had been formed, and this was an important development in the history of the Alliance. The fact that these two sections worked independently of each other (though there was some co-ordination) was to bring difficulties in later years. But for the present those who had planned the Alliance must have been grateful for what was in fact a great progress.

In the Geneva Archives of the Alliance (WPA-EA1) we have the minutes of the European Commission since 1884. Though little business was transacted at the beginning, they show that the Alliance was anxious to develop its activities and become a positive influence in the life of its member Churches. The meetings of the European (or Eastern) Section normally took place in Edinburgh, and this quickly gave a Scottish flavour to the sessions of the Committee. There were, at the beginning at least, three meetings every year, each meeting lasting only a few hours. On several occasions, the problem of appointing a General Secretary was raised, but no provision had been made for this post by the Belfast Council, and Dr Blaikie kindly agreed to remain the honorary secretary of the Section, giving as in the past much time to the affairs of the Alliance.

From the Minutes of the Eastern Section we hear that Rev. Dr J. I. Good, Convener of the American Section of the Committee on the European Continent, and Dr Mathews, American Secretary, travelled to Germany in 1884 and that they had valuable contacts with representatives of the Reformed Churches there. In years to come the name of Dr Good was due to appear constantly in relation to the Continent of Europe. He was a member of the Reformed Church in the United States (later to become the Evangelical and Reformed Church and later still the United Church of Christ) and had an extremely keen interest in the Continent of Europe; moreover, he did more than any one else to make the Churches of the Western Section aware of their responsibilities towards their weaker brethren on the Continent. For him Inter-Church Aid was a normal part of the life of a Christian Church.

In 1885, the Churches of the Continent were asked by the Eastern Section (called at the time European Section) if they were in favour of having a Continental Section. The answers were mostly in the negative, and this is not surprising, as the Alliance had not yet become a reality to these Churches.

1886 saw an important development in the work of the Alliance. Readers will remember that *The Catholic Presbyterian* (the monthly so ably edited by Dr Blaikie) had to suspend publication at the end of 1883. This decision had been regretted and in January 1886 a new quarterly with the not very inspiring name of *The Quarterly Register* was started. Once more Dr Blaikie had agreed to become the editor of the journal, and was to continue until a full-time secretary of the Alliance was elected in 1888. It was a much more modest publication, each issue having 16 or 20 pages. But it 'put the Alliance on the map' once more and made it possible for the young organization to keep in touch with far distant Churches which otherwise knew very little of the Alliance or of its activities.

In the first year of its publication the journal, in an article entitled 'Is a Presbyterian Alliance necessarily sectarian?' refutes this thesis; the editor writes: 'Its aim has ever been to make the instrument in its hand for the advancement of the cause of Christ more efficient . . . First consolidate your Presbyterian Alliance; then the spirit of Christian brotherhood will become so strong as to desire facilities for a wider fellowship.'[1] History was to prove Dr Blaikie right; for the leaders of the Alliance, in later years, were also to become the most enthusiastic supporters of the ecumenical movement and of the cause of Christian unity.

We have already noted that Co-operation in Foreign Missions was from the beginning one of the most important fields of work of the Alliance. *The Quarterly Register* of January 1887 gives an account of an important Conference on Co-operation in Foreign

Missions, which was held in Edinburgh in October 1886. The resolutions adopted clearly show the direction into which the Alliance desired its member Churches to go. They insist on:

1. The necessity to encourage the Mission Churches in any territory.

2. The desirability of having but *one* Presbyterian Church in any territory.

3. The undesirability to have the Native Churches represented in the Courts of the Presbyterian Churches at home.[2]

Another such Conference, held in Edinburgh in November 1887, was even more insistent on the subject of unity.

*　　*　　*

1888 was to be the year of the Fourth General Council, which met in London from 3 to 12 July. It is worth noting that the Alliance Councils were more frequent then than they are now, in spite of the fact that journeys were much longer and, in many cases, much more difficult than today. One has to remember that the Alliance was at that time one of the few world organizations in the Christian world. Church leaders were not requested to attend innumerable meetings as is now the case and they enjoyed the fellowship they had in the Alliance.

The volume of *Proceedings* was edited by Dr Blaikie. In an Introduction, he noted with satisfaction:

'2. The remarkable progress which this volume records in measures for securing co-operation, and in some cases, more than co-operation, in Foreign Missions. This is one of the most substantial achievements of the Alliance.

'3. The applications for admission to the Alliance, especially from Churches and congregations in the European Continent.

'4. The appointment of Dr Mathews as permanent secretary.'[3]

Like its predecessors, the Fourth Council had no theme, but many subjects were discussed. Let us mention a few: 'How best to work the Presbyterian System', 'Intellectual Tendencies bearing on Faith', 'Social and Commercial Life', 'Church Worship', 'Aggressive Christian Work', 'Women's Work', 'The Church's Duty to the Young'. And of course there were reports of the different Committees (Foreign Missions, Continent of Europe, etc.).

c.s.—3

One of the criticisms of this Council, voiced by delegates, was that there were too many addresses and too little time for discussion. The Council always met in plenary sessions, and it was not possible to work as efficiently as would have been the case if the assembly had divided into sections. But it is not for us to criticize methods which were generally accepted at the time; and there is no doubt that with all its limitations this Council, like other Councils of the same period, helped the Alliance to play a very positive role in the life of the Reformed Churches and of the Christian Church generally.

It is good to know that this Council devoted some of its time to social problems, and that the speakers were all concerned with the conditions which existed then. Listen to what Principal MacVicar, from Canada, was saying: 'Christian nations have, for the sake of gain, corrupted and depraved Pagan lands by an infamous rum and opium traffic . . . The directors of great commercial and manufacturing enterprises have united to form huge monopolies, which have trampled under foot the laws of God and man, and which have deprived honest toilers in many instances, of a fair share of the fruit of their labour . . . The Church . . . must boldly lift her voice in God's name.'[4] But the speaker added rightly: 'The Church is not blameless in the matter under discussion. She has too much allied herself with the rich, and sought their favour, instead of trusting in God . . . She needs a baptism of the Holy Spirit that she may herself be purified . . .'[5] Other speakers were equally strong in the condemnation of the state of society and of the unfaithfulness of the Church.

A whole day was devoted to Co-operation in Foreign Missions, and it is evident that while the Council was intent on developing co-operation between Alliance member Churches, the Alliance leaders had already in mind a much larger unity. Proof of this is given by a resolution which was approved unanimously by the Council, on the recommendation of the Committee on Co-operation in Foreign Missions: 'That the Council, while pursuing its special object of promoting union in the Mission Field among the Presbyterian Churches connected with the Alliance, expresses its earnest hope that all Evangelical Churches in each foreign field may ultimately unite in one and that, where incorporation is not yet practicable, co-operation be increasingly sought.'[6]

The Council was reminded once more that Mission was not the

work of a minority, but the work of all Christians. Said Rev. J. Buchanan, Foreign Mission Secretary of the United Presbyterian Church of Scotland: 'It is time we were done with the idea of having a missionary society connected with a Church, or with a congregation; it is each congregation as a whole, it is the Church as a whole, that is to be a missionary society.'[7]

People who do not belong to our tradition often criticize the worship of our Churches. This was already the case last century, and it is why the Alliance leaders had put the problem of Reformed worship as one of the subjects to be discussed. The great Reformed liturgist, Pasteur Bersier, of Paris, gave the main address, and he was very frank: 'People complain that our form of worship is too cold and dry, that it does not leave room to the soul for pure adoration . . . They add that pure worship is too much like a long monologue, that the personality of the preacher is too prominent . . . the celebration of the Lord's Supper must be its real center', and further: 'it is a great error . . . to ignore systematically all that belongs to the past history of the worship of the Church. All that is evangelical in the Catholic Church before the Reformation belongs to us also, and we have the right to claim it as our own property.'[8] These ideas must have been new to many representatives of Presbyterian Churches, but it was necessary for them to hear Dr Bersier's criticism; there is no doubt that in this field also the Alliance was doing pioneer work.

Though the Fourth Council, like its predecessors, was mainly a British and American affair, ten addresses were given by representatives of the Churches of the European Continent on the state of their Churches; and four representatives from Australia, New Zealand and South Africa made people realize that the Church was expanding in many areas of the world.

The delegates to the Council were not only concerned with the progress of the Gospel; they knew that there were many hostile forces at work, and they were ready to face realities. One of them was the sale of liquor in the Congo, and indeed in all of Eastern and Western Africa. Rev. Dr F. F. Ellinwood, who was later to play such an outstanding role in developing ecumenical co-operation in Foreign Missions, was adamant in his condemnation of this traffic. The Council passed a resolution asking its member Churches to take the matter up with their respective governments in order to stop this scandalous traffic.[9]

Though international peace did not seem menaced at that time, the Council gave full support to a Memorial received from the Society of Friends, asking that arbitration be substituted for war in all conflicts. This was to remain a resolution!

Having learnt that the Lambeth Conference of Anglican bishops was presently convening in London, the Council voted an amicable resolution affirming the desire of the Presbyterian Churches 'to maintain friendly relations with their clergy and people all over the world'.[10] Speaking of this Motion before its adoption by the Council, Dr Philip Schaff, a great prophet of unity, said: '. . . The subject of reunion of Christendom is in the air. We are all believers in the one flock and the one Shepherd . . . I have not wisdom enough to say when and how the solution of this great problem is to be accomplished, but I know that it is to be brought about before the world can be converted to Christ.'[11]

The Council took some very important decisions to improve the organization of the Alliance. At long last it was decided to elect a permanent Secretary. Rev. Dr G. D. Mathews, who had moved to Quebec, Canada, after his ministry in New York, was unanimously appointed General Secretary of the Alliance (July 1888). The same Council also appointed Rev. Dr Wm H. Roberts, Stated Clerk of the Presbyterian Church in the U.S.A., as American Secretary, an honorary post to this day. Then the European and American Sections were officially re-named 'Eastern' and 'Western' and were so called until the 1954 General Council at Princeton.

Taking leave of Dr Blaikie in his capacity as honorary Secretary of the Alliance and Editor of its Journal was a solemn and moving moment. Many speakers spoke of his great abilities, his vision, his earnestness, tact and loving spirit. Added to this the amount of work undertaken by this one man is incredible. The motion adopted reads as follows: 'When the history of this great organization, which has already been productive of so much good, comes to be written, no name will hold a more honourable place in it than that of Dr Blaikie.'[12] The writer of this present history, having carefully studied the archives of the formative years of the Alliance, cordially agrees with this.

In expressing his thanks it was typical that Dr Blaikie should remind the Council that it was Dr McCosh, the venerable father on the other side of the Atlantic, who was the real originator of this movement. Happily for the Alliance this was not to be the end of the services of Dr Blaikie to the organization.

Before separating, the members of the Council voted that each of the two Sections of the Alliance should have a Chairman, elected until the next General Council, and that the chairman of each Section should hold the office of President of the Alliance alternatively. And so, in July 1888, Dr Blaikie was unanimously elected as the first President of the Alliance.

* * *

While the London Council was still in session, the two Sections met to decide on the first diplomatic mission undertaken by the Alliance. The sections voted to send a deputation to King Leopold of Belgium to bring to him the Alliance's concern on the question of the liquor traffic in the Congo. The deputation finally went to Brussels in February 1890, during the International Anti-Slavery Conference held in that city and expressed the views of the Sections on the questions under consideration to the British and American Ministers there as well as to the President of the Conference, Baron Lambermont.

On the suggestion of Dr Mathews, the two Sections voted in 1890 to exchange Minutes of their respective meetings. However the American and British Churches had very different interests. They were of course both concerned with the welfare of the Reformed Churches on the Continent of Europe and in both sections Mission Committees were pushing for an ever closer co-operation between the Churches of the Alliance. But it will soon be seen that each Section went its own way, and that the Western Section took initiatives which were well in advance of the Eastern Section.

Religious problems were not the only concern of the Alliance at that time. We have already seen that a deputation was sent to Brussels at the time of the Anti-Slavery Conference. This was not the end of the Alliance's interest. In the November 1890 issue of *The Quarterly Register* there is a very strong article on some of the decisions taken there. 'Five of the European nations . . . have stepped forward and cooly divided amongst themselves nearly two-thirds of the vast continent of Africa; at first this reads like a huge joke, for on what plea or right could any of these parties base their conquest? The present inhabitants of Africa have not asked them to do this, and unquestionably, the native rulers and princes will not thank them for it. One is almost reminded by it of the division of Europe by Attila or by Alaric among their followers: Might being held to make RIGHT.'[13]

It is good to know that at a time when most Europeans were unconcerned with these problems or accepted annexations without hesitation the Alliance General Secretary protested against this immoral policy of the great European Powers.

At about the same time, the name 'New Hebrides' begins to appear frequently in *The Quarterly Register* and in the Minutes of the two Sections. The reason is explained in the February 1891 issue of the journal. 'Great uneasiness is felt in Australia in reference to the New Hebrides. In these islands we Presbyterians have a most interesting and efficient mission; but the natives are still being taken away in vessels, owned and sailed by white men, into what is practically slavery. The new Caledonian authorities and colonists are steadfastly advancing on lines that point out to annexation as their ultimate object . . . At its last meeting, the Eastern Section of the Alliance determined to move in the matter.'[14]

The fate of the Jews in Tsarist Russia was miserable, and the Alliance joined hands with other organizations to try and secure some relief for these persecuted people. The February 1891 issue of *The Quarterly Register* mentions a great meeting which had recently taken place in London, at which it had been decided to send a petition to the Tsar. The Eastern Section of the Alliance had been represented at this meeting. A Memorial was adopted and forwarded to Russia for presentation to the Tsar. The Editor sadly comments: 'This memorial has been returned to England, not having been even presented.'[15]

*   *   *

We are now in 1892, the year of the Fifth General Council of the Alliance, which took place in Toronto from 21 to 30 September. As this Council was held in the Western Hemisphere, representatives from the Continent of Europe were again very few; so were those from Asia and Africa; only from Australia was there a fair number of delegates. For the first time the Council had a President, the well loved Dr Blaikie who, having been in charge of the work of the Alliance for the last four years, was 'au courant' with all the difficulties and problems past and present.

The Council did some good work, and we shall mention it in the coming pages. But the present writer cannot resist recounting an incident which had nothing to do with theology, but must have been remembered for a long time by all the participants in the Council.

Inevitably, the Canadian Committee had organized a trip to the Niagara Falls. This took place on Saturday, 24 September. The Minutes of the Council indicate that on Monday morning, 26 September, a motion was adopted, which reads as follows: 'The Council hereby records the expression of its admiration for the courageous conduct of the Rev. J. Ramsay, LL.B., one of its delegates [from Ballymoney, one of the delegates of the Presbyterian Church in Ireland, *Ed.*] who, under God's providence, prevented the excursion to Niagara Falls from being saddened by a very melancholy accident.'[16] In a footnote, there is the following explanation: 'it should be stated that Mr Ramsay, his Toronto hostess, Mrs Grimson, and her two daughters were among the Council excursionists to Niagara. Walking across the Upper Suspension bridge, Mrs Grimson slipped, and, falling forward, fell through an opening in the railing. Providentially, at that moment she struck one of the guys that connect the bridge with its great cables, and was thus thrown back, falling on a girder that was about a foot wide, and about ten feet below the flooring of the bridge. This she instantly seized and clang to it for her life, for there was nothing between her and the deep boiling river that one hundred and seventy feet below was hurrying down to the Rapids. Mr Ramsay at once climbed over the railing, seized the guy that Mrs Grimson had struck, climbed by its means down to the girder to which she was still clinging, and catching hold of her almost lifeless body, sustained it till they were both rescued from their frightening position,'[17] This of course made headlines. Commenting on this action the *Toronto Globe* wrote: 'A false step, a faint heart or a weak head, and he would have been precipitated into the angry, rushing river nearly 200 feet below, and Mrs Grimson would have been his companion into death. But there was no faltering, fainting or weakness, and Mr Ramsay came back to Toronto the hero of the day.'[18]

Apart from this courageous exploit, the Council was content to devote its energies to less dangerous exercises.

In his Presidential address at the opening of the Council Dr Blaikie struck a note which was to reappear more than fifty years later in the Basle Statement on 'The World Presbyterian Alliance in the Present Ecumenical situation' (1951). The Alliance President, speaking on the achievements of the Alliance, said: 'If it has made us more Presbyterian, it has made us more catholic too . . . the more you have of union, the more you desire to have, and, for my part, I think the day may not be very distant when something will be accomplished in the direction in which our friend, Dr McCosh, has lately been working—when a federal union may be established among the great evangelical Churches . . .'[19]

The report of the Committee of the Western Section on Co-operation in Foreign Missions, presented by its convener, Rev. Dr F. F. Ellinwood, went in the same direction. It recommended that 'it be the constant aim of our missions . . . to promote the broader co-operation among all Protestant missions.'[20]

The report also demanded that at a meeting of the Executive officers of the various Mission Boards of the Western Section, which the Committee wanted to organize, 'during one day they invite a broader conference with representatives of the missionary boards and societies of other Protestant Churches.'[21] This decision, as we shall see later, was to have important consequences for the whole missionary movement.

Dr Ellinwood was a Presbyterian, but he was first of all an Evangelical Christian. In his report, he said: 'we hail with delight the evidence that all Protestant denominations are drawing together in their missionary work, and that Presbyterians are everywhere among the first in the promotion of this broader movement.'[22] No doubt the Alliance was beginning to influence the thinking of our Churches.

Dr Ellinwood was not only concerned with unity; the racial problem also preoccupied him greatly. Speaking of the Indians in the U.S.A. he said: 'If you leave the Indian alone to the laws of the survival of the fittest . . . he will certainly go to the wall . . . I should dread the coming of that day when the American people shall become so dead to sentiment as to forget that they have entered upon the noble heritage of this people without rendering any just return.'[23]

Along with racial problems the Council was also concerned with social questions. One of the speakers at the Council, Principal Grant, of Canada, said things which are strangely contemporary and which, had they been accepted at the end of the nineteenth century, would have meant a more harmonious development of the capital-labour relations than has been the case. Speaking on 'The Wage Question' Principal Grant said: 'When all charges have been met, justice demands that the profits should be divided equitably between employers and employed. In other words, the employed . . . must be regarded as partners, instead of being classed with machinery . . . The wage system, then, must be supplemented by PROFIT-SHARING.'[24] Dr Grant then launched a passionate appeal to the Churches of the Reformed family: 'Let us go on to full growth; that is, let us apply our principles to the making of men and to the reconstruction of Society. A Church may call itself Holy, Catholic, Apostolic, and Presbyterian, but if it cannot apply its principles to the questions of the day, it is dead.'[25] Did the 'Church and Society' Conference gathered in Geneva under the auspices of the World Council of Churches, in 1966, speak differently?

In reply to an overture from the Reformed Church in America the Council decided to add to the existing Committees of the Alliance a Committee on Co-operation in Home Missions. This Committee was to render good services in developing a more active co-operation between the member Churches in their respective countries, and especially in the U.S.A.

Before the close of the Council the Special Committee on the Bohemian Commemoration Fund was able to report that over £5,500 Sterling had been raised to help the Reformed Church of Bohemia and Moravia.

For the first time President McCosh had been unable to attend the Council, on account of age and ill-health; the Council had sent him a very cordial message. At the end of the Council a formal farewell was given to Dr Blaikie, the retiring President of the Alliance and its most active agent during the formative years. A new President was elected in the person of Rev. Dr Talbot W. Chambers, of New York, a minister of the Reformed Church in America.

New men made their appearance in the Alliance but the aims of the organization remained the same; and if the leaders could

look backwards with gratitude on the first achievements, they
knew that tremendous tasks lay ahead for them to tackle.

*   *   *

The General Secretary of the Alliance, Dr Mathews, was a great
traveller. Of necessity, he was often away from the Alliance
Office, which had been established in London. Before the Toronto
Council he had already visited several Churches on the Continent;
in 1893 we find him in Egypt, Syria and other parts of Asia
Minor, as well as in Cyprus, Greece and several countries of
Western Europe. This led the Eastern Section to discuss the
possibility of holding an Alliance meeting or a General Council
on the Continent. Times however were not yet ripe for such a
venture, and one has to wait until the twentieth century before
seeing the Alliance launching out on the European Continent.

At the Western Section meeting of April 1893 Dr Ellinwood
was able to report that the hope he had expressed at the Fifth
General Council had become a reality. A Conference of the
representatives of the Mission Boards of several Evangelical
Churches had been held in New York on 12 January 1893,
'when many important points of mission policy had been discussed, with great profit and much interest to those present . . .
it was in contemplation to hold similar conferences in the
near future'.[26] In 1895 Dr Ellinwood was able to report to the
Section that 'it had been agreed to hold these conferences
annually'.[27]

Co-operation in Home Missions had become an important item
on the agenda of the Western Section, and in 1895 the Special
Committee arranged for a meeting with representatives of Home
Mission Boards attending the Section meeting. This was to
prepare a statement of general principles of co-operation, though
the representatives of the different Churches agreed that a considerable amount of co-operation was already taking place. In
1896 the Section adopted a plan for increased co-operation and
had it sent to the Synods and General Assemblies of the member
Churches in the U.S.A. and Canada.

At the same time the Western Section was trying to sponsor the
creation of a Federation of the Reformed Churches in America
(U.S.A.). The meeting of October 1894 expressed its gratification
'that the subject of the Federation of the Reformed Churches

holding the Presbyterian System, is now under consideration by the several Churches'.[28]

In 1894 Dr Mathews undertook a four month visit to the Churches of the Reformed family in Southern Africa, and especially in South Africa, though he also travelled to Mozambique and to Basutoland (now Lesotho); he had numerous contacts with Churches and Missions established in those lands. He particularly wished to attend the Synod of the Dutch Reformed Church of Cape Colony, in October 1894; he brought them the greetings of the Alliance. This journey was important, as it assured the Churches of South Africa, and especially the Boer Churches, that they were really part of the Alliance. Unfortunately the Boer War was soon to destroy the goodwill created by this visit, and, as a result, the Dutch Reformed Churches were shortly to end their membership.

*   *   *

A glance at *The Quarterly Register* during those years shows that the problem of religious liberty was still one of the main concerns of our organization. In May 1892 an attack had been made on the building of the Evangelical Church in Athens. The November issue of the same year reports persecution of the Methodists in Austria, and especially in Vienna. It is good to know that the Alliance was as concerned by these persecutions as by the attack on the Evangelicals in Greece. In 1894 *The Quarterly Register* gives facts about the persecution of Russian Stundists; they were devoted Christians whose only offence was to have left the official Russian Church. The article ends: 'For us, all that is certainly possible is prayer, prayer to the God of the persecuted, that He would sustain our brethren . . . and restrain the wrath of the persecutor . . .'[29]

The February issue of 1895 deplores the death, at the end of 1894, of President James McCosh, at the age of 83. The Editor pays tribute to this great man: 'To Dr McCosh belongs the credit of having set before the American Churches the idea of a great Confederation of Reformed and Presbyterian Churches . . . His name and labours secured support for it in those early days when friends were comparatively few, and when its present range of practical work still lay far beyond the vision of even its promoter.'[30]

Soon afterwards, the President of the Alliance, Rev. Dr T. W.

Chambers, died, and the May issue of the *Quarterly* reminds readers of the active interest taken in the Alliance by the great New York pastor.

*   *   *

The Sixth General Council of the Alliance took place in Glasgow, Scotland, from 17 to 26 June 1896. The Chair was occupied by Rev. Dr W. H. Roberts, American Secretary, who was at the same time President of the Alliance, having replaced Dr T. W. Chambers, who had died shortly before the Council.

In his Preface to the volume of *Proceedings* the General Secretary, Dr Mathews, notes the concern of the Council for:

1. The Continent of Europe and especially the smaller, struggling Churches.

2. The Younger Churches. This is the first time this term appears in the annals of the Alliance and it is significant. For, as Dr Mathews wrote: 'Another object of the Alliance is the caring for the Younger Churches rising on the Mission Field, the aiding in the formation of such Churches, and then the taking of them by the hand and formally connecting them, as independent organizations, with the Presbyterian household . . . and at the Council itself the Alliance formally recognised native Christians in Formosa . . . as an independent Church, a portion of the common family, and as such entitled to take their place in the brotherhood of the Alliance.'[31]

Mission problems again played an important part in the life of the Council. The reports of the two Committees (Eastern and Western Sections) make very interesting reading. Dr Ellinwood was of course able to report about the annual Conferences of representatives of the Boards of Foreign Missions of the U.S.A. and Canada, which the Alliance had initiated. These conferences had proved such a success that it had been deemed unnecessary to continue holding conferences of Presbyterian representatives only.

The first fruits of these conferences in the field of unity were beginning to become apparent. Rev. Dr J. Gillespie, of New York, reporting on these conferences, was able to write: 'It is hoped that the suggestion made by the Conference at its recent session, that an Ecumenical Council be held in America within the next five years, may meet with favour. Thus while others are discussing the subject of Christian unity, almost before we know it, it will be an accomplished fact through co-operation at home and abroad in the great work of world evangelisation.'[32]

Once more the concern for religious freedom was apparent at the Council. The fate of the Armenians was becoming more difficult in the Ottoman Empire. The Council felt compelled 'to record their protest against the relentless oppression and barbarity which has devastated many scenes of peaceful industry and desolated many thousands of homes'. The resolution further said: 'The Council feel constrained to urge on the Christian Governments of Europe and America . . . to concert measures to bring such inhuman misgovernment to a speedy end.'[33]

The Stundists of Russia were not forgotten either, though the Alliance knew that they had no power to interfere in the affairs of the Tsarist Empire. They passed a resolution of sympathy, exhorting these brethren to 'remain faithful to their Evangelical position'.[34] This was little indeed, but there is no doubt that the Alliance was watching for every opportunity to help.

Social problems were again in the forefront. The delegates were aware that the society in which they lived was far from Christian and that they could not accept it as it was. This was made plain by Rev. Dr Donald MacLeod, when he addressed the Council: 'No conquering army ever left in its track a more terrible legacy of desolation and death than has the pressure of competition in its march towards wealth and success . . . The Church may have only an indirect relationship to such matters as the supply of decent accommodation for the housing of the poor, sanitation, underpaid labour, with consequent poverty . . . and yet, these matters have a close connection with the elevation of the people.'[35]

The problem of peace once more occupied the minds of the delegates and the Council adopted a Memorial on Arbitration which both Sections were requested to present to the Governments of their areas. The Memorial says: 'We, the representatives of the Presbyterian Churches . . . humbly memorialise the Government of . . . in support of peaceful Arbitration as the wise and Christian method of settling disputes between nations . . .'[36] One could point out that they were not very successful; but the fact remains that the Presbyterian representatives of the end of last century were aware of the growing danger of international tensions and were anxious to find a peaceful solution to these tensions.

Rev. Dr J. Marshall Lang, of Glasgow, was elected President of the Alliance and the Council came to an end.

* * *

We have already noted that Dr Mathews, the General Secretary of the Alliance, was a great traveller. But what he had done up till now was little compared to the long, strange and arduous journey which he was due to undertake in 1897, when he was nearly 70, and which would take him, by train, boat and horseback, to Russia, through Armenia and as far as Persia. The Eastern Section had 'instructed him to make full enquiries into the condition of the Stundists in Russia, and into the condition of the Armenians. He was also directed to attend the annual Synod of the Native Evangelical Church in Western Persia'.[37]

The story of this journey, as written by Dr Mathews, appears in several issues of *The Quarterly Register* of 1898 and 1899. It is really fascinating and the present writer's only regret is that shortage of space does not permit large quotations from Dr Mathews' report. One cannot resist however giving a few extracts from his diary. After having travelled through Russia and visited the Stundists Dr Mathews went to Tiflis. He writes: 'My stay in Tiflis was unwillingly prolonged by a severe illness consequent on the singularly stifling heat. When recovered . . . I started for Western Persia, taking a somewhat unfrequented route that I might visit some Armenian relief stations in rather out of the way localities.

'One leaves Tiflis by the Baku train to Akstafa, a station of few hours distant, and here,—Good-bye to Western civilisation . . . The modes of travelling are not numerous. There are three classes of vehicles; . . . every ten or twelve miles one finds a "post house" at which the horses are changed . . . At every one there is a common waiting room with a couple of sloping board beds on which the traveller can rest his limbs, oftentimes sharing the bed with its numerous residents.'[38]

After reaching Erivan, Dr Mathews went to Etchmiadzin, the famous monastery of the Catholicos of the Armenian Church, where he spent two days, before continuing his journey to Persia. His impressions of the country are not those one normally finds in the prospectus of a tourist agency: 'In an instant scales fell from our eyes, and we knew that the beliefs of a lifetime as to the orient splendor had been dreams . . . it was squalid filth and poverty that came before us.' His first experiences of Persian officialdom were not encouraging, but Dr Mathews was a sturdy Scot, and the following incident shows that he did not easily lose his head. 'Our passports had been collected by a man who reported himself to be the representative of the Shah, that they might be "visaed", which meant, of course backshish. Just before going to sleep he returned, demanding ten Pounds Sterling as his fee, when he was told to keep the passports. Most politely he assured us that we could not leave the village without them . . . We said it was too late to discuss business . . . Next morning a messenger came to receive the ten Pounds when we replied we would dispense with the passports, and proceed to mount our horses. Before we had got a dozen yards, the man himself arrived with the passports, the backshish [Dr Mathews had agreed to give five shillings, *Ed.*] was duly paid over, and hands shaken all round, with a warning not to attempt such extortion again.

'The reputation of the district not being too good, we had obtained a couple of soldiers for protective purposes . . . At last darkness came on, leaving us with several hours' travel before us. Our horses were tired, and their riders not less so, when we entered the remarkable gorge that leads to the town of Maku . . . It was soon so dark that the reins were left on the horses' necks, while every now and then a soldier would make a rapid gallop round some huge boulder to see if there were gathered near it any persons likely to be dangerous . . . Suddenly we found ourselves in a city . . . where we found shelter for the night, glad indeed to lie down after some twelve hours continually in the saddle.'[39]

I doubt if many General Secretaries of world organizations ever undertook such a trip and accepted as cheerfully as Dr Mathews the hazards of the journey.

Dr Mathews had not gone to Persia for touristic purposes; he had been commissioned by the Alliance to visit the Nestorians, or rather the Evangelical group which had come out of the historic Nestorian Church in 1862 and was known as the Syriac Evangelical Church of Persia, a Church with 36 organized congregations, nearly 40 pastors and 2,500 communicants. His visit was deeply appreciated by this small evangelical minority and he was able to give them real encouragement.

* * *

There is no doubt that at the end of the nineteenth century many British and American Presbyterians were unhappy about the state of affairs in the Evangelical Churches of Europe. They had the feeling that there was a great deal of 'infidelity' and that it would be good to start evangelizing Europe as if the Reformed Churches there did not exist. As a matter of fact, at the beginning of this century, one American Church was seriously thinking of starting a Presbyterian Mission on the Continent. It is probable that, had the Alliance not intervened this would have happened, with results which might have been disastrous for the cause of Reformed unity. *The Quarterly Register* of November 1897 was already discussing the problem in an article entitled 'Helping the Continental Churches', and the words of wisdom in this article were not superfluous: 'plainly, in seeking to be of service to these brethren, we must not so act as to convey a censure on them, or to derogate from their position. They are our brethren, our equals, and remembering the golden rule, we must carefully avoid anything that would savour of our being more righteous than they, or as if they were objects of pity or of blame.

'In seeking to aid these brethren, the first thought with many is—Oh, let us commence a Mission . . . Yet nothing could be better fitted to defeat the object sought than such a proposal.

'. . . It amounts to helping existing Churches by planting another in their midst, and one composed of people drawn from their own congregations . . .'[40] The article ends by reminding Presbyterians of Britain and America that the best way to help is to give more assistance to the Continental Churches, as the Alliance is already trying to do. There again we have one of the principles of modern Inter-Church Aid clearly expressed; it is good to know that in this field also the Alliance was doing pioneering work.

On 10 June 1899, Rev. Dr William Garden Blaikie passed peacefully on to a fuller life. In the August issue of *The Quarterly Register* the Editor rightly stated that 'by the death of Dr Blaikie, the Alliance has lost not merely one of its earlier supporters, but one to whom it is indebted practically for its very existence . . . At the close of the Edinburgh Council . . . the burden of guiding the new association devolved on Dr Blaikie. During the next dozen of years, Dr Blaikie *was* the Alliance, and by the influence of his name, the wisdom of his counsels, the abundance of his labours, secured for it the co-operation of all our Churches . . .

'At the time of his death he was preparing a report on the Religious Condition of the European Continent for the Washington Council and had agreed, at the request of the Eastern Section, to write a paper for the Council on the history and work of the Alliance for the first quarter-century.'[41] We can only regret that death prevented Dr Blaikie from writing this important chapter of the history of the Alliance. But if the history is unwritten, his work remains, and the Alliance will never forget this remarkable and devoted leader.

*   *   *

The Seventh General Council of the Alliance met in Washington, D.C., from 27 September to 6 October 1899, only three years after the Glasgow Council. There was a good British representation, but the Continental Churches of Europe were practically unrepresented; only one delegate of the Waldensian Church of Italy had made the journey across the Atlantic.

The Council was grateful to God for the first quarter-century of the existence of the Alliance and the General Secretary reminded the Council of the encouraging achievements of the first 25 years.

As in former Councils, the work in the Mission field and its implications for the Churches at home were in the centre of the discussions. At the time of writing the history of the Alliance, when China is being recognized as a great nation, it is good to read what was said about China at the Washington Council, when China was being humiliated and many people had nothing but disdain for this land: 'The Chinese Government may be said to be breaking up . . . What we are persuaded of is that it is a great nation, and has a great future before it.'[42]

We have seen that the Council expressed its joy at the achievements of the Alliance in the first quarter-century of its existence. But the delegates assembled at Washington knew that more could be done and the General Secretary spoke on 'Methods for increasing the efficiency of the Alliance'. He thought that the Council might address 'words of counsel, request, or even censure to kings, governors and men in high places in our lands.'[43] Dr Mathews also wanted the Alliance to make its voice heard in problems related to the conduct and the social life of people.

Dr Mathews ended with words which sound strangely up to date: 'The closing century has placed our Churches amid conditions they never saw before. Our Council might aid them in learning from the methods of business . . . One of the notable features of modern times is the prominence of SPECIALISM in every department of secular business. This very feature we may soon have to deal with inside the Christian Church. Our huge modern congregations call for a combination of organizing power, of pastoral oversight, of preaching gifts, and of public leadership, that but few men are ever found to possess. Hence we may soon require to choose between our ordinary system of medium-sized congregations with an individual bishop, and one in which, like the cathedrals previous to the Reformation, or in the Collegiate system of some Continental Protestant Churches today, there is a two-fold, a three-fold, or even a four-fold ministry of men of special gifts with separate departments of work . . . What the world demands is not men born and brought up in the spirit and life of a century ago, but men . . . who belong to the century which is to come; men that will lead the Church into new activities.'[44]

The Washington Council was also seriously preoccupied by social problems. Rev. Dr E. B. Coe, of New York, reminded the delegates that 'it is high time that the mutual antagonism of Christianity and Socialism should come to an end . . . The Church must regain the confidence of the masses of the people by manifesting an active interest in the efforts which these are making to secure better economic and industrial conditions. It must show itself fearless and faithful in rebuking the iniquitous measures by which the poor are often defrauded and crushed. It must enforce, not the doctrine only, but the ethics of the New Testament.'[45]

The international situation gave rise for anxiety. The tension between the Boers and the British was growing and war was to start soon after the Washington Council. Delegates were aware of the responsibilities of the Alliance, as the Dutch Reformed Churches of South Africa as well as the British Churches were involved in the conflict. The Council passed a resolution, expressing 'the earnest hope and prayer that a peaceful solution of the present difficulties may be reached'.[46]

On the whole subject of peace, the Council heard an address by a Scottish delegate, Professor Dr Paterson, of Edinburgh, 'Arbitration in the light of Christianity'. Dr Paterson was certainly ahead of his time, and of many Christians, even today, when he said: 'Christian nations have not yet realized the position they ought to take up in relation to war. But Christians have now reached such a stage of development that inconsistency, if henceforth persisted in, will require to be described by a harsher term, and characterized as deliberate disobedience to the Prince of Peace . . . "Unquestioning obedience" is just what no free Christian ought ever to pledge himself to give; for if he is ordered to fight in an unjust cause, he is always bound to disobey his superior officer.'[47]

This did not prevent our forefathers from being proud of their time and of the achievements of the nineteenth century. Listen to these words of Rev. Dr H. Duffield, of New York: 'Whatever may have been the length of the creative days, the last one hundred years have witnessed a practical re-creation of the world. By mechanical invention, by commercial development, by romantic and heroic exploration, by daring and scientific investigation, the earth has become a new planet, and the conditions of earth-life are largely transformed.'[48]

Analysing the progress of the Christian Church during the nineteenth century, the speaker saw it along three lines: Missionary activity, Ecclesiastical fraternity and Spiritual intensity. He was optimistic for the future. Events in the twentieth century were to show that this optimistic vision was not entirely justified. But on one point it was. 'Today,' he said, 'reverent students are on their knees before the pages which tell of the Spirit's mission. Eager hearts are watching for the manifestation of His presence as they do watch for the morning. There is a deepening thirst for a present-day experience of the fullness of His power . . . The longing in the heart of Christendom for a repetition in our time of such displays of the Spirit's presence is a vast step onward and upward in the direct line of the grandest progress.'[49]

This 'repetition' was not to take place immediately in the Churches of the Reformed family. But the beginning of the twentieth century was to see the birth and development of the Pentecostal Churches, which have already played a significant role in the life of Christendom. With the development of the neo-pentecostal movement in the classical Churches, since 1960, one can hope that the 'vision' of the New York pastor may become a blessed reality.

Rev. Principal Dr Wm Caven, of Knox College, Toronto, a minister of the Presbyterian Church of Canada, was elected President of the Alliance, and the Council came to an end.

REFERENCES

1. *The Quarterly Register*, vol. I, no. 3, p. 33.
2. Idem, vol. I, no. 5, p. 72.
3. *Proceedings 4th General Council*, pp. XIV and XV.
4. Idem, p. 144.
5. Idem, p. 145.
6. Idem, p. 186.
7. Idem, p. 175.
8. Idem, p. 217 et seq.
9. Idem, p. 312.
10. Idem, p. 360.
11. Idem, p. 363.
12. Idem, p. 368.
13. *The Quarterly Register*, vol. II, no. 8, p. 122.
14. Idem, vol. II, no. 9, p. 137.
15. Idem, vol. II, no. 9, p. 137.
16. *Proceedings 5th General Council*, p. 157.
17. Idem, p. 157.
18. *The Quarterly Register*, vol. III, no. 4, p. 71.
19. *Proceedings 5th General Council*, p. 30.
20. Idem, appendix, p. 98.
21. Idem, appendix, p. 99.
22. *Proceedings 5th General Council*, p. 102.
23. Idem, p. 182.
24. Idem, p. 358.
25. Idem, p. 360.
26. Western Section Minutes, April 1893, p. 3.
27. Idem, April 1895, p. 3.
28. Western Section Minutes, October 1894, p. 3.
29. *The Quarterly Register*, vol. III, no. 9, p. 145.
30. Idem, vol. IV, no. 1, p. 1.
31. *Proceedings 6th General Council*, p. VII.
32. Idem, p. 238.
33. Idem, pp. 227–228.
34. Idem, p. 464.

35. Idem, p. 330 et seq.
36. Idem, p. 443.
37. Eastern Section Minutes, May 13, 1897, p. 2.
38. *The Quarterly Register*, vol. V, no. 3, p. 47.
39. Idem, vol. V, no. 5, p. 86.
40. Idem, vol. IV, no. 12, p. 227.
41. Idem, vol. V, no. 7, p. 126.
42. *Proceedings 7th General Council*, p. 139.
43. Idem, p. 204.
44. Idem, pp. 205–207.
45. Idem, pp. 270 and 277.
46. Idem, p. 257.
47. Idem, pp. 322 and 326.
48. Idem, p. 373.
49. Idem, pp. 380–381.

CHAPTER SIX

The Dawn of a New Century

The delegates to the Washington Council had expressed the desire to start the new century with new men and new methods. What was to be the result of these decisions?

In Scotland, the year 1900 was marked by the union of the Free Church of Scotland and of the United Presbyterian Church, under the name of United Free Church. A small fragment of the Free Church dissented, but the great majority joined the new Church. This was a great step forward in the bringing together of the different segments of Scottish Presbyterianism and there is no doubt that the Alliance contributed to this reunion. During the meeting of the Western Section held on 15 November 1900, the American Secretary, Dr Roberts, said: 'The highly auspicious movement which resulted in this union of the Free Church and of the United Presbyterian Church of Scotland was felt by your officers to be so vitally related to the work and influence of the Alliance, that they forwarded to the accredited representatives of both Churches, on behalf of the Section, a letter of congratulations.'[1]

1901 saw the formation of the Presbyterian Church of Australia, and if the problem there was only the union of the different State Churches, the result was the same; and there again it is certain that the Alliance encouraged our Australian brethren to go ahead with their plans for greater unity. So much so that the General Secretary had been commissioned by the Washington Council to attend the union meeting of the Australian Churches; and only a severe illness at the time prevented him from discharging this duty.

The Western Section also had cause for rejoicing. At the meeting of 15 November 1900 of the Executive Commission, the Foreign Missions Committee was able to report: 'It had been extremely gratifying to the Foreign Missions Committee, and equally so, we are sure, to the Commission, to know that the splendid Ecumenical Conference in New York, with its inspiring influence, was a practical result of the work of the Alliance.'[2]

In other fields the Alliance was less successful. The Boer war had aroused much agitation among the Reformed Churches of the Continent, who were favourable to the Boers. A letter had been received from Switzerland by the General Secretary, 'asking the Alliance to use its influence with the British Government to obtain "a prompt and fair settlement of the South African war" '.[3] In its meeting of 24 October, the Eastern Section (which was in fact British) answered 'that it is not within the sphere of the Alliance to intermeddle in political questions'.[4] A strange answer indeed when one thinks of the declarations of the Washington Council about arbitration and about the necessary refusal for the Christian to obey his government in an unjust war. But the men of the Alliance were men of their time; and more than that, they were British and it was difficult for them to see the injustice of the South African war. Christians who, during the First—and even the Second—World War sided so completely with the government of their country should think twice before passing too hard a judgment on our British brethren of 1900; we can only regret that the Alliance, on this occasion, missed the possibility of speaking prophetically.

1900 was also the year of the Boxer rising in China. Here again we find little real Christian spirit and little understanding on the part of the Alliance. This may have been due to bad information (the August 1900 issue of *The Quarterly Register* speaks of wholesale massacres of diplomats and missionaries which were later proved not to have taken place, though many people were killed); but today, it is hard to accept what was written in the November issue of the same magazine: 'The Chinese must be led to know that the might of Europe is greater than theirs, but to deal with the strong hand would be branded by our sentimentalists as barbaric cruelty, while to deal leniently in hope of securing co-operation in reorganising their country and their Government would be regarded by the Chinese themselves as timidity and fear, and so our Government have to make a momentous choice.'[5]

At the beginning of the century the Western Section showed great activity and the minutes of the meetings of the Executive Commission have many interesting facts to report. In the meeting of 23 April 1902, the Foreign Missions Committee reported on the Conference held in Shanghai in October 1901, at which ten different Missions belonging to five Presbyterian Churches were represented. The Western Section passed a strong resolution in favour of the union of all these groups; it further voted to recommend 'that all Presbyterian Churches to be formed in future [in China, *Ed.*] be organized as Chinese Churches, independent of the Home Churches'.[6]

The Section was also interested in the unity of Presbyterian Churches in India, and the Section heard with interest that the 7th Council of the Presbyterian Alliance of India, which met in Allahabad in December 1901, had 'decided to submit to the various Presbyterian bodies in India proposals for a United Church'.[7]

The Committee on Home Missions of the Western Section did not remain inactive either. On its recommendation the Section resolved in April 1902 'that special attention be called to the necessity for the adaptation of the Home Mission work to the changing conditions of our population, and for more systematic efforts to reach all classes and all communities with the Gospel.'[8]

The year 1903 saw the withdrawal from the Alliance of the Dutch Reformed Churches of South Africa. The Clerk of the Synod of Transvaal explained this withdrawal 'on the ground that the Alliance seemed to the Synod to have become an Alliance of English-speaking Churches and was therefore not answering the expectations which that Church had cherished when joining it'.[9] While regretting this decision we fully understand it. It was to be over twenty years before the Dutch Reformed Churches of South Africa again became part of the world family of Reformed Churches.

During all these years the Alliance General Secretary, Dr Mathews, who celebrated his ministerial Jubilee in 1904, visited many Churches and was frequently on the Continent of Europe, apart from journeys to the Western Hemisphere. Especially important was his visit to the Decennial General Synod of the Reformed Church of Hungary in 1904, as it helped the Alliance develop further contacts with that great Church. During the same trip Dr Mathews also went to Prague in order to have preliminary discussions about the possibility of organizing the first Continental Conference, which was to take place in 1906 in this historic city.

During the first years of the century the Alliance was constantly concerned with the problem of religious freedom and always ready to come to the assistance of persecuted minorities. There are frequent references to Russia; they are not concerned with the politics of the Russian Empire, but with its lack of the most elementary freedom. In an article devoted to 'The Land of Oppression', *The Quarterly Register* of February 1903 writes: 'We have before us copies of the proceedings in a number of recent Justice of Peace courts of Southern Russia, mainly in the Kieff and Odessa districts. On examining them we find that during the last 18 months about 814 persons have been brought before these courts accused of "having attended Prayer meetings", and thus having shown themselves of being members of the Stunds . . . In no country under the sun calling itself either civilised or Christian, other than Russia, would such an outrage be possible; while so carefully are these proceedings guarded from the public eye, that not one in a million of the Russian people have any knowledge of what is going on *to-day*; and as for those outside Russia, men in their ignorance shrug their shoulders and turn away in unbelief, when one speaks of "Russian persecutions".'[10]

Does this report not remind us of certain situations today and is not the reaction of many of our contemporaries to such situation the same as in 1903?

        *   *   *

1904 was the year of the Eighth General Council of the Alliance, which took place in Liverpool from 28 June to 7 July. Critics of former Councils, and especially the Seventh General Council, had complained that there were too many papers, that they were too long and that there was consequently too little time for discussion. But little was to change in Liverpool. This was almost inevitable, for long discussions in plenary sessions were difficult. It was not until the 1948 Council in Geneva that a completely new method of work was adopted and the Council subdivided in sections or groups, each with the responsibility of studying a special aspect of a Theme and of reporting to the plenary. Another factor which made real discussions difficult was the fact that English was the only official language of the Alliance. Councils were attended by delegates of the Continental Churches of Europe who did not always master this language; and consequently, they could not take an active part in the discussions, with the result that the thinking of these Churches did not really influence the deliberations. For the smooth running of the Council it was much easier to have papers read by distinguished representatives of the member Churches, and the system was continued for many more years.

In spite of the Council being held so near the Continent, only eight delegates from European member Churches were present, while six represented the 'Associated Churches' of Hungary and of France. British and American (including Canadian) Churches sent full delegations to Liverpool, but this did not minimize the fact that the Churches of the Continent of Europe were once more practically unrepresented. As for Asia, the only delegate was a missionary from the Presbytery of Tainan, in Formosa; Africa had also a single delegate, from the Presbyterian Church of South Africa. There were four representatives from Australasia, while Mexico sent a National as delegate of the Presbyterian Church; the two delegates from the Presbyterian Church of Jamaica were also missionaries.

In his Preface to the volume of *Proceedings* of the Council, the General Secretary has this to say: 'Many questions, which were wholly or in part unknown to our fathers, are at present occupying the mind of our Churches and for their examination, ordinary Church meetings give no suitable opportunity. Hence, any open and simple examination of such is a real service, and likely to be followed by the most beneficial results. At the Liverpool Council, a number of these questions were considered, and we have reason to believe that the statements then made have contributed not a little to the calming of anxieties which were arising in many a bosom. The Council did not charge itself with furnishing a solution of these difficulties; sufficient for it to indicate the lines along which a solution should be sought, and by doing this, it has rendered such service to our Churches as fully to justify its own existence.'[11]

It has already been clearly stated that though the Alliance was a fellowship of Reformed Churches, it helped its members to have a clearer vision of the Church of Christ, Catholic. This was repeated by the Alliance President, Principal Dr Caven, in his presidential address to the Council: 'How greatly we should rejoice to see the visible Church reflect more perfectly the unity which of necessity, belongs to the Church invisible! . . . for whilst the Reformed

Alliance has aimed primarily at bringing the Reformed Churches of the Presbyterian Order nearer one to another, I venture to affirm, that it has helped us to realize more perfectly the unity of the Church of God, and to dwell more on the things in which the followers of Christ are one, than upon those which separate them.'[12]

Once more, social problems occupied the minds of the delegates; they lived in a society where the worker was still exploited and they were aware of the injustices which existed in their countries. How could they have remained silent? Rev. Dr J. B. Gold, of the U.S.A., expressed the mind of the Council when he said: 'The Church, like her divine Head, must take heed to the bodies as well as minister to the soul of the human family . . . It must, like her divine Lord, hear the cry of the blind, the withered, the homeless, the workless and hungry ones of this earth or perish like a rudimentary appendage for lack of use . . . The Church must plant itself squarely on the side of the human right and against human wrong and then will men believe it to be the honest champion of mankind and the friend and servant of God.'[13]

This was not a 'social Gospel'; for the delegates to the Liverpool Council were aware that there were other needs, and Rev. Dr George Wilson expressed it clearly when he said: 'The Church today has many needs, but her supreme need is a fresh endowment of the Spirit of God. The Church of today has many perils, but her supreme danger is deadness within and not assault from without.'[14] Times have changed since the beginning of the century; but the problems seem to remain the same!

In the field of Foreign Missions, the Committees were able to report steady progress in the cause of unity. The Committee of the Western Section reported that on 15 December 1904 a United Church would be formed in India, being the result of the coming together of at least twelve different Presbyterian bodies.

The Home Mission Committees were also able to show that the work started by the Alliance was beginning to bear fruit. The Western Section Committee reported 'that the plan of co-operation in Home Missions work . . . has proved to be very satisfactory . . . the spirit of brotherly love prevails, and the right of priority in new fields is recognized much more than formerly. In connection with this we may refer to the increasing desire for closer relations, unions between those now substantially one, and co-operation, or federation, between others.'[15]

*   *   *

We have already seen that, so far, the Alliance had been a 'Men's organization'. This was to continue for a long time, though the Council recognized that the Church could not exist without women. 'The history of the Church', said Rev. E. B. Cobb, of the U.S.A., 'from Apostolic days is largely the history of woman's work. There are probably, in all our Churches to-day, more women than men . . . women are more thoroughly organized than men for missionary work. Upon the Mission fields, they are entering doors which are barred to men and are accomplishing therefore a work which men could not accomplish.'[16]

Once more the problem of the Reformed Churches of the European Continent took a considerable place in the deliberations of the Council. We have already seen that some of the Churches of the Anglo-Saxon world were not too happy about the state of affairs in the Continental Churches and that, but for the existence of the Alliance, they would probably have started work on the Continent and created a further split among the already weak Churches there. This problem was again raised by the General Secretary when he reported on behalf of the Eastern Section of the 'Committee on Work on the European Continent': 'Every year a large amount of money is spent on the Continent in support of what are called "individual missions". But such are not the kind to bring forth any permanent fruits. What is wanted is assistance that shall encourage and stimulate the native pastors and congregations, that shall be linked to some Church, be under direction, be continuous and self propagating.'[17]

The same note was struck by the Convener of the Western Section of the same Committee, Rev. Dr J. I. Good, a man who knew the Continent intimately and had a real love for the Reformed Churches there: 'Rationalism is a great foe to be reckoned with in Continental work . . . How to aid our brethren is a difficult and delicate problem. It is not for us to interfere with the ecclesiastical status of those Churches.'[18] Wise words indeed, and it is good to know that, through the judicious counsel of the Alliance, any assistance to be given to the Reformed Churches of the Continent was to be channelled through the existing Churches so as to strengthen them instead of bringing division among their followers.

The Alliance has sometimes been criticized for perpetuating divisions between the different members of the Church of Christ. Nothing is further from the truth. The Liverpool Council was to show once more how groundless were such accusations. Both the General Secretary and the American Secretary were asked to address the Council on the subject of 'Work for the Alliance'. Dr Mathews said: 'It has been my privilege to visit some of these fields [mission fields, *Ed.*] and two points have been borne in upon me as a result: First, I saw the necessity, not merely of co-operation between our mission agencies and the native converts of the Reformed and Presbyterian Churches on those fields, but of organic union, so that there might be but one Church of Christ standing out in the midst of overflowing heathenism.

'My second point is, that there should not only be union among the converts on the field, but *union of the Mission Boards at home* . . . A general Mission Board, consisting of the representatives of all the Churches, would be an object lesson to the world, especially to the Churches at home, that Foreign Missions are not a matter of mere denominational activity but the very distinctive work of the Church as a whole, that in carrying on of such, every trace of denominationalism should be effaced.'[19]

Dr Roberts then challenged the Alliance to take 'a more vigorous attitude in regard to the living issues of the day' and went on to say: 'I speak for many when I say that we long for the day when there shall be but one Church in the U.S.A. holding the Reformed Faith and the Presbyterian System . . . And this Alliance through its Councils, and especially through its agencies, can in the future, as in the past, effectively aid the forces which make for the union of our Churches.'[20]

The Council also transacted a certain amount of Alliance business, as its predecessors had done, and new officers were chosen. The President elected by the Council was a man who had long been associated with the Alliance, Rev. Principal Dr J. Oswald Dykes, of Westminster College, Cambridge, and former pastor of the Regent Square Presbyterian Church in London. It was he who had welcomed the delegates to the historic London Conference of 1875, when the Alliance was founded.

*   *   *

At the Liverpool Council, Dr Roberts, the American Secretary of the Alliance, had mentioned his hope to see but one Church of the Reformed family in the U.S.A. But this did in no way indicate that he was only concerned with Reformed unity; the opposite is true. For at the 15 November 1904 meeting of the Western Section, Dr Roberts reported that at least twelve of the leading denominations in the U.S.A. 'have either appointed or authorized the appointment of delegates to a General Convention of the American Protestant Churches, to be held in the city of New York, in November 1905'.[21] Dr Roberts added that he had been invited to act as chairman of the Committee on Arrangements for this Convention, whose purpose was to organize, if deemed advisable, a National Federation of the Protestant Churches.

*   *   *

In 1905 a new name begins to appear in the annals of the Alliance, the 'Russian Molokans' or 'Molokani'. The November 1905 issue of *The Quarterly Register* gives the following information: 'On the 30th of last August we received a letter from the Continent inviting us to attend a "Centennial Jubileum" to be held in South Russia during the first week of September. Deeply to our regret, other engagements did not allow of our being present. We have, however, great pleasure in laying this invitation before our readers, that these may learn something of that "underground" [already then, *Ed.*] religious movement which is in progress in Russia.'[22]

The letter of invitation indicated that their fathers had received their first religious freedom on 22 July 1805 and that they had decided to hold a Centennial Jubileum to celebrate the occasion. The Molokans were to meet in conference at Astrachanth from 2 to 4 September, and the New Molokans (Presbyterians) were to have a conference of their own from 4 to 8 September.

But who were these Molokans, and how was the Alliance related to them? The letter of invitation gave some information on their history: 'Somewhat like the Plymouth brethren, they base all their religion on the Bible. They have neither pope, bishop nor priest, no Master save Christ, every believer being a priest unto God. They hold that the Church is an assembly of devout believers, and have no church buildings, but meet in each other's house where their worship consists in reading the Scriptures, repeating the Lord's prayer, and singing psalms and hymns.'[23]

A participant in the centennial celebrations then gave the following account: 'The number of Molokans in the whole of Russia amounts to nearly 200,000. Among these a reform movement arose which divided them into two camps, the "Old Molokans" and the "New Molokans". They received the name of 'Molokans' in the following manner. When they commenced to search the Scriptures, they did not find therein anything to support the teaching of the Orthodox Church that milk must not be used during Lent. They broke the teaching of the Church, and using milk during Lent, came to be called "Milk Drinkers" (from "Moloko", milk).'

How did the 'New Molokans' become Presbyterians? The story is a very strange one, as told by the same reporter: '. . . the agent of the British and Foreign Bible Society in Russia, Mr Melville, threw in his lot with the Molokans and engaged in mission work among them, being assisted by a Syrian . . . who was also a Presbyterian; and it is through these men that the impetus was given to the movement.'[24]

One could use this story to show how ridiculous confessional affiliation can be. But one ought not to take the 'Presbyterianism' of these Russian brethren too seriously. What they wanted above all was fellowship with other Evangelical Christians, and though Dr Mathews could not attend their centennial celebrations, it is certain that he was able to give the Molokans the assurance that they had friends in other countries.

*   *   *

A year later Russia was again on the Agenda of the Alliance at the meeting of the Eastern Section held on 5 January 1906. The persecution of the Jews, which had for so long been sporadic in Russia, had again grown in intensity. This prompted the Eastern Section to send a strong resolution of sympathy. It was sent to the Procurator General of the Holy Synod of the Russian Church, as well as, for information, to the Chief Rabbi of Great Britain. We have no information about the result of this step; one can only but think that, like former resolutions, it did not directly affect the policy of the Russian State or the attitude of the Russian Church towards the Jews.

*   *   *

We have already seen that the Western Section gave whole-hearted support to the idea of a National Federation of Protestant Churches in the U.S.A. The meeting of the Western Section on 11 April 1906 heard an enthusiastic report of the New York Conference of November 1905, which was presided over by the American Secretary of the Alliance, Dr Roberts. He reported that the plan prepared by this Conference provided for the assembling of a Federal Council in December 1908. The report further stated: 'Of the Churches already enlisted in this movement, seven are members of the Western Section of the Alliance of Reformed Churches. This attempt to express the fellowship and catholic unity of the Christian Churches makes an era in the history of the times in which we live.'[25] This leaves us in no doubt about the Alliance's attitude towards the movement for greater Christian unity. We can be grateful that Presbyterian solidarity, instead of creating a confessional bloc, helped our Churches to become more active in the movement for true catholic unity.

1906 was an important year in the life of the Alliance, for it saw the first of the 'Continental Conferences' which were to help the Alliance understand the problems of the Reformed Churches of the Continent, and which were, at the same time to get these Churches more thoroughly involved in the total life of the Alliance. The Conference was held in Prague on 14 and 15 August. It is interesting to hear the comment of the General Secretary of the Alliance, as it appears in the 15 November 1906 issue of *The Quarterly Register*: 'The Prague Conference of 1906 has unquestionably been the most important "Forward Movement" that our Alliance has yet undertaken . . . We have gone to the homes of our brethren, and grasping each other's hands, have then walked before the world side by side—one body in Christ. The Conference has thus been an historic event of great significance in the life of our Church, and which may lead to results we are yet unable to estimate . . . To the Bohemian Church and to the Protestant cause in Bohemia generally, we believe that the recent Conference means a great "uplift" socially as well as spiritually. A Roman Catholic Community has seen Protestant theological professors, pastors and others, come to Prague, not merely from other European countries, but from Great Britain, from Canada and from the United States, to attend a two days' religious Conference in fellowship with a small Protestant Church which is just recovering from centuries of most cruel persecution. That Community must realize that the great Protestant world attaches to that Native Church an importance much greater than its numerical strength might seem to justify; and seeing that, it must feel bound to treat that Bohemian Church and the Protestantism for which it stands, more equitably in the future than it has done in the past.

'For the Alliance itself, that Conference has pointed out a new line of action for the future. It has distinctly shown that as the Continental Churches cannot come to its General Councils held by the English-speaking Churches, there must be added a series of Continental Conferences. At each of these, the Churches of the Alliance must be represented by delegates, sufficient in numbers to exhibit our actual Brotherhood, while the natural leadership on such occasions of the native Churches must always be acknowledged.'[26]

I have already mentioned that there was little communication between the Eastern and the Western Sections of the Alliance. Of course, minutes of the meetings were exchanged; there was a constant flow of correspondence between the General Secretary and the American Secretary. On several occasions Dr Mathews went to the U.S.A. and Canada and attended meetings of the Section as well as General Assemblies of the Churches of the U.S.A. and Canada. American leaders also came to Europe and kept in touch with Alliance member Churches there as well as with the Eastern Section when they visited Great Britain.

The fact however remained: there were two Sections with their Executive Commission and their officers; as long as there was not a World Executive Committee at the head of the Alliance, it was natural that a certain lack of unity should be felt and that at times tensions should develop within the Alliance.

The General Secretary paid one of his visits to the Western Section and to its Churches in 1907. In his report to the meeting of the Eastern Section held on 17 October of the same year, Dr Mathews made this comment: 'The Church mind in the Western World seemed to be much occupied with questions of Church Union, Church Federation, and Inter-denominational Federation, so that the distinctive mission of the Alliance is much discussed.'[27]

This is the first official mention of the different interests of the two Sections. Their different attitudes were natural and need not

c.s.—4

be overemphasized. The Churches of the Western Section were naturally more concerned with Protestant unity whereas in Scotland at that time the main problem was the reconstitution of Presbyterian unity.

In the report given to the Western Section meeting of 11 February 1908, the American Secretary was able to inform the Section officially that 'the Council of the Reformed Churches in the U.S.A. holding the Presbyterian System has been duly organized. The Council met in the Marble Collegiate Reformed Church, New York, December 3, 1907.'[28] Dr Roberts was elected Stated Clerk of this Council. The purpose of this new organization was 'to evince and develop their spiritual unity, and to promote closer relations and more definite administrative co-operation among the Churches.'[29]

The missionary interest of the Western Section at that time seems to be greater than the interest of the Eastern Section, though both Sections were very active in this field and encouraged increasing co-operation between their member Churches. At the meeting of the Western Section on 11 February 1908, the Committee on Co-operation in Foreign Missions noted that: 'Among Christians, both at home and abroad, the consciousness deepens, that first and foremost the Christian Church is a Missionary Church, that its missionary activity is not merely one of its functions, but the very breath of its life.'[30] The Committee also noted that 'from the mission fields continue to come the most powerful impulses toward Christian unity. Where men are engaged in the same great work, under the same conditions . . . they get a true perspective of the relation of essentials and non-essentials . . . Our Foreign Mission Boards are working under the conviction that the object of the foreign missionary enterprise is not to perpetuate on the mission fields the denominational distinctions of Christendom.'[31] And the Foreign Missions Committee of the Section had the right attitude, when it further said in its report: 'The time seems already at hand, in some foreign mission lands, when our Foreign Boards and our Foreign missionaries must be ready to decrease, in order that the native Churches in those lands may increase.'[32]

A real ecumenical spirit animates the whole report of the Foreign Missions Committee and this must be emphasized. 'The annual Conference of the Foreign Mission Boards', continues the report, 'which the Alliance of the Reformed Churches throughout the world inspired, continues to aid our Churches greatly in the work of co-operation in Foreign Missions. This Conference, in no small measure, made possible the Laymen's Missionary Movement. More important still, the Conference within the past year created a Central Committee of Reference and Counsel . . . to further the spirit of co-operation and union.'[33]

The missionary interest in some of the Churches of the Western Section was so great that the General Assembly of the Presbyterian Church in the U.S.A., in 1907, instructed the Board of Foreign Missions 'to make enquiries about its commencing Mission work on the European Continent'. In the preceding chapter, the present writer mentioned that a similar desire had already been expressed in the 1890s (see p. 64). Once more, the Alliance was able to prevent a false step which would have had serious consequences. In his reply to the Western Section, Dr Mathews, the General Secretary 'had very earnestly hoped that there would be no "Mission" organized in any country in which a Native Reformed Church was already in existence'.[34] The American Churchmen agreed and nothing came of it. The Eastern Section, in its meeting of 16 January 1908, gave its full approval to the action of the General Secretary.

* * *

Among the numerous ecumenical relations of the Alliance, special mention should be made of those with the International Congregational Council. Dr Blaikie had represented the Alliance at the Founding of the ICC in London, in 1881, and since then there had been several exchanges of what we now call 'fraternal delegates' between the two organizations. One is the more surprised in reading in the Minutes of the Meeting of the Eastern Section of 8 October 1908 'that owing to the pressure of engagements, the Congregational Council lately meeting in Edinburgh had found itself unable to receive the Deputation which had been appointed to attend its meeting, and had expressed great regret for this inability'.[35]

* * *

So far, no mention has been made of Calvin in this volume, though the Churches gathered in the Alliance are considered by many—even today—as Calvinist Churches. The fact is that our

Churches claim to be 'reformed according to the Word of God', and, while grateful to God for the witness of the great Reformer, we must remember that we are the disciples of the One who was Calvin's Master, Jesus Christ. However, as we approach the year 1909, the fourth centennial of his birth, the name of Calvin begins to appear more frequently in the records of the Alliance. A Calvin Commemoration was to be held in 1909, and the Alliance was naturally interested in it. But there was no desire to glorify the Reformer. In the November 1908 issue of *The Quarterly Register*, the Editor says: 'John Calvin was one of the greatest gifts bestowed on the Christian Church since New Testament times . . . May we hope that the coming meetings and addresses will not be such a "building of the sepulchres of the prophets" as may tempt men to think that by these things they are paying the debt they owe to Calvin. The best use of the Commemoration will not be so much to speak about the man, for we have in print all that is known about him, but to show how we of the present day may in our lives follow him in his consecration to God and in his service to men.'[36]

A look at the Minutes of the Section meetings of the year 1909 clearly indicates that the Calvin Commemorations did not prevent the Alliance from giving its attention to the problems of the day. The meeting of the Western Section, on 9 February, was concerned with the problem of European and American residents in foreign seaports. An Alliance Committee had been formed to try and help in this field. They had the feeling that too little was being done for these people; and they were also concerned because many of them, by their licentiousness, were hindering mission progress in the great cities of Asia. The Committee wanted to send the best possible men to influence American and European business men living in these seaports; and they demanded 'Union Churches' for they realized that the work to be done there was not denominational, but Christian.

The same meeting heard with gratitude that the first meeting of the newly formed Federal Council of Churches in America had taken place at Philadelphia [at Witherspoon Building, the headquarters of the Presbyterian Church in the U.S.A., *Ed.*] from 1 to 8 December 1908 and that all the member Churches of the Alliance in the U.S.A., with the exception of the Reformed Presbyterian Church, had joined the organization.

The meeting also paid a tribute to a man who had played an outstanding role in the life of the Alliance, especially in the Foreign Missions Committee of the Western Section, and who had possessed an ecumenical vision which was far from common at the time. This man was Dr F. F. Ellinwood, Secretary of the Board of Foreign Missions of the Presbyterian Church in the U.S.A. 'It was largely through Dr Ellinwood's influence, at the Council of the Reformed Churches in Toronto 1892, that there was held, in the following January, the first Conference of the officers of the Foreign Mission Boards in the U.S.A. and Canada. Since then these Conferences have been held annually, and they inspired largely the Ecumenical Missionary Conference of 1900 [in New York, *Ed.*] which was the forerunner of the World Missionary Conference, to be held in Edinburgh in 1910.'[37]

The same meeting clearly indicated that the Alliance stood in favour of closer co-operation of the Protestant Churches, and passed the following resolution: 'While rejoicing in the progress of the Kingdom of Christ in these latter times, through the co-operation of various branches of the Church, believing that a more thorough union is not only desirable and possible, but that it also would mean a multiplication of the Christian forces, this Commission joins in the appeal for prayer in behalf of the World Missionary Conference, to be held in Edinburgh, in 1910.'[38]

*   *   *

New York welcomed the Ninth General Council of the Alliance, which was held there from 15 to 25 June 1909. Once more it was a British–American Council, although many papers were devoted to Calvin. Only two delegates from the Continent of Europe had travelled to New York; there were no representatives from either Asia or Africa; no Latin American delegate was present, and there was but one Australasian representative; the New Hebrides had sent one missionary; so had the Presbyterian Church of Jamaica.

As already said, there were many addresses on Calvin: 'John Calvin: Salient features of his life', 'Calvin and the Reformation', 'Calvin as Expositor of Scripture', 'Calvin and the Doctrinal System (The Institutes)', 'Calvin and Church government', 'Calvin and the Christian Ministry', 'Calvin and his Ethical System', 'Calvin and the case of Servetus', 'Calvin the Theologian'. The list ended with three lectures on 'Calvinism and Liberty', 'The Influence of Calvinism in the World Today' and 'The World-wide Mission of Calvinism'.

At the beginning of the twentieth century men were optimistic about human progress, and this was clearly expressed in the presidential address of Principal Dr Oswald Dykes: 'The old order has given place to a new one. Altered social conditions call for novel applications of the ancient remedy that saves . . . One material revolution in our methods of communication has, of course, become too obvious not to become commonplace. In a very few years the inhabited earth has contracted before our eyes at the magic wand of science, till now its remotest inhabitants look comparatively close at hand, and distant lands can literally hear each other speak . . .'[39] But the President of the Alliance was greatly preoccupied by the existing poverty of so many, and added: 'If even worldly society, frankly irreligious, can no longer retain its indifferent attitude to social evils, much less can Christian men or Christian societies be indifferent . . .'[40]

Although delegates from the Reformed Churches of the Continent of Europe were conspicuous by their absence, the Continent was not forgotten. There were substantial reports from the 'Committee on Work on the Continent of Europe' (Eastern and Western Sections). The Eastern Section report mentions the opening of Russia to evangelistic work, as the Tsar had proclaimed absolute religious freedom in his Empire, while the report of the Committee of the Western Section emphasized the fact that 'Europe needs a new Reformation'.[41] Ties with the Continent were strengthened, for among the Churches admitted to membership we find the Reformed Church of Hungary; this was the first large Continental Church to join the Alliance.

Dr Mathews, in his report on behalf of the Committee on Work on the Continent of Europe (Eastern Section) reaffirmed the position of the Alliance on the problem of evangelistic work by British or American Churches: 'A Reformed Church . . . has no moral right, under the plea of a desire for evangelistic work, to enter a land in which a Reformed Church already exists.'[42] This must have been finally understood by the British and American Churches, for this is the last time the problem is mentioned in the records of the Alliance.

As in former General Councils, Foreign Missions occupied an important place. The tone of the reports of the Foreign Missions Committees is optimistic: 'There is abundant evidence', says the Eastern Section Committee, 'that the century will be one of continued progress and great missionary enterprise.'[43] The delegates did not realize that five years later the First World War would break out; but we can certainly not blame them for that!

The Committee of the Western Section dealt at length with the problem of unity: 'We rejoice in the many evidences that all Protestant denominations are drawing together in their foreign missionary work. We are happy in the knowledge that the Reformed Family of Churches has been among the first in the promotion of this great movement.'[44] And it is clear that, once more, the Alliance stood for independent and strong Younger Churches. The aim of mission work was 'to plant a Church of God which shall grow of itself, its own inner life continually nourished by the Spirit of God, a Church which shall not be a foreign, but an indigenous Church, addressing itself to men and women and children of its own race, whose innermost feelings they can understand, with whose aspirations they can enter, and whose upward path toward the light of the eternal kingdom they can smooth, because they have trod that path themselves'.[45]

World problems were not forgotten in New York. Once more, the problem of forced labour in the Congo came for discussion at the Council, and a resolution was passed: '*Whereas* we learn with profound regret that the inhuman exploitation of the Congo natives continues essentially unabated, and that the guarantees demanded have not been given: *Therefore* this Council . . . appeals to the Governments of both Great Britain and the United States to take such action as will secure without further delay on the part of the Belgian Government the abolition of forced labour, the restoration to the natives of their rights in the soil, and the institution of those human conditions which ought to accompany all civilized government.'[46] This appeal was to be transmitted to the governments of Great Britain and of the United States.

Two other resolutions were adopted. One dealt with the oppression of the Jews in Romania, the second with the Armenian massacres. It said: '*Whereas* the time has long gone by for the passing of resolutions: This Council . . . urges the Governments of Christendom, particularly the signatory Powers of the Berlin Treaty, to take united, radical, vigorous and persevering action for the protection of Armenians and other Christians residing in Turkey.'[47]

Rev. Dr David J. Burrell, of New York, a minister of the Reformed Church in America, was elected President of the Alliance. The Council seems to have ended on an optimistic note, the spirit of which seems strange to us. The American Secretary, Dr Roberts, said: 'If only Britain and America can stand together shoulder to shoulder, and act heart to heart, in the interests of religion and humanity, the day will soon come when Christ shall be hailed as Lord of all.'[48] And the retiring President added: 'The closer these two great divisions of Anglo-Saxon Christianity shall stand together in the days to come . . . the better it will be for civilization, and the better for the redemption of the races of mankind.'[49]

*   *   *

1910 saw the great Ecumenical Missionary Conference of Edinburgh, and we have already seen that the Alliance was fully behind this venture. The New York Council of 1909 had passed a resolution saying in particular: 'It looks forward to more complete realization at this Conference of the Prayer of the Master for the unity of believers, and of obedience to His Command to disciple the nations . . . And this Ninth Council commends the World Conference to the attention and prayers of Churches and Congregations.'[50]

At about the same time the reports of the Alliance indicate that another great movement towards unity, what is now known as the 'Faith and Order' Movement, was beginning its activity. During the year 1911, both the Eastern and the Western Section had to take position in relation to that movement. But the reaction of the two Sections was entirely different. At the Western Section meeting of 7 February 1911, after a paper had been read on 'Christian Unity', representatives of the Protestant Episcopal Church submitted to the Section proposals for a World Conference on Faith and Order. It was resolved by the Western Section 'that the Commission cordially approves of the proposed Conference'.[51]

On 18 May 1911, the Eastern Section held a meeting. The

General Secretary, Dr Mathews, told the members that he had received a letter 'from Mr Gardiner, secretary of a New York Committee, proposing to hold in that city, a World Conference for a consideration of the different systems of Faith and Order held by the different Christian organizations, with a view to a closer apprehension of these to one another, and with a request that he would bring the proposal before the different Presbyterian Churches of Great Britain. The correspondence having been read, the Section agreed that as the Alliance was permitted to address the Supreme Courts of these Churches, only as reporting on the work of the Alliance, it would not be in order for it to deal with other matters, and directed the General Secretary to so inform Mr. Gardiner'.[52]

A strange answer indeed. It may have been technically correct that the proposed Faith and Order Conference was not within the scope of the Alliance's responsibilities, but a way could certainly have been found to show greater open-mindedness. One wonders if the negative reaction of what was really the 'British' Section of the Alliance was not caused by the fact that relations between the Church of England and the Presbyterian Churches of the British Isles were not always as cordial as they could have been? In any case, the reaction of the Eastern Section seems to be in contradiction with the resolution of the Ninth General Council regarding the Edinburgh Conference which looked forward to more complete realization at this Conference of the Prayer of the Master for the Unity of believers (see p. 88).

*   *   *

For the Alliance 1911 was a year of further 'Continental Conferences'. One was held in Prague and one in Budapest. Reporting on these Conferences in *The Quarterly Register* of November 1911, the General Secretary of the Alliance says: 'Our two Conferences, that in Prague, when the British Delegation met with the representatives of the Bohemian and Moravian Churches, and that in Budapest, when it met with the representatives of the Hungarian Church, have closed under most happy conditions. The Delegation consisted of some thirty-five elders and ministers, appointed by seven different Churches. Our relations with Bohemia and Moravia have been so intimate, and date so far back that we hardly regard their Churches as "Foreign"; but this was the first occasion

of our meeting the Hungarian brethren, and so a special importance was naturally attached to the Deputation . . . the Hungarian
Church is very far from being dead. She is rather a young giant,
who is beginning to show her strength, and may be relied on as
about to fill an important part in the evangelizing of Eastern
Europe.'[53]

Between the Prague and the Budapest Conference, the British
Delegation spent ten days visiting colleges and theological seminaries of the Hungarian Reformed Church, and the British
delegation were greatly impressed by what they saw.

A comment on these 'Continental' Conferences is certainly not
out of place here. They were not 'Continental' in the sense we
now give to this term. The Reformed Churches of the Continent,
with the exception of the Churches visited, were not represented.
The Alliance was in fact a British Delegation. This is not to
contest the value of these meetings; they were significant for the
Churches of Bohemia and Hungary and they helped our British
brethren to understand some of the problems of the Continental
Churches. But there was still a long way to go until the Alliance
could understand that the Continental Churches needed more than
visits by British Churchmen and that the different Churches had
to come together to discuss their own particular problems.

*   *   *

The Tenth General Council, meeting in the lovely Scottish city
of Aberdeen from 18 to 26 June, was to be the last Council of the
first period of the Alliance. Before looking at the Council let us
see what the Alliance was like in 1913, almost 40 years after it
was founded.

The 1875 preparatory Conference in London had brought
together representatives of 22 Churches. At Edinburgh, 27
additional Churches were received into the Alliance fellowship.
What was the situation in 1913? The volume of *Proceedings*
indicates that 52 Churches were members of the Alliance, but this
figure seems incorrect, as Churches which had withdrawn, like
the Dutch Reformed Churches of South Africa, are still on the
list of the member Churches. Twelve Churches from the U.S.A.
and Canada are listed, ten from Great Britain, twelve from the
European Continent, seven from Asia, three from Australasia.

Africa was in fact represented only by the Presbyterian Church of South Africa.

Up till now finances have not been mentioned. At the first General Council it had been agreed that half the expenses would be paid by the British Churches and the other half by the Churches of the Western Section, and this had not been changed. The proportion was to be altered after World War I, when the Churches of North America agreed to be responsible for a larger proportion of the expenses. Whatever the proportion, the Alliance's spending was very modest. The General Secretary was then the only paid official, and the financial burden on the member Churches was not very heavy.

*   *   *

Once more, the Council was almost entirely British–American; the Continent of Europe had eleven delegates, eight coming from Hungary; there was but one delegate from Asia (Persia), none from Africa or Latin America, and two from Australasia.

The main preoccupation of the Council was evangelism. This was already the dominant note of the Presidential address at the beginning of the Council. It was repeated in the report of the Committee on Evangelistic Work of the Western Section. The convener of the Committee, Rev. Dr D. J. Burrell, reported that in 1910 the Western Section had appointed a Committee of Cooperation in Evangelistic Work. This Committee had contacted other Protestant Churches throughout the world. The Council approved the report, together with these recommendations:

'(1) That pastors of the Churches represented in the Alliance be urged to present more earnestly and more constantly, both in their preaching and in personal conversations with members of their congregations, the vital necessity of repentance for sin and faith in Jesus Christ as the conditions of pardon and eternal life.

'(2) That the Tenth General Council hereby commends to all the Churches represented in it the World-wide Movement for Evangelization, as it has relation to evangelistic effort within their own bounds, and the cultivation, in their ministry and membership, of the evangelistic spirit . . .

'(3) That this Council sends out to the Churches a solemn call for a year of intercession, beginning 1st October 1913, for the outpouring of the Holy Spirit throughout the world, in both home and foreign fields.'[54]

The problem of the Faith and Order Conference also came before the Council. The American Secretary, Dr Roberts, reported on behalf of the Business Committee and submitted a resolution which proposed positive action.

The minutes of the Council indicate that 'on careful consideration of the terms of the Committee's recommendations, part of it appeared to be somewhat in advance of what a considerable number of delegates were prepared to adopt in the present state of their information on the subject of the proposed Conference. On motion, therefore, it was agreed to recommit the matter to the Business Committee for further consideration and report . . .'[55]

The Council finally approved the following Resolution:

'*Whereas,* there has been submitted to this Council a proposal by the Joint Commission of the Protestant Episcopal Church in the United States for a World Conference on Faith and Order of all Christian Churches which confess our Lord Jesus Christ as God and Saviour, for the purpose of study and discussion, without power to pass resolutions; and

'*Whereas,* a Conference of said Commission with Co-operating Commissions and Committees of other American Churches has submitted the same proposal through General R. E. Prime of New York, a duly appointed delegate; and

'*Whereas,* the Western Section of the Executive Commission has commended this proposal, and it has been approved by a number of its constituent Churches, therefore

'*Resolved* (1), that this Council places on record its sympathy with all these wise measures which have for their object the restoration of the unity of Christendom and the fulfilment of our Lord's prayer for His Church.

'*Resolved* (2), that the invitation to join in the proposed Conference concerning Faith and Order be transmitted to the constituent Churches composing the Alliance, with such information as shall secure an intelligent consideration of the whole matter.

'*Resolved* (3), that the necessary information, so far as this Council is concerned, be furnished through the Eastern and Western Sections of the Executive Commission.'[56]

The decision of the Council not to adopt a more positive line towards the Faith and Order Movement may be in part the result of the General Secretary's reaction. A few months before the Council, in the February 1913 issue of *The Quarterly Register*, Dr Mathews had spoken very plainly: 'Speaking now only for ourselves and in no way committing the Presbyterian Alliance in this matter we must at once confess, that we take no interest whatever in any of the varied schemes for the promotion of so-called Church Unity or Organic Union, which have lately been floated out so abundantly . . . We fail to see why the proposed Conference should be held.'[57]

The Council spent also considerable time hearing reports about the Continent of Europe and the Mission Field. The delegates rejoiced in the growing unity of the 'Younger' Churches and the growing co-operation of the Mission Boards in Europe and America.

Though Europe was still at peace in 1913, rearmament was in full swing, and the Council once more adopted a Resolution on arbitration:

'This Council is of opinion that most of the disputes which lead to war might be settled by properly constituted Courts of arbitration which would command the confidence of the various countries of the world.

'The Council therefore rejoices in the proposals for treaties in favour of Arbitration between different nations, providing for the submission of disputed questions to such Courts before appealing to the arbitrament of the sword, and would encourage the Statesmen of the world to seek to secure the acceptance of such treaties wherever possible.'[58]

A new President, Rev. William Park, of Belfast, was elected. In his valedictory address, he said: '. . . Many of our numbers are growing visibly older and less fit to bear the burden and the heat of the day.'[59]

This was unfortunately true. The last Council of the nineteenth century had expressed the hope that the twentieth century would bring new men and new methods. In fact, there were still too many who were 'growing visibly older'. Both the General Secretary and the American Secretary had been in their posts for 25 years; but the General Secretary, Dr Mathews, had been connected with the Alliance for 40 years. Now, at the age of 85, he had no intention of retiring. But the extra work connected with the Aberdeen Council must have been too much for him, and on 5 July 1913 he died in his London home, in his 86th year.

This really marks the end of the first period of the Alliance. The man who was to be appointed his successor, Rev. Dr R. Dykes Shaw, fully recognized the debt the Alliance owed to its first General Secretary. 'Gifted with high business ability, great force of character, and many endowments of nature and grace, Dr. Mathews never spared himself in abundance of labours during those long, strenuous years.'[60]

The delegates to the 10th General Council had decided to meet again in Pittsburgh in 1917. Little did they know that in 1917 most of the nations of the world would be engaged in an atrocious war and that many of the Aberdeen delegates would not attend another Council.

REFERENCES
 1. Western Section Minutes, Nov. 15, 1900, p. 2.
 2. Idem, p. 7.
 3. Eastern Section Minutes, Oct. 24, 1900, p. 2.
 4. Idem, p. 2.
 5. *The Quarterly Register*, vol. V, no. 12, p. 235.
 6. Western Section Minutes, April 16, 1902, p. 8.
 7. Idem, p. 9.
 8. Idem, p. 26.
 9. Eastern Section Minutes, Nov. 26, 1903, p. 2.
10. *The Quarterly Register*, vol. VI, no. 9, p. 161.
11. *Proceedings 8th General Council*, pp. VI and VII.
12. Idem, pp. 29–30.
13. Idem, pp. 163–166.
14. Idem, p. 162.
15. Idem, Appendix, p. 62.
16. *Proceedings 8th General Council*, p. 233.
17. Idem, Appendix, p. 94.
18. Idem, Appendix, p. 98.
19. Idem, pp. 300 and 301.
20. Idem, p. 304.
21. Western Section Minutes, Nov. 15, 1904, p. 4.
22. *The Quarterly Register*, vol. VII, no. 8, p. 394.

23. Idem, p. 395.
24. Idem, pp. 397 and 398.
25. Western Section Minutes, April 11, 1906, p. 9.
26. *The Quarterly Register*, vol. VII, no. 12, p. 478.
27. Eastern Section Minutes, October 17, 1907, p. 2.
28. Western Section Minutes, Feb. 11, 1908, p. 5.
29. Idem, p. 6.
30. Idem, p. 9.
31. Idem, p. 9.
32. Idem, p. 10.
33. Idem, p. 10.
34. Eastern Section Minutes, Jan. 16, 1908, p. 3.
35. Idem, Oct. 8, 1908, p. 1.
36. *The Quarterly Register*, vol. VIII, no. 8, pp. 169 and 171.
37. Western Section Minutes, Feb. 9, 1909, p. 12.
38. Idem, p. 13.
39. *Proceedings 9th General Council*, pp. 44 and 45.
40. Idem, p. 46.
41. Idem, Appendix, p. 75.
42. Idem, Appendix, p. 65.
43. Idem, Appendix, p. 57.
44. Idem, Appendix, p. 116.
45. Idem, p. 277.
46. Idem, p. 356.
47. Idem, p. 409.
48. Idem, p. 439.
49. Idem, p. 447.
50. Idem, p. 457.
51. Western Section Minutes, Feb. 7, 1911, p. 8.
52. Eastern Section Minutes, May 18, 1911, p. 2.
53. *The Quarterly Register*, vol. IX, no. 9, p. 457.
54. *Proceedings 10th General Council*, p. 158.
55. Idem, p. 162.
56. Idem, p. 216.
57. *The Quarterly Register*, vol. X, no. 1, p. 12.
58. *Proceedings 10th General Council*, p. 216.
59. Idem, p. 396.
60. Idem, Preface, p. VI.

CHAPTER SEVEN

The Alliance and World War I

The sudden death of Dr Mathews compelled the Alliance to take immediate action. Rev. Dr Robert Dykes Shaw, a minister of the United Free Church in Edinburgh, who was one of the delegates to the Aberdeen General Council, was asked to act as Interim General Secretary. At the Eastern Section meeting of 3 October 1913, Dr Shaw was unanimously appointed General Secretary of the Alliance, the Western Section concurring.

Dr Shaw, having been released for this post by his Presbytery, became General Secretary on 2 December 1913. By decision of the Eastern Section, Dr Shaw was to have his office in Edinburgh. If this was understandable, as the meetings of the Eastern Section already took place regularly in Scotland, it meant that the Alliance was to be more isolated from the Continent than before; in later years, this was to have serious consequences. Meantime, Dr Shaw started his work with enthusiasm and ability. He had a good knowledge of French and German, and this was important, as the Alliance was very anxious to develop its contacts with Churches outside the Anglo-Saxon world.

Strangely enough, 1914 seems to have begun on an optimistic note. The Western Section meeting of 10 February heard a report of the Foreign Mission Committee saying: 'The sufficiency of each of these great non-Christian systems, as they are, is no longer believed in. They are crumbling . . . This is the indubitable and significant fact. Through rifts that will multiply the way is opening for the light of Christ to penetrate the darkest depths . . .

'Cooperation, not competition, is the significant spirit of present day progressive missionary endeavour.'[1]

After speaking enthusiastically about the Edinburgh Conference of 1910 and its Continuation Committee, '40 men chosen without regard to section or denomination, solely because we all believe that they are Christ-endowed for the sole task of inspiring and directing the world-wide missionary activity of the Protestant world',[2] the report has strong words about the Church at home: 'The Church must cease playing at missions. The whole Church must be brought into the line of conflict.'[3]

In spite of their distance from Europe, the Western Section were well aware that a more active participation of the Continental Churches was essential for the Alliance, and General Prime made this point strongly in a paper on 'The need of a Continental Section'. Alas, less than six months later, the Continent of Europe was to be on fire, and members of the Churches of the Reformed family fighting against each other.

The same meeting was reminded that the Alliance had played an important, if indirect role, in the formation of the 'Reformierter Bund', the German Reformed Alliance. Dr Brandes, a German Reformed leader, had attended the Belfast General Council in 1884; he had become enthusiastic about the World Alliance of Reformed Churches and had said: 'We must have such an Alliance in Germany.' The first meeting took place at Marburg in 1884. 'Now the Reformierter Bund is a strong organization',[4] added Dr Good, the Chairman of the Europe Committee.

We live in an age of statistics, and some of the specialists tend to frighten us when they speak of the world population in a few decades. It is therefore interesting to hear that the people attending the Western Section meeting of February 1914 were told that 'Canada and the U.S. have passed the 100 million mark ... Within the next fifty years, it is calculated we will have about 500 million'.[5]

Though the U.S.A. were still expanding at the time, Church leaders realized that their responsibilities were changing. The Committee on Home Missions could report that 'The old order of Home Missions has seemingly passed away. It is no longer the frontier which appeals, but the congested city, the disintegrating country Church, the helpless mountaineer, the confusing Babel of foreign tongues, the mining camps, the lumber mills, the commercialized and wordly nominal Christianity, and the degraded negro, demoralizing whole communities'.[6]

Last, but not least, evangelism occupied an important place in the deliberations of the 1914 Western Section Meeting. 'There is a growing conviction,' said Dr J. Ross Stevenson, chairman of the Committee on Evangelistic Work, 'that the work of evangelism must be put on a permanent basis. We believe that our pastors and communicants should be admonished that the fullness of time has come to push the primary business of the Church and "make disciples".[7]

In 1914, our Reformed leaders in the Western Section were also concerned with the problem of unity. Dr Roberts, together with two representatives of other Churches, visited Great Britain early in the year, in order to bring to the Churches invitations to attend a Conference on Faith and Order. Dr Roberts was able to attend the Eastern Section meeting on 15 January. But the Section remained noncommittal, as they had been at the Aberdeen Council.

✽   ✽   ✽

August 1914. The First World War had broken out. The whole of Europe, with the exception of a few small nations, was involved in it or was soon to be. It was a real tragedy. 'Civilized' nations, which claimed to be Christian, were fighting savagely against each other. Belgium and France had been invaded; the war was raging in Eastern Europe, with untold miseries for both soldiers and civilians.

The first reaction to the war from the Alliance is found in an article written in the November 1914 issue of *The Quarterly Register* by the Editor, Dr Shaw, the new General Secretary:

'A great war is raging among the European nations . . . In human history there has been nothing to compare with the volcanic outburst, and unhappily the grim spirit of the struggle seems to be such that it is feared there will be no end save the end brought about by sheer exhaustion on one side or on both. Even after the war a sad heritage may be anticipated, of prostration, of distrust, of crippled resources, retarded civilization . . .

'The saddest feature of it all is that it is a war of Christian nations. Members of many Reformed Churches within the Alliance are ranged as combatants in the opposing armies. And each side is blaming the other. It is natural to ask self-justification, for the responsibility to the Christian conscience is too crushing to be borne; but amid the cloud and smoke of battle it is scarcely possible to see with clear eyes, or to agree in judgement on the same facts. Good men on both sides are busy arguing that theirs alone is the cause of righteousness . . .

'One thing is clear . . . All Christians throughout the world are

called on as they never were before to heart-searching and prayer
. . . We need to humble ourselves under the mighty Hand of God.
We need to pray more earnestly for the Spirit of Christ, to look
not only on our own things, but also on the things of others . . .
And along with the prayers we can strive with a new generosity
and fervour to alleviate the distress of stricken hearts, to heal the
havoc that man's inhumanity has made, and to lay the foundations
for better and saner methods of solving things in the future. It
may be that God will be pleased to use the Alliance in the great
work of a healing ministry. The ties that bind us must become
closer and more vital. The sorely tried Reformed Churches of
Europe will never appreciate our fellowship more than when the
time comes, and it will come, to prove to them that in heart we
were never severed, and that our fraternal relations with them
cannot be broken.'[8]

And in the same issue, the President of the Alliance, Rev. Dr
William Park, of Belfast, had an article on 'The War—And After':

'Our first feeling, surely, as Churchmen and as Christians, must
be that of shame . . . If we as Churches had done our duty to our
Saviour and to our fellowmen, would not some better way than
this have been found ere now for settling the disputes of nations ?

'To shame must be added intense sorrow that Christian people,
in the countries that are at war, have for a season been so alienated
that even members of the great Presbyterian family are to
be found, it may be in opposite camps, drawn against each
other . . .

'And when the war is over—God grant it may be soon!—the
case of the Churches in our Presbyterian fellowship which have
suffered most must be carefully and generously considered, so
that they may be comforted and strengthened, and fitted, as soon
as possible, to take up the broken threads of their work again.
There is nothing that will do more to heal the wounds this war
has caused in the family of Christ on earth than such sympathy and
kindly care . . .

'Our last word must be one of hope . . . The Gospel of Peace,
far and near, is slowly but surely doing its work. A new day is
breaking—perhaps the very war with all its horrors may hasten
it—a day of universal peace, of brotherhood, of love. We will
live and labour in the hope of its speedy appearing.'[9]

If I have quoted at length from these two articles, it is because they show that the Alliance leaders were not the victims of the mad nationalism which invaded even the Churches at that time. It is good to know that they realized the madness of war and saw in it the real enemy.

*   *   *

The same note was struck in the February 1915 issue of *The Quarterly Register*. At the end of November 1914, the Alliance General Secretary had sent a letter to the General Curator of the Hungarian Reformed Church, Count Joseph Degenfeld: 'Even if it is impossible at the present time, in the different nationalities, to have a common view as to the human causes and responsibilities for the war, it is still possible for good men in all the Churches to cherish feelings of regard and sympathy for one another, feelings alone worthy of Him who is the Lord of us all.'[10]

The Quarterly Register quotes the text of the answer received a few weeks later by the General Secretary, in the form of a letter signed by the Presiding Bishop, Bishop Baksay, and the General Curator to whom Dr Shaw had sent his letter: 'All our hearts are filled with a deep sorrow that we are in conflict with nations towards whom we have always had the feeling of regard . . . But it is a true joy for us to know that, in our great conflict, there are many, also in your country, who do not forget that even if we are enemies as members of our earthly countries, as members of our common heavenly fatherland we must remain brethren.'[11]

And the General Secretary of the Alliance expresses his joy at this exchange of correspondence. He knew nothing of war-hatred, and for this we can thank God.

The Eastern Section meeting of 5 November 1914 was also deeply concerned by the war and passed the following resolution: 'The Executive Commission, Eastern Section, desires to record its grief at the war now raging among the European nations, and its deep sympathy with the Reformed Churches affiliated with the Alliance that are enduring acute distress at the present time owing to the havoc of military operations. It profoundly laments that so many members of the Protestant evangelical faith are opposing one another on the field of battle, and earnestly prays that there may be a speedy and righteous issue, and that men may be set free again to devote themselves to labours and ideals worthy of their civilisation and of the religion of Christ. It calls on the Churches within the Section to continue in fervent supplication . . . that the nations of the earth may perceive their deep need of Christ, and seek an outpouring of that Divine Spirit which alone can secure the true peace and blessedness of the world.

'The Section also desires to commend to the Christian liberality of the Churches the cases of their brethren who may be enduring special hardships.'[12]

*　　*　　*

During the first year of World War I the American Churches went on with their business very much as usual. They knew of the war in Europe and we shall see that they were anxious to help those suffering from it. But their preoccupations were still those of peacetime. The meeting on 5 February 1915 of the Western Section showed that our American brethren were anxious to define more clearly the duties of the new General Secretary of the Alliance and his relations to the Sections. The American Secretary reminded the meeting that Dr Mathews never asked the concurrence of the Western Section as to the use of his time and that he was really a member of the Eastern Section. This should not be so. The General Secretary 'should be at all times an officer and servant of the whole',[13] as the Rules adopted at the London Council of 1888 clearly indicated.

Soon afterwards the General Secretary, Dr Shaw, visited the United States and Canada. He met the leaders of the Western Section and they spoke quietly and frankly together. The difficulties which had sometimes arisen between Dr Mathews and Dr Roberts are not mentioned during the period Dr Shaw was General Secretary. But there is no doubt that differences of opinion were bound to arise as long as the two Sections lived practically independently from each other. Not until the reorganization in 1948 would the Alliance really become *one* world organization.

The 1915 meeting of the Western Section was concerned about the way in which the Continental Missions were affected by the war. German missionaries could no longer operate in many territories and this put a new responsibility on British and American Churches. The Committee called for 'new larger sacrifices'[14] on the part of the Churches of the Western Section.

1915 should have been observed in the Reformed Churches of Europe as the 500th anniversary of the death of John Hus and celebrations should have taken place in Prague. However the war made this impossible, but the American Churches of the Alliance decided to observe 6 July as 'John Hus Day'.

Dr Good, the active Chairman of the Committee on Work in Europe of the Western Section reported on the effects of 'the awful war on our member Churches there'[15] and appealed to the American Churches to give help to French Protestants.

A 'Committee on an Appeal to the Nations at War in behalf of Peace' had been appointed by the Section. Its report is as follows:

'The Western (American) Section . . . deplores the dreadful loss of lives of multitudes of our fellow-beings caused by the war now raging in Europe, the serious injuries to myriads who have been maimed for life, and the ruin of great numbers of homes that have been overwhelmed by death and sorrow. In view of this catastrophe, we appeal most earnestly to all the Churches concerned with this Alliance to implore Almighty God to influence the warring nations that a righteous peace may be speedily secured.'[16]

The war continued, and instead of a settlement, there were soon new nations involved in the deadly struggle. Sufferings increased and destruction mounted. The Eastern Section (which was virtually British) could not do much, except try to help the Churches which were suffering. This she did most earnestly, and the Minutes of the Section, as well as *The Quarterly Register,* insist on the responsibilities of British Christians and British Churches in the field of what we now know as Inter-church Aid. There is no doubt that the constant appeals of the Alliance helped the Churches of Britain respond generously to the needs of the distressed Churches of the Continent.

It would be wrong to think that even at that time, the only preoccupation of the Churches was the war. We have already seen that at the beginning the American Churches and the Western Section continued living as heretofore. Even in Europe, Churches realized that they had to plan ahead. On both sides of the Atlantic, the Faith and Order movement was active, and the new General Secretary of the Alliance seems to have taken a more friendly attitude toward the movement than was the case of his prede-

cessor. *The Quarterly Register* of May 1916 has an article entitled
'World Conference on Faith and Order. Two Preparatory Movements'. The article reports on an important Preparatory Conference of representatives of North American Commissions, held
near New York on 4–6 January 1916, for the purpose of considering further procedure in connection with the proposed World
Conference. Rev. Dr W. H. Roberts, American Secretary of the
Alliance, acted 'in the important capacity of Convener of the
Business Committee . . . the atmosphere was one of brotherly
conciliation, and harmonious conclusions were always arrived at.

'In connection with a particular statement the use of the phrase
"the sin of schism" was objected to, and it was pointed out that
there are Churches wholly in sympathy with the movement, which
yet have no apology to offer for the Protestant Reformation.'[17]

Especially interesting, in view of later reactions of the Roman
Catholic Church to the Ecumenical Movement, is the mention, in
The Quarterly Register, that a 'Letter was read from Cardinal
Gasparri expressing the Pope's sincere desire for the success of
the proposed Conference.'[18]

'The other preparatory movement has taken place in England
in the form of a Conference of the Committee appointed by the
Archbishops of Canterbury and York and of certain members of
the Commissions of the Free Churches of England chosen for the
purpose . . .'[19] No mention is made of representatives of the
Churches of Scotland.

*   *   *

1917 was the year of the Russian Revolution. *The Quarterly Register*
of May 1917 has a paragraph on this revolution in 'Notes on
Current Events'. One has to remember that the Communist
revolution of November 1917 had not yet taken place. But it
shows how difficult it is to prophesy.

'The Russian Revolution was carried out in a few days, and
with remarkable little bloodshed . . . It is impossible to forecast
future developments, but the general opinion seems to be that
the men at the head of affairs are strong enough to maintain the
position, and that a permanent addition has been made to the
democracies of the world. A free Russia is certainly an omen of
tremendous portent, and its emancipation will send waves of
influence far beyond its own borders. Above all, it promises

gloriously to redeem the Russian people from their long night of
oppression, and friends of civil and religious liberty throughout
the world will join the American President in hailing Russia as
"a fit partner in a league of honour".[20]

1917 was also the year of the 400th anniversary of the Lutheran
Reformation, and it is good to read in an article by Rev. Professor
Stalker, of Aberdeen, in the May issue of *The Quarterly Register*:

'The situation reminds us painfully of the failure of Protestantism to be a uniting bond strong enough to curb the passions
provoking war; and it illustrates the necessity for a far more
world-wide organisation of the connection between Church and
Church for the promotion of which the Alliance exists; for one
foundly hopes that, if the Churches of the different countries had
found their voices the War might not have happened . . .'

And the article ends: 'For our own sake we ought to remember
Luther . . . we do well to recall the light-bringers of the Reformation—Luther and Melanchthon, Zwingli and Calvin, Cranmer and
Knox—for it is only as long as we remain true to the light
vouchsafed through them that we can expect the light we need
on the problems and tasks of our time.'[21]

*   *   *

In 1917, the United States also entered World War I. The meeting
of the Western Section held on 7 March mentions that over
$100,000 U.S. had been received for the French and Belgian
Churches. The Committee on Work on the Continent of Europe,
after analysing the situation on the Continent, asked the question
'What about the end of the War?' and answered: 'One thing is
evident—religion will be somewhat different . . . The old lines of
division, which have so often and so long produced friction will
be broken down. It will be easier for the Churches of the different
lands to draw together than for the different peoples. The Church
must begin the movement.'[22]

During their meeting, the members of the Western Section sent
a telegram to President Woodrow Wilson, 'to express to President
Wilson, a founder member of this Section, their profound sympathy in this time of strain and stress'.[23]

*   *   *

In the middle of war problems, it is strange to read in *The
Quarterly Register* of November 1917 that the Reformation Monu-

ment in Geneva (begun in 1909, the 400th anniversary of the birth of Calvin) was, without 'any ceremony of solemn inauguration, formally handed over to the custody of the Geneva City authorities'.[24] A reminder that in the midst of destruction Switzerland was still a haven of peace.

✳   ✳   ✳

1918 was to see the end of the war, but not before terrible battles had raged and more blood was shed, mainly the blood of young men who had so much to contribute to the welfare of humanity.

In the midst of war, Alliance leaders were already concerned with reconstruction. The Minutes of the Eastern Section of 17 January 1918 indicated that a Deputation from the Presbyterian Church in the U.S.A. was hoping to come to Great Britain 'for the purpose of conferring on the religious conditions created by the war, and the best methods by which the Presbyterian Churches throughout the world might unite in dealing with them'.[25] Later, the meeting of 7 November of the Eastern Section —a few days before the Armistice—made it clear 'that during the reconstruction period after the war the Presbyterian Churches in this country should give financial and moral assistance to the Churches of the Continent'.[26]

As for the Western Section, the report of the Committee on Co-operation in Foreign Missions shows that American Presbyterians, though deeply concerned about the tragedy of the war, were hopeful that good would come out of it. We read: 'In some ways this incomparable cyclonic struggle will be made to minister to the enlargement of His Kingdom. War has been the explosive used to remove obstruction, open doors, and establish international relationships upon foundations more sure and lasting.

'It [the war, *Ed.*] has compelled the conviction that the hope of the world does not lie in armies and navies, or in commercial prosperity. Surely that has been tasted and found wanting . . .

'That is the supreme lesson to be learned . . . that our civilization is built on materialism, and that the witness of the Church has been so feeble, so pervaded with the spirit of the world, so corroded with selfishness and rivalries and suspicions that she has failed to interpret to the world the Spirit of Jesus Christ.'[27]

✳   ✳   ✳

11 November 1918. The fighting had ended, but it was not yet
the end of the war. Hatred still existed between the nations, and
if Great Britain and America were among the victors, the Alliance
leaders could not forget that millions of their own people were
amongst the defeated nations, and that their fate was difficult and
even cruel. Hungary, the home of the largest member Church on
the Continent of Europe, was to be broken up, or at least deprived
of large portions of its territory.

The Alliance could not remain indifferent; and we see that soon
it was to be faced with new and heavy responsibilities, especially
in the diplomatic field. The Eastern Section meeting of 16 January
1919 had before it an appeal from the Hungarian Reformed
Church. The General Secretary indicated that he had already
prepared a Draft Memorial for submission to the British Government, and that he was going to The Hague to meet three representatives of the Hungarian Reformed Church.

The February 1919 issue of *The Quarterly Register* in an article
'Appeal from Hungary' explains the Hungarian point of view on
the question: 'Grave anxiety exists in the Reformed Church of
Hungary regarding the possibility of the Peace Conference trans-
ferring portions of Hungary to the dominion of other Powers.
Such a transference, it is stated, would mean the loss to the
Reformed Church . . . of a thousand congregations and two
Colleges . . .

'The Hungarian Reformed Church is a member of the Alliance
. . . and the Appeal will undoubtedly at the earliest opportunity
receive the attention of both the Eastern and Western Sections of
the Executive Commission. It is plain that, whatever political or
territorial changes the Peace Conference may judge right to make,
it is the duty of the Alliance to do all in its power to safeguard
the interests of religious liberty among its members.'[28]

The Western Section did not remain behind. The Minutes of
the meeting of the Section on 25 February 1919 indicate that on
1 February the American Secretary, Dr Roberts, had sent a
Message to President Wilson, then at the Paris Peace Conference
'on behalf of religious freedom, especially with regard to Transylvania and Romania'.[29] The problem of Transylvania was to
remain for many years an Alliance responsibility.

*   *   *

Hardly had the war ended when the Alliance was to lose the man who had been directing its activities with devotion and intelligence. On 17 February 1919 Rev. Dr Dykes Shaw died after only one week's illness. In the May 1919 issue of *The Quarterly Register,* Rev. Dr R. J. Drummond pays tribute to this distinguished Presbyterian. After his theological studies at the Theological Hall of the United Presbyterian Church, he had gone to the University of Heidelberg and then to the Theological Seminary of the Free Church of Neuchâtel. He was inducted in his first charge, in Hamilton, in 1880. 'A perusal of the Minutes of the Eastern Section since he entered on his duties conveys a vivid impression of the range, and importance of the work he did on behalf of Presbyterianism . . . At the time of his death he was engaged in most important negotiations bearing on the future of the great Reformed Church of Hungary.'³⁰ Dr Shaw's death was a great loss to the Alliance.

Fortunately for the Alliance the 'young veteran' of the Western Section was still active. On 31 January 1919 Dr Roberts celebrated his 75th birthday. He had been Stated Clerk of the Presbyterian Church in the U.S.A. for 35 years and American Secretary of the Alliance for over 30 years.

*   *   *

We have already seen that the Alliance was very active on behalf of the Hungarian Reformed Church. On 29 December 1919 the Eastern Section sent a 'Memorial to the Allied Council, at Paris regarding the Reformed Church of Hungary, and in the interests of Religious Liberty in Transylvania, Slovakia, the Banat, and other Territories of Eastern Europe'. After reminding the Allied Council that a Memorial had already been sent on 3 February 1919, the Second Memorial goes on to say:

'It is with deep regret that we have now to represent that the course of events since then has more than justified the fears entertained, and that the situation in many parts of the territories in question warrants grave concern as to the future in these regions of all forms of Christianity which do not command themselves to Rumania and other powers in military occupation or possession. In particular, we have been shocked by the reports which have reached us, on credible authority, of what is happening in Transylvania . . .

'At this stage we ask no more than an impartial and thorough investigation of the facts. We realise that this is a broad question involving far more than sectional or sectarian interests, and though our Presbyterian communion is very largely concerned, we recognise that a satisfactory settlement must depend on co-operative and representative effort. We therefore very respectfully, but very urgently, request the Allied Council to appoint a Commission of Inquiry to visit Transylvania and other occupied districts, and that there should be associated with its political members ecclesiastical commissioners represented and nominated by allied branches of the different Churches concerned, these being the Roman Catholic, the Reformed, the Lutheran, the Unitarian. We are strongly of opinion that this course will yield the best results, and will be instrumental in preparing the way for the establishment of those international conditions of religious freedom and equality that the Allied Council desires to promote . . .'[31]

The Eastern Section, in its annual report to the Churches, sent in April 1920, mentioned the Memorial of December 1919 and added: 'Should any grievance remain unredressed, we may find it necessary to bring their case before the League of Nations.'[32]

*   *   *

The annual report of April 1920 was signed for the first time by the newly appointed *interim* General Secretary, Rev. Dr J. R. Fleming, of London, who was to be a worthy successor to Dr Shaw.

The Minutes of the first post-war meeting of the Western Section on 2 February 1919, make interesting reading. The report of the Foreign Missions Committee mentions that ' "the New Era" is the slogan of today. Old things are passing away and all things are becoming new.'[33]

China of course occupies a large place in this report. 'The Chinese have always had a genius for organization . . . One naturally shrinks from the ever increasing multiplication of machinery, so often lacking in spiritual dynamic and results.' The same report shows that Presbyterians were anxious for a greater degree of unity with other Christians: 'The challenge to the Church is appalling . . . What else can be done but to cooperate, to get together and seek by united efforts to measure up to the requirements of the times?'[34]

The Committee on Work on the European Continent, after having expressed its concern at the success of Bolshevism, put before the Section what we now call a world strategy of Inter-Church Aid. 'We must save Europe in order to save ourselves . . . The Continental Churches need help and the help that America alone can give . . . War has produced a condition that the European Churches are unable to meet. Unless it is met, we too, will suffer. Shall the Churches of America save at this crisis the Churches of Europe, and in doing so save themselves and the world? We therefore urge that the Reformed-Presbyterian Churches aid not only the French and Belgian Churches at this moment . . . but that they take measures to aid permanently the European Churches of our Faith from year to year.'[35]

Dr Good, the convener of the European Committee, decided to visit the Continent in the summer of 1919 in order to see the situation with his own eyes. This visit was going to have far-reaching consequences, for soon the member Churches of the Western Section of the Alliance were to play a major role in the first organized Inter-church Aid action undertaken on behalf of the Protestant Churches of Europe.

REFERENCES
1. Western Section Minutes, Feb. 10, 1914, pp. 14 and 15.
2. Idem, p. 15.
3. Idem, p. 16.
4. Idem, p. 18.
5. Idem, p. 26.
6. Idem, p. 27.
7. Idem, p. 36.
8. *The Quarterly Register*, vol. X, no. 8, p. 169.
9. Idem, p. 172.
10. Idem, vol. X, no. 9, p. 194.
11. Idem, vol. X, no. 9, p. 194.
12. Eastern Section Minutes, Nov. 5, 1914, p. 6.
13. Western Section Minutes, Feb. 9, 1915, p. 4.
14. Idem, p. 14.
15. Idem, p. 38.

16. Idem, p. 50.
17. *The Quarterly Register*, vol. X, no. 14, p. 316.
18. Idem, p. 316.
19. Idem, p. 318.
20. Idem, vol. X, no. 18, p. 409.
21. Idem, pp. 412 and 414.
22. Western Section Minutes, March 7, 1917, p. 43.
23. Idem, p. 25.
24. *The Quarterly Register*, vol. XI, no. 2, p. 45.
25. Eastern Section Minutes, Jan. 17, 1918, p. 3.
26. Eastern Section Minutes, Nov. 7, 1918, p. 4.
27. Western Section Minutes, Feb. 27, 1918, p. 12.
28. *The Quarterly Register*, vol. XI, no. 7, p. 158.
29. Western Section Minutes, Feb. 25, 1919, p. 7.
30. *The Quarterly Register*, vol. XI, no. 8, p. 170.
31. WARC Archives Geneva, Memorial, pp. 1 and 2.
32. WARC Archives Geneva, WPA/EA2.
33. Western Section Minutes, Feb. 25, 1919, p. 12.
34. Idem, p. 15.
35. Idem, p. 22.

CHAPTER EIGHT

The Alliance and the
New Ecumenical Situation

For the first 45 years of its existence the Alliance had tried to bring together the Churches of the Reformed family; though it had remained practically a 'Presbyterian' Alliance of the British and North American Churches, it had however never lost the vision of a 'world' Alliance and our fathers had shown constant interest for the Continent of Europe and for the Younger Churches developing on the Mission Field.

From the beginning the Alliance leaders had made it clear that the unity they were trying to achieve among the Reformed Churches was not intended to create a 'bloc' against other Churches. This had been affirmed in the Preamble to the 1875 Constitution and time and again Alliance spokesmen had affirmed their desire to achieve greater unity with other Churches. They had quickly come to realize that unity within the family of Reformed Churches would make their members hungry for more unity.

We have also seen that these were not mere words; the Western Section, for instance, was very active in helping to develop agencies for interdenominational co-operation, especially the Annual Conference of representatives of Foreign Mission Boards in the U.S.A. and Canada and the Federal Council of the Churches of Christ in the U.S.A.

Some Christian leaders wanted to go further, and the Protestant Episcopal Church in the U.S.A. had launched the idea of a Faith and Order Conference as early as 1910. The Western Section, under the leadership of its Secretary, Dr W. H. Roberts, had been an enthusiastic supporter of the scheme, but the Alliance as a whole had been more reserved.

Now, in the 1920s, many Christians felt that the time had come for all Christian Churches to come more closely together. The First World War had shown the tragedy of the separation between Churches and it was felt that only a greater unity would prevent the recurrence of such a tragedy. While the Faith and Order Movement continued to develop, other Movements, of a more practical nature, made their appearance. The World Alliance for Promoting International Friendship through the Churches, born on the eve of the 1914 war, was anxious to become a force in the post-war situation; and what was to be known as the 'Life and Work' Movement was becoming a reality.

This meant that the Alliance was faced with a totally new situation. We hope to show in this chapter that, far from preventing the Reformed Churches from playing a useful role in these movements the Alliance helped them to become fully involved as it had already encouraged them to take an active part in interdenominational co-operation.

*   *   *

This was not the only task facing the Alliance in the 1920s. We have already seen that the War had left the Churches of the Continent of Europe, or at least the majority of them, in a pitiful state. Devastation was great and financial resources for reconstruction very slender. New countries had been formed, in which Reformed Churches were struggling to exist. The largest Church of the Continent, the Hungarian Reformed Church, had been broken up by the Peace Treaties. Its members were now scattered in four countries: Hungary, Romania, Czechoslovakia and Yugoslavia, and contacts between these four sections of the Church were difficult because of the political situation.

It is quite remarkable to see that the Alliance, in which the Continental Churches had not yet really taken their place, played so important a role in the reconstruction work and gave these Churches moral support which was of the greatest importance at the time, even if efforts undertaken on the diplomatic level were not very successful. But how could they have been? The decisions taken by the Peace Conferences were irreversible and the Alliance could only try and limit the damages and make sure that minorities were given the rights which had been assured to them in the Peace Treaties.

As we look at the activities of the two Sections in 1920 we see that the Continent of Europe is now the main preoccupation of the Alliance. On 15 January, the Eastern Section had already decided that there should be a Continental Conference before the end of the year. This was to be remarkably organized by the two Sections, in order to give the Alliance the possibility of becoming really well acquainted with the problems of the Continental Churches. A few weeks later the Western Section heard Dr Good, who had visited Europe in 1919, plead for a strategy of Inter-Church Aid and for a continuing effort on the part of the Churches of the Western Section. In his report to the Western Section, Dr Good mentions a man who was to play a major part in the developing of modern Inter-Church Aid, Rev. (later Dr) Adolf Keller, pastor in Zurich. Pastor Keller had visited the U.S.A. in 1919 and had pleaded on behalf of the weakened Churches of the Continent. Dr Good noted that Pastor Keller wished to bring the Swiss Churches into 'closer touch with the Churches of other lands' and that, on his initiative, the Swiss Churches showed 'a greater desire to come in some way into closer relations with our Alliance and its Churches'.[1]

However Europe was not the only concern of the Alliance. Asia and Africa had also been affected by the war and new situations had arisen there which demanded new and urgent solutions. We have already seen that for several decades Alliance leaders had insisted on the necessity for the Churches in Britain and in America to work toward the formation of Young and Independent Native Churches, with Native leadership. Alas, these warnings had not been heeded or at least had not been taken seriously in the majority of cases. Now the need was more urgent than ever and the Foreign Missions Committee, reporting to the Western Section meeting of March 1920, said: 'the spirit of nationalism already existing has been intensified. There is a revolt against foreign control . . . the reins must be transferred to other hands'.[2]

The Alliance was also deeply concerned about infringments of religious liberty in Korea; the Presbyterian Church there, the largest in the land, was passing through difficult days. The 1 April 1920 meeting of the Eastern Section noted that the situation in Korea [then under Japanese domination, *Ed.*] called 'For action by the Alliance'.[3] The facts were bad indeed, and *The Quarterly Register* of May 1920 noted: 'What they [the Japanese troops, *Ed.*]

C.S.—5

did in the great cities like Seoul and Pyang-Yang was bad enough, but the culminating horrors came in the country villages . . . In one case all the Christian men were called into the village church. The door was closed, the men were shot down and then the church was set on fire.'[4]

The Alliance tried to act through the usual diplomatic channels; but there again success was very limited; Japan was an ally of Great Britain, who was not anxious to intervene. And so the martyrdom of Korean Christians went on unabated for years to come.

*   *   *

We have already mentioned the decision of the Eastern Section to hold a Continental Conference in 1920. This Conference took place in Lausanne from 5 to 11 August and was attended by 40 representatives from 30 Churches and Societies. The November issue of *The Quarterly Register* contains a very full report of the Conference. The Editor notes: 'It is rather remarkable that during the 43 years of its existence the Presbyterian Alliance had not held a *general* Conference on the Continent until this year . . . Lausanne, 1920, will be memorable as the scene of the first attempt of the Alliance to take a complete view on the Continental situation by meeting in a central place and receiving and discussing reports from as many as possible of the Churches of our order. The experiment was a success in every way . . . And while the gathering was chiefly concerned with the needs of the European Continent, America, India and New Zealand joined hands with Great Britain in sympathetic welcome to our brethren of the war-ravaged countries.'[5]

The Reformed brethren who met in Lausanne were not only concerned with their own interests; they knew that the peace of the world was as important to them as Church matters, and they passed a resolution on the League of Nations, which was soon to meet in Geneva for its first session: 'The Continental Conference . . . desires to place on record the feelings of gratitude and hope which have been awakened in the hearts of its members and the Churches they represent, by the formation, under the auspices of the leading statesmen of the world, of the League of Nations to prevent war . . . The Conference expresses the earnest hope that those Nations, which are not yet within the League, will soon become members of it.' There was realism in the resolution voted in Lausanne, for it went on: 'It is well aware of the tremendous difficulties which lie in the way of such a League and which must be overcome before its tasks can be successfully accomplished.'[6] The future was to show how true this was.

The Conference also tried to define the attitude of Reformed Christians towards movements for larger unity, and *The Quarterly Register* reports as follows: 'It was fitting that the last session of the Lausanne Conference should have been largely devoted to a consideration of this subject. For the last few years these movements have been much in evidence. The war seems to have accelerated them.

'Not much was said about the "Faith and Order" Movement ... but the interest taken in it by the members of our Conference was shown by the fact that no fewer than 25 of the 40 delegates [including the Alliance General Secretary, *Ed.*] went on to Geneva from Lausanne to attend the great gathering there from August 12th to 19th ...

'Another Conference held in Geneva took the first steps towards holding another kind of world-congress, which is perhaps more likely to yield definite results than the one just mentioned. Its main promoter is Archbishop Söderblom, of Uppsala.

'Professor Curtis and the Secretary attended by special invitation another important conference that took place in Switzerland in August—that of the World Alliance for Promoting International Friendship through the Churches.

'Meanwhile we have a good deal to do to achieve unity within our own borders ... By making our present Alliance more real we pave the way best for the Holy Catholic Alliance of the future.'[7]

✳   ✳   ✳

In the middle of these international and inter-denominational pre-occupations we have to record the death of another important leader of the Alliance, Rev. Dr W. H. Roberts, who passed away on 26 June 1920, in his 77th year. In the August 1920 issue of *The Quarterly Register*, the Editor could well write: 'The General Presbyterian Alliance has lost one of its outstanding figures, and America one of its foremost religious leaders ... His great work was done as Stated Clerk of the General Assembly [of the

Presbyterian Church in the U.S.A., *Ed.*] . . . and as a strenuous promoter of union both within and beyond the bounds of Presbyterianism . . . As American Secretary of the Alliance since 1888 . . . he did much to shape the policy and lay down the lines of its organisation . . . He was an enthusiast for the Faith and Order Conference . . . and the closing year of his life was largely devoted to planning an organic union of the Protestant Churches in America.'[8]

*   *   *

In 1921 it became very clear that peace and harmony were not yet established, and that the whole world was in a state of turmoil. This affected the work of the Alliance and the report of the Foreign Missions Committee to the 16 February 1921 meeting of the Western Section is revealing:

'The word "unrest" in varying degrees of intensity characterizes world conditions today . . .

'In some quarters these conditions are so acute as to imperil the very existence of Missions . . . The drift is strongly against the white man and what is believed to be the white man's religion.'[9]

Speaking of Europe, the report says: 'A nationalism more narrow, more bitter and more selfish than before the war has replaced the fleeting hope of a real League of Nations based upon the brotherhood of man.'[10]

Concerning the Orient, the same report writes: '. . . the disease is even more insidious and malignant, and if less disruptive is more difficult to heal . . . The brutality of Japan's treatment of the Koreans is unique in modern times. It is comparable only to Turkish massacres in Armenia.'[11]

'Even docile Africa, oppressed and exploited so long and regarded with pity rather than respect, has caught the spirit of the New Age and is demanding recognition.'[12]

At the same meeting, Dr Good, Convener of the Committee on Work on the Continent of Europe, presented a remarkable survey of the situation. After having noted the extraordinary vitality of the Roman Catholic Church and its activity all over the Continent, as well as the danger of 'Boshevikism', Dr Good was able to report that $200,000 had been raised for Europe in 1920 by the constituent Churches of the Alliance in North America. However he was not satisfied, and he added: 'Brethren, it is time that we consider the real situation in Europe. We have too long been working at it in a haphazard way. We should consider a broad and comprehensive plan, a program by which Europe can be quickly helped and helped permanently.'[13]

If conditions described by the Foreign Missions and the European Committees were gloomy, the Home Missions Committee of the Western Section were more optimistic. There were difficulties, of course, and the report notes: 'Perhaps the most prevalent of these is the backsliding of our people from the high ideals of two years ago . . . The reaction came like a flood; the reaction of selfishness and greed and profiteering . . .'[14] But the Churches had not remained inactive, and the report noted the success of the 'Forward Movements' launched by the member Churches. 'However,' adds the report, 'the most striking and possibly the most important achievements came under the head of Interdenominational Cooperation. The Church . . . is feeling . . . the urgency of world conditions so serious that loyalty to Christ requires a sacrifice of denominational prejudices . . . the denominations are recognizing more clearly their kinship and interdependence as members of the same spiritual universal Church, with the same Divine Head.

'The plan of Federal Union proposed by the Council of Reformed Churches and which is now under consideration by the Churches united in the Alliance is a strong expression of this growing desire for some kind of closer relations.'[15]

*   *   *

For the Alliance, 1921 was essentially the year of the Eleventh General Council, originally planned to take place in 1917, and which finally met in Pittsburgh from 17 to 25 September 1921.

In the Preface to the volume of *Proceedings*, Rev. Dr J. R. Fleming, who at Pittsburgh had become General Secretary, after having been Interim Secretary since 1919, writes: 'All who were present at Pittsburgh in September 1921 felt that the Great War and its consequences were compelling the Alliance, like every other institution, to set its house in order for the new era. And the outstanding thing about this Council was its determination, while holding fast to the Eternal Verities, to march forward with the times, to get rid of obsolete traditions that have hindered its influence, and to cultivate a wide outlook on the world's present needs. The hopefulness that characterized a gathering held at a time when there was much to depress, was the best omen for the years ahead . . .'[16]

But what happened at Pittsburgh? And first of all, was the Council really representative of the Reformed Churches of the world? Alas, we have to answer once more in the negative. The list of delegates indicates that the Churches of the Continent of Europe had only nine delegates, while there were three representatives of 'associated Churches'. Asia had only two representatives, while none was present from Australasia. There was one delegate from South Africa and no other from the rest of the great black Continent. Brazil had sent one delegate. There was of course a large British delegation, together with full delegations from Canada and the United States.

Financial difficulties partly explained the fact that the Council was predominantly an Anglo-Saxon affair; but there is more to it than that. The Councils of the Alliance at that time had only one official language, English, and it was not easy for delegates of Churches coming from other cultures to feel at home in such Councils.

*   *   *

Happily, the Council had among its members some men who had a perfect knowledge of conditions in Europe and on the Mission Fields of the world. They saw to it that the delegates gathered at Pittsburgh did not get lost in the problems of the Anglo-Saxon Churches.

Naturally, the problem of Christian unity was in the centre of the deliberations. The Lambeth Conference of 1920 had issued a call to other Churches, and the President referred to it in his presidential address: 'The proposal that for the united Church the form of government should be episcopal is a matter which needs to be calmly and carefully discussed in all its various aspects . . . For, after all, our Saviour and His Apostles, in the Gospels and in the Acts, seem to attach comparatively little importance to the form of government which the Church of the future might adopt.'[17] And Professor Dr G. W. Richards, a future President of the Alliance, spoke in the same vein: 'The time has come when we see more clearly than Hildebrand, and more clearly than the Protestant Reformers, the ideal of Christian fellowship, and in that light we must advance beyond what Catholic or Protestant has yet attained. If we fail to be obedient to the heavenly vision of which we are now catching glimpses, then failure becomes sin . . .

'This work of Christian union is not the work of man alone. It is the work of God. And until Christianity has undergone a regeneration under the power of God's Spirit and has experienced a new conception of what Christianity is, we cannot reach the consummate ideal of unity in diversity.'[18]

The Council took position with regard to the Lambeth proposals; it is interesting to note that the position then taken has been followed by most Reformed Churches ever since. Here are a few extracts of the resolution adopted by the Council:

'1. This Council . . . recognizes and welcomes the earnestness of purpose and brotherliness of spirit manifested therein, and it cordially responds to the call for closer fellowship among the various branches of the Church of Christ.

'2. . . . This Council is not a legislative body; but it may and does express the hope that the Churches it represents will be able to meet in conference with our brethren of Lambeth in the spirit of prayer and willingness to learn together the mind of Christ concerning the peace and unity of His Church on earth.

'3. The Council records its opinion that any such conference must be as between Churches meeting on equal terms, and must be unrestricted as to all questions of ecclesiastical order. Further, its members are at one in declaring their conviction that there will be substantial progress towards reunion only when the conferring Churches are ready frankly to recognize one another's Church standing, and to accompany words of unity by acts of unity in the fellowship of the Lord's table and in co-operation in the Lord's work.

'4. This Council . . . appeals to the members of all the Churches which it represents to promote the great end of unity by avoiding and discouraging all divisive speech and action among Christians and by co-operation with members of other Churches in worship and work, that it may be made manifest that the Church is one in Jesus Christ.'[19]

Naturally, the problem of the ministry was discussed before the Council as it had been raised by the Lambeth appeal. And the speaker who addressed the Council on 'The conception of the ministry in relation to the Church', Professor Dr Carnegie Simpson, of Cambridge, England, took the same line as the Council was to take in answer to the Lambeth appeal: 'If we start by making the ministry the primary issue and if we say we cannot recognize the Church standing of Communions which have not ministerial order as we hold it, then Reunion has no future . . . But if we start . . . with the Church rather than with the Ministry, and if . . . we are able to recognize one another's communions as branches of the Church, and to treat them as such—by, particularly, the act of intercommunion—*then* we can go on to discuss such a subject as the ministry, in which some communions are clearly defective in their ordering, and can discuss it quite in another spirit and on quite a different plane.'[20]

*   *   *

But the problem of unity was not the only one which occupied the minds of the delegates to the Pittsburgh Council. Europe, and by this we mean the Continent, was present throughout the Council, and this in spite of the very meagre continental representation. The Committees of the two Sections on Work on the Continent of Europe came before the Council with full reports and proposals. These Committees realized that some of the Churches of the Continent needed more than financial assistance or brotherly care; they were in need of diplomatic assistance. Dr James Good, the Chairman of the Western Section Committee, said: 'I trust this Council will either appoint or give authority to appoint a diplomatic commission. There are cases that need looking into over there, and we must agitate and agitate until some of those governments get light.'[21] And the Council finally adopted a resolution presented by the Committee of the Eastern Section, proposing 'the diplomatic representation of the Alliance, as need may arise, before the League of Nations and in conference with the governments concerned.'[22] If this representation never materialized, the fact remains that the diplomatic activity of the Alliance in the years following the First World War was considerable, and constant representations were made by the General Secretary to the British Foreign Office and by the American Secretary to the State Department.

Among the few Europeans present at Pittsburgh was Rev. Dr

Adolf Keller, of whom we have already spoken (see p. 113). He was there in a double capacity: as the delegate of the Free Church of French Switzerland and as a fraternal delegate of the Federation of the Protestant Churches of Switzerland, which was to be admitted to associate membership at Pittsburgh, before becoming a full member four years later. Speaking chiefly to American delegates, Dr Keller said: 'The centre of Protestantism has shifted towards the Western World. And when we are looking toward you, we wish to see, in spite of our brotherly feeling for this or that Church, the Protestant unit, the co-operating power of American Protestantism as a whole . . .

'Your denominationalism means nothing for us in the great need of our time. Only the united forces of such great bodies as the Alliance, and even larger bodies, can meet adequately the difficult problems with which European Protestantism is confronted now . . .

'We in Switzerland have come to the conclusion that European Protestantism is in need of common concerted action by the whole Evangelical world . . . In studying the situation of these Churches we were made aware that relief work done from a merely denominational standpoint is not suited to the condition of these Churches and has even done harm to the common Protestant cause.'[23] This was fully accepted by the Council, which voted to 'give special attention until the next Council'[24] to the Churches of the Continent of Europe in need of assistance.

Dr Keller not only spoke about Inter-Church Aid, with which he was soon to be so closely associated. He brought to the Council a message from the Executive Committee of the proposed 'Universal Conference on Life and Work' and declared: 'We Protestants are busy here and there with movements towards more perfect unity, having different principles as their basis. . . . We should not forget that there is something greater in Christianity than the Reformed tradition of the past.'[25]

His appeal was heard, and the Council voted the following resolution: 'The Council records its gratification that progress is being made for a Universal Conference of the Church of Christ on Life and Work, and that so many communions in both Europe and America, including many of the constituent Churches of the Alliance, are co-operating and are represented on the Committee on Arrangements. The Alliance commends the

Conference to the sympathetic interest and the earnest prayers of all the Churches.'[26]

The Faith and Order Movement did not come up for discussion before the Council, but it was not forgotten. Bishop Charles H. Brent, of the Protestant Episcopal Church, and the main promoter of Faith and Order, was received by the Council and addressed it. He spoke about the Faith and Order Conference and his spirit won the hearts of the delegates. He said: 'We are looking for peace, not through victory, but for peace without victory. There is no urgent demand for surrender, but a humble petition or appeal that there may be a mutual sharing of one another's wealth . . .'[27] This was exactly what the Council wanted.

We have seen that in past Councils Foreign Missions occupied a large place. If the time given to the Missions was not as large at Pittsburgh, the Alliance again reaffirmed its desire to see the autonomy of the Younger Churches. The Moderator of the Presbyterian Church of Formosa, Rev. Dr T. Barclay, said: 'There is one lesson which I think at least we Presbyterians have learnt, viz. that the Churches which we set up in foreign lands are from the beginning to be regarded as indigenous Churches of the various countries, and not extensions into these lands of the Mother Church at home.'[28]

The Council did not forget Industrial and Social Problems, and Rev. Dr R. J. Drummond of Edinburgh expressed the mind of many delegates when he said: 'Is it not plainly the duty of Christian men to apply the principles of Christ to all social and industrial relations? . . .

'We live in a day when we are industrially the heirs of "laissez faire" . . . it revealed terrible openings for abuse and wrong . . .

'Christian men are not to stand still, sing dumb, do nothing . . . Christian men should play a mediatorial part, breaking down walls of partition between class and class, Capital and Labour, rich and poor . . .'[29]

Pittsburgh was the first Council since the end of the war. Widespread destruction caused by the war was still apparent, and it is not surprising that the Council should have passed a Resolution concerning the approaching Washington Disarmament Conference. 'This Council . . . being deeply interested in the grievous character of the burdens imposed on the world by excessive armaments . . . expresses its satisfaction at every proposal made and put forth for the lifting of the burden. In especial it regards with gratitude the important and auspicious step taken by the President of the United States in initiating the Conference of the nations for considering this weighty matter . . . the Council hopes that the approaching Conference at Washington may result in the securing of such lessening of armament as will remove many of the evils which arise from their continuance and open the way for the fuller establishment on earth of the reign of the Prince of Peace.'[30]

*   *   *

A Committee of the Eastern Section had prepared a report on 'The future Organization of the Alliance'. Commenting on this report the General Secretary emphasized the need for Continental Conferences between the General Councils, the necessity to revise the boundaries of the Sections and to organize new Sections, the need for a greater financial support of the work of the Alliance, without which it would be impossible to develop the work of the organization, and the need for more publicity. The report was adopted, but no action was taken, apart from the appointment of a committee of three members from each Section, together with the President and General Secretary. This committee was to consider the revision of the Constitution and Rules.

Concerning Inter-Church Aid, the Council voted 'That all payments of money [for the Continent of Europe, *Ed.*] be made by the Treasurer of the Alliance',[31] and this on behalf of all the member Churches of the Alliance, so that their benevolence be co-ordinated. This was a step in the right direction. Others were soon to follow.

*   *   *

We have already seen that the Alliance was a 'men's organization'. Some wives of delegates were present at each Council, but they were not delegates. Since the Toronto Council, in 1892, there existed an 'International Union of Women's Foreign Missionary Societies of the Presbyterian and Reformed Churches'. This International Union had a 'one day meeting' during each Council and the report of their deliberations is to be found in each volume of *Proceedings*. But they could not as yet be members of the Council. Therefore their contribution was very limited. The new General Secretary, Dr Fleming, fittingly wrote at the bottom of the minutes of the International Union at Pittsburgh: 'In any reorganization of the Alliance, the place of women in our scheme of work must be recognized more distinctly, and their range of interest must not be limited to co-operation in Foreign Missions, wide and urgent though that field may be. We are still only at the beginning of woman's share in the work of the Alliance.'[32]

The Council closed with the election of a new President, Rev. Dr John M'Naugher, a minister of the United Presbyterian Church of North America in Pittsburgh.

*   *   *

The Quarterly Register of November 1921 gives the impression of some delegates to the Pittsburgh Council. Dr Adolf Keller certainly expressed the opinion of all the continental delegates, when he wrote: 'A continental delegate could in the first days hardly escape the impression that the Presbyterian Alliance would be an Anglo-Saxon concern. But looking back to what the Alliance has been, and seeing with what problems she is concerned actually, the continental delegates from Europe had to admit that a significant change was taking place in this regard.

'Then the fact that the Alliance felt so deeply concerned about the Protestant situation in Europe and tried to examine it from the high standpoint of a great common interest, secured for it at once a new and unanimous sympathy and collaboration on the part of the European delegates and surely also from the Churches they represent. We feel no longer that we are left alone with our struggles and problems, but feel that a great family is participating in our cares and tasks and is ready to help where help is needed.'[33]

*   *   *

The Pittsburgh Council did not only elect Dr Fleming as General Secretary of the Alliance. It also elected Rev. Dr Henry B. Master, of Philadelphia, who had acted as Interim American Secretary since the death of Dr Roberts, as American Secretary. These two men were to have a harmonious and fruitful collaboration.

*   *   *

1922 saw the birth of the first organized interdenominational Inter-Church Aid, and we are glad to note that from the beginning the Alliance was fully behind this great venture. Here are the facts, as reported in the November 1922 issue of *The Quarterly Register*.

After having spoken of the Conference of the World Alliance for Promoting Friendship through the Churches, which took place in Copenhagen from 6 to 10 August, the Alliance General Secretary goes on to say: 'On the Thursday afternoon [10 August, *Ed.*] farewell words were spoken in three languages . . . but a good many of us remained, and some new guests arrived for a second conference that began that evening. It was called by the Swiss Evangelical Federation in conjunction with the Federal Council of Christian Churches in America, to devise, if possible, a common policy of help for Continental Protestantism in its present crisis of need . . . Of the delegates present, 18—one fourth of the whole—were more or less representing our Alliance . . .

'The result was the unanimous passing of the following resolution:

'This Conference, consisting of 72 representatives of 37 European Churches or Church Federations, in 20 different countries, considers it desirable, that a united relief action for European Protestantism be organised, and for this purpose considers itself as representing the Protestant Churches of Europe. It therefore elects an Executive Committee, consisting of the representatives of the Churches who have issued the invitation to the present conference, and authorizes this Council to appoint additional members.'[34]

The General Secretary of the Alliance was the first to be co-opted as a member of the Executive and this clearly shows the active part taken by the representatives of the Reformed family of Churches. Never was there any doubt that the Alliance was in favour of a wide Protestant Inter-Church Aid, rather than a narrow Presbyterian one.

The General Secretary further comments: 'This decision . . . will do much to unify and draw together the too long divided Evangelical Churches of Europe . . . In Dr Keller of Zurich the new organization has as its mainspring a man of business-like abilities and wide outlook, who seems to have been raised by

Providence for this special task. Nor can we grudge to Switzerland, with its central position and philanthropic record, the
honour of being chosen as headquarters.'[35]

The Alliance did not only speak; it acted. At the meeting of
the Eastern Section on 2 November 1922 the members 'hailed
with satisfaction the action of the Bethesda Conference at
Copenhagen in drawing together the various Protestant Churches
of Europe into a common organisation for the relief of distress
prevailing among them.' Further 'The Section authorized the
raising of a fund—if possible not less than £1,000 Sterling—for
special continental relief . . . This, of course, is only an emergency
measure, preliminary to direct and more comprehensive action
later by the stronger Churches.'[36] Later, at the meeting of the
Western Section on 14 February 1923, the Chairman of the
Committee on Work on the Continent of Europe reported that
in October 1922 an organization had already been formed,
consisting of the chairman of the European Committee [of Inter-
Church Aid, *Ed.*] of the constituent Churches. 'This committee
aims to bring our denominations more closely together in this
work.'[37]

*   *   *

Some of the Alliance spokesmen thought that Churches were too
slow in their search for unity, and at the meeting of the Western
Section on 14 February 1923, Dr W. I. Wishart said: 'Almost
every individual Christian leader is now ready to admit that our
system of competing denominations is entirely out of harmony
with the spirit of Jesus and the spirit of present progress, and is
daily becoming more intolerable . . . We all magnify the spirit
of cooperation, and write singularly beautiful resolutions about
unity, and the union of Churches, but when it comes to action
we are not willing to lose our denominational identity nor to let
our denominational rush-lights be swallowed up in the glory of
the united Church of Jesus Christ.'[38] How true these words are
still today!

The Alliance was nearing its Jubilee and some of its members
felt that a record of its activities should be written. At the 1922
meeting of the Western Section, Dr Richards, chairman of the
'Committee on Presbyterian and Reformed History' of the Section
proposed that 'the Section consider the advisability of preparing

a history of the Alliance as well as of the Western Section'.[39] This was approved with enthusiasm; a Committee was formed under the chairmanship of Dr D. S. Schaff, of Pittsburgh; but a year later the Committee reported that no history would be written and that instead special addresses would be given at the 12th General Council, scheduled to be held in Cardiff in 1925.

*   *   *

1922 had been an important year, as it had seen the birth of the first Protestant Inter-Church Aid Organization, under the leadership of Dr Adolf Keller. The Alliance had given it full support and the 1923 meeting of the Western Section decided to ask the Churches of the Section 'to raise $150,000 for the Churches of Continental Europe this coming ecclesiastical year'.[40]

In 1923 the most comprehensive Continental Conference organized to date by the Alliance was held in Zurich in July.

In *The Quarterly Register* of November 1923, the General Secretary says: 'We are inclined to think that "Zurich 1923" will be an even more memorable date in our history than "Pittsburgh 1921" as indicating a new stage in the development of the Reformed consciousness on the European Continent, especially on the practical side.

'One of the acts of the Zurich Conference of the Alliance was to send a message of greeting to the Pan-Lutheran Congress held at Eisenach in August. To this, a very warm and friendly reply was received.'[41]

Altogether 17 Continental countries were represented at the Zurich Conference including six or seven Churches which had never been represented at any previous Conference or Council. But Zurich was a Conference of the whole Alliance, and apart from Great Britain, Canada and the U.S.A., Australia and New Zealand, Egypt, India and South Africa had sent representatives. Among the subjects discussed, we note 'The Protestant Crisis in Europe', 'Common action for Church Aid', a subject on which Dr Keller spoke at length. He asked the Churches of the Alliance to give full support to the Central Bureau established in 1922 and this was naturally agreed to. The problem of Minorities also came for discussion. For, as *The Quarterly Register* writes: 'No Church problem . . . in Central or Eastern Europe, is so urgent as that of the treatment of Religious Minorities . . . We cannot and will not let this question rest till our statesmen and the League of Nations grapple seriously with it.'[42]

The problem of peace was also discussed at Zurich. The Resolution adopted on this point says: 'This Conference of the Alliance . . . views with grave anxiety the present unrest in Europe, and the spirit of hate, suspicion and mistrust, so sadly prevalent among the nations, and deplores the vast sums that continue to be spent on armaments and preparations for war.

'This Conference calls on the member Churches of our Order, here represented, and on all the members thereof, to seek ever for the settlement of all disputes between nations by methods of conciliation and arbitration.'[43]

The Conference gave its full support to the approaching Conference on 'Life and Work' and commended it to the Churches of the Alliance.

Giving his impressions on the Conference, Dr Keller wrote: 'The Conference has not only drawn nearer together the Reformed Churches on the Continent, but was for the first time a real meeting place between Continental and Western Protestantism, where the delegates of the Continental Churches could explain to their Western brethren their needs and problems without having the feeling that the Alliance was mainly an Anglo-American concern, or that they were in the background. They felt for the first time that the Alliance is their own affair and that they are concerned with its tasks in the same way as the Western brethren.'[44]

The Conference also discussed the future organization of the Alliance and voted 'that a new subsection be formed for the Continent of Europe, with Geneva and Zurich as alternate centres'.[45] This, though insufficient, would have been an improvement, but it never materialized, and for another 25 years the Continental Churches were to continue to have little influence on the decisions of the Alliance. But the work was increasing, and it became more and more difficult for the General Secretary to accomplish all the tasks which were required of him. It was therefore very welcome that the Conference decided on the appointment of a lady assistant in the Edinburgh office.

Though the Zurich Conference had been concerned with the future organization of the Alliance, nothing had been changed as regards the method of representation, one of the great weaknesses of the Alliance. Each General Council elected the 'members' of the Sections, and the Eastern Section co-opted a great many more men; they naturally represented the different Churches of the Section, but only in an indirect way, as they had not been chosen by the Supreme Courts of these Churches. The Western Section saw to it that the representatives to the Section were really proposed by the constituent Churches, but this was not the case for the Eastern Section; the Section meetings were a kind of 'closed club'. There were many distinguished Presbyterians among the members, as the leaders took great care in filling vacancies; but the fact remains that this was not a representative system and that the Churches did not feel directly concerned by decisions taken by people whom they had not appointed. Not until the 1948 reorganization of the Alliance in Geneva was the system to be completely abolished.

*   *   *

Readers will remember that the Dutch Reformed Churches of South Africa had withdrawn from the Alliance early in the century, as they felt, after the Anglo-Boer war, that the Alliance was an Anglo-Saxon affair. The Alliance regretted the decision and did all in its power to maintain some ties with the Churches of the Reformed family there. The Presbyterian Church there had of course remained a member of the Alliance, but it could hardly claim to speak in the name of the Reformed family in that country.

After the end of the First World War the Alliance leaders again tried to bring the Dutch Reformed Churches into their fellowship, and it was decided by the Eastern Section that the General Secretary should pay an extensive visit to South Africa. Dr Fleming went there in 1924 and his visit was fruitful; the Synod of the Reformed Church of Cape Province decided to join the Alliance again, while the other Synods decided to study the question. The newly formed Bantu Presbyterian Church also decided to affiliate with the Alliance. In the course of his visit, Dr Fleming also visited the Church of the Paris Mission in Basutoland, now the Evangelical Church of Lesotho and one of the newer members of the Alliance.

Some time before Dr Fleming's visit there had been an important meeting in Johannesburg to discuss the racial problem. In the February 1924 issue of *The Quarterly Register*, Dr Fleming

makes the following report: 'The most representative gathering
that has ever yet discussed the native problem in South Africa
assembled lately in Johannesburg. Called together by the Dutch
Reformed Church, it included delegates from all the leading
Christian bodies (except Roman Catholics), from the nine native
welfare associations functioning in the Union, from the Universi-
ties, and from the various native organisations. One good thing
the Conference has done was to dispel the false idea that the Dutch
Reformed Church is firmly prejudiced against native advance . . .
The resolutions, adopted either unanimously or by large majori-
ties, were of a decidedly liberal tendency . . . By an emphatic
majority the principle of the complete segregation of the races was
rejected, while the independent development of each race along
its own lines in a spirit of amicable co-operation was strongly
advocated . . . The Archbishop of Cape Town hailed the Conference as an "epoch-making event, the commencement of a new
era".'[46] In view of the harsher attitude taken later by many
representatives of the Dutch Reformed Churches in South Africa,
it is interesting to note that this has not always been their official
policy. Pray God that they may still remember what they decided
in 1924.

*   *   *

In 1924 the Alliance lost one of the men who did most to make
the Churches of the European Continent feel part of the Alliance.
Born in 1850, Dr Good had been closely associated with the
Alliance since the Belfast Council of 1884. He was a member of
the Reformed Church in the U.S. [later the Evangelical and
Reformed Church and now the United Church of Christ, *Ed.*] and
became President of its Synod. He was, at the time of his death,
and for many years before that, the chairman of the Committee
on Work on the Continent of Europe of the Western Section. As
such, he visited the Continent of Europe almost every year, and
he was acquainted with all the problems of the Reformed Churches
there. He was the man who developed the Alliance's strategy of
Inter-Church Aid and he gave strong support to the work of the
Central Bureau started by Dr Adolf Keller. His last visit to
Europe was in 1923, when he attended the Zurich Conference and
took a prominent part in the deliberations and resolutions of the
Conference.

Dr Good passed his enthusiasm on to the members of the Western Section, who continued to show interest and understanding for European Protestantism. At the meeting held on 26 February 1924, Dr Adolf Keller was present and spoke about the needs of the Continent and the work of the Central Bureau. The meeting then voted 'that the Western Section of the Alliance greatly recommends the raising of $500,000 for work on the Continent of Europe'.[47] It further decided that contributions should be sent, not to the Churches directly, but through the Central Bureau.

*   *   *

In December 1907 a 'Council of Reformed Churches in America' (U.S.A.) had been organized, whose aims were to bring a closer co-operation between the member Churches of the Alliance in the U.S.A. In the course of the years, it was seen that the Western Section was already fulfilling this function and that no other organization was necessary. Consequently, a joint meeting of the Western Section and of the Council of Reformed Churches took place during the Western Section meeting of 17 February 1925. The meeting moved that the General Council of Reformed Churches go out of existence. This was voted. The Western Section then decided to bring this action to the attention of the General Council in Cardiff [1925, *Ed.*] 'to secure, if the way be clear, necessary changes in the Constitution:

'a. Regarding the election of the members of the Western Section of the Alliance by the Supreme judicatories.

'b. Regarding the assumption by the Western Section of the specific powers, embodied in the Constitution of the General Council.'[48]

The Cardiff Council took action along the lines suggested and this was the end of an organization which had become superfluous.

*   *   *

For Christendom, 1925 was the year of the great Stockholm Conference on 'Life and Work' and the Alliance Churches, the majority of them at least, took an active part in it. But for Presbyterians, 1925 was also the year of the Twelfth General Council, which took place in Cardiff, Wales, from 23 June to 2 July.

If delegates from the Younger Churches were still very few, there was considerable progress with regard to the representation from the Continent of Europe; 42 delegates represented 23 Churches at Cardiff. For the first time the Swiss representatives sat as delegates of the Federation of Swiss Protestant Churches, after the admission of the Federation as a full member of the Alliance. Eleven other Churches were admitted by the Council, mainly from the Continent of Europe.

The Cardiff Council met exactly 50 years after the organization of the Alliance in London, in 1875, and though it had been decided that no history of the first 50 years should be written, the Council listened to the General Secretary speaking about 'The founding and achievements of the Alliance'[49] with great interest.

The Council devoted a whole day to the question 'Is a Common Statement of Faith (Creed or Confession) desirable and practicable for the Presbyterian World?'[50] Among the addresses on this subject there was a paper prepared by Professor Karl Barth, then at Göttingen, but unable to be present at the Council. The German text would have taken over two hours to read; the address was therefore given in an abridged translation by Dr A. Mitchell Hunter of Edinburgh. The Council voted 'that this Council favour the appointment of a small committee to draw up a common Statement of Faith to be presented to the Council for consideration'.[51] The Council then unanimously voted that the Eastern and Western Sections be instructed to take steps towards the realization of this resolution, and to appoint Committees to correspond with each other and to report to their respective Sections with a view to the presentation of a Joint Report to the next Council. Four years later, at the Boston Council, the Committees of the two Sections had to report that they had failed to agree and that consequently they could not propose to the Council any Statement of Faith. Once more the Alliance had to realize that it had to remain a fellowship, and not an organization bound by a common Statement of Faith.

*   *   *

The Council was also concerned with Europe. After hearing Dr Keller speak of the situation of many minority Churches there, and especially in Central and Eastern Europe, the Council voted to continue to give its support to the work of the Central Bureau and through it, to the Churches in need of assistance. Special attention was given to the developing evangelical witness in the Ukraine (then part of the Polish Republic).

The Council also passed another Resolution on peace. But no special action was taken.

Special problems were also in the minds of the delegates and Rev. J. Morgan Jones, from Wales, speaking on 'The New Social Outlook', reminded the delegates that the Church 'does not shrink from criticism of the *forms* of social life, or of established political and social institutions. It judges the Capitalist System, on the one hand, by its fruits; the monstrous toll it takes in human values, in human life and human happiness and human virtue . . . under this system in our land today, multitudes are doomed from their cradle to a narrow, empty, joyless existence, scarcely higher than that of the animal . . . On the other hand the system is judged by its principle, which is unfettered individual pursuit of individual gain . . .'[52]

Dr Fleming was reappointed as General Secretary until 31 December 1927. It was also decided that his successor should be a man not over 55 and that the said successor should work for a few months with Dr Fleming before taking up his post.

The Very Rev. Dr J. N. Ogilvie, of Edinburgh, was elected as the new President of the Alliance, and for the first time one of the two vice-presidents was a representative of the Continent, Rev. Dr Ch. Merle d'Aubigné, of Paris.

Less than a year had passed when the President of the Alliance, Dr Ogilvie, died suddenly, at the age of 66, and Dr Merle d'Aubigné became President of the Alliance.

*   *   *

China was in a state of ferment. In 1925 Chinese citizens were shot down by the police of the International Settlement of Shanghai. There was a sharp reaction by the Synod of Manchuria, representing 20,000 Christians who had been brought to the Faith by missionaries of the United Free Church of Scotland and of the Presbyterian Church in Ireland. In their declaration they said: 'We firmly believe that the root cause of this tragedy is to be found in the defective form of government of the International Settlement of Shanghai, as well as in the unequal treaties at various times concluded with China. We therefore declare the necessity of a fundamental revision of the regulations of the Shanghai Municipal Council, as well as of all treaties which are unfair to China.'

The Synod further requested the Conference of Missionaries 'voluntarily to relinquish the former treaties securing protection for mission work, and to be content with the protection afforded in the Constitution of the Chinese Republic, and it asks the Home Churches to make that request to the British Government.'[53]

Fortunately this was also the opinion of many missionaries of the Reformed family, and the Foreign Missions Committee of the Western Section, reporting to the 1926 meeting, said: 'Some missionaries disclaim the benefits of treaty protection. They regard it as a disadvantage . . . This is in a measure true, and the time may have come when all Christian work should be withdrawn from political control.'[54] Once more missionaries were in advance of the Churches of Europe and America, and one can only regret that their advice was not heeded immediately.

An Alliance meeting took place for the first time in Geneva in 1926. *The Quarterly Register* of November 1926 reports on this meeting as follows: 'All the world flocks to Geneva in September for the Assembly of the League of Nations. In concordance with a decision of the Cardiff Council last year it was agreed to hold at the same time a meeting of representative Continental Presbyterians with a small contingent from Great Britain and America "for mutual encouragement and counsel and for the discussion of questions affecting the life and progress of the Continental Churches . . ."

'Ever since the war one great object of our Alliance had been to strengthen and encourage our brethren in the lands so grievously hurt and disrupted by that disastrous conflict, and Switzerland has proved itself to be a most convenient centre for such efforts. Lausanne and Zurich have already done their part . . . Now it has been the turn of Geneva . . . It is rather remarkable that the Alliance has waited more than fifty years before paying an official visit to the city so famous in our Presbyterian tradition.

'We were forty in numbers, and the list of those present will show how representative our gathering was, covering 18 countries and 25 Churches . . .

'It was also a happy omen that we met just a week after the admission of Germany to the League of Nations . . . We had some reason to be proud of the fact that we were a few years ahead of the diplomats and politicians in our reconciling endeavours . . .'

The group came to discuss the name of the Alliance and *The Quarterly Register* continues: ' "Alliance Universelle des Eglises Réformées" in French and "Reformierter Weltbund" in German seem to find more favour abroad where the word "Presbyterian" is not in common use.'[55]

*   *   *

1925 had seen the great Stockholm Conference on 'Life and Work', and we have already seen that the Alliance was fully behind this endeavour to bring all Churches closer to each other in the field of practical Christianity.

The year 1927 saw another great Conference, the Lausanne Conference on 'Faith and Order'. What position did the Alliance take with regard to this movement towards Christian Unity? *The Quarterly Register* of May 1927, in an article signed by Professor W. A. Curtis, of Edinburgh, gives the answer:

'At the Geneva Conference in September 1926, no subject aroused greater interest or livelier discussion than the relation of the Churches of the Alliance to the Faith and Order Movement . . . Not a few of the Reformed Churches of the Continent had hesitated to take part in the Lausanne Conference, and some had practically resolved to abstain. The Conference finally decided to recommend cordial participation in the movement, and there was a strong demand for guidance from the Alliance. Indeed the demand was unanimous from the delegates present.

'It was arranged that the Continental Committee should prepare suggestions and offer them to all whom it might concern through *The Quarterly Register*. These suggestions are now available, and have been approved by the Eastern Section. They are as follows:

'1. Our Churches should be as strongly represented as possible, and take an active and cordial part at Lausanne.

'2. . . . their delegates should arrange to meet at Lausanne as a Presbyterian group.

'3. Delegates should carefully guard against the adoption of any resolutions or any programme which would seriously divide the Churches of our Alliance . . .

'4. In any scheme of reunion for Christendom a reasonable freedom should be conserved (a) in respect of the Church's constitutional autonomy and liberty to develop its life through orderly progress: and (b) in respect of the thought and action of its individual ministers and members.

. . . . . .

'6. Delegates should exercise vigilance, in connection with the formulation of any understandings of a doctrinal or constitutional nature, to see that a place be found with them for Reformed Principles which we deem essential . . .

'7. It is suggested that care should be taken to secure that adequate definition be obtained of the representative and constitutional character of the episcopate as a proposed element in the future organisation of the Church; and that in the light of history and scholarship it be acknowledged openly as a basis for reunion that the Church of the future is not pledged or bound to hold that the episcopate is in itself necessary to the *esse* of the Church.'[56]

This is a long quotation, but it seems important that readers should know the official position taken at that time by the Alliance. The point of view expressed by our fathers has been defended again and again by leaders of the Reformed Churches in more recent times. What is more important however, is the fact that the Alliance helped its member Churches to become fully involved in the Faith and Order Movement.

The meeting of the Eastern Section, on 13 June 1927, called Rev. W. H. Hamilton, a minister of the United Free Church Greenock, Scotland, to succeed Dr Fleming on his impending retirement. Mr Hamilton was to begin his work with Dr Fleming on 1 October and become his successor on 1 January 1928. This appointment was ratified by the Western Section.

*   *   *

On 6 July 1927 a Jubilee Service was held at St Giles', Edinburgh, where the delegates to the First General Council had met for worship in 1877. It was a great occasion and the President of the Alliance, Dr Merle d'Aubigné, was present.

The same year saw another Continental Conference, the Budapest Conference, which lasted from 4 to 14 September; representatives of 22 countries were present at Budapest and the Conference spent a good deal of time on the problem of religious minorities and their difficulties. The Conference also expressed its heartfelt sympathy with the Reformed Congregations in Russia and resolved 'to take such steps as it can, along with its constituent Churches, so that the congregations which are still able to carry on their existence may be maintained, may be able to keep their property and may be able again to get pastors'. The Conference recommended that where this was not possible 'individual members of congregations should join the Lutheran communions'.[57]

*   *   *

The end of 1927 saw the retirement of the very much appreciated General Secretary of the Alliance, Dr J. R. Fleming. In the February 1928 issue of *The Quarterly Register*, Dr R. J. Drummond could well write: 'world-wide travel had brought him into touch, in a way enjoyed by few, with sections of the Presbyterian Church in every part of the globe. His mastery of languages opened the door for easy conference with men of many nations.'[58] Dr Adolf Keller added that Dr Fleming had really brought together the Churches of the Continent of Europe and of the English-speaking world.

*   *   *

The work begun by Dr Fleming, that of bringing closer together the Anglo-Saxon and the Continental Churches, did not stop with his retirement. The Continental Churches were now members of the Alliance and wished to come together to discuss common problems. 1928 saw another Continental Conference, more modest than the Budapest Conference. It was a 'Group Conference' and the wish was expressed that the continental organization of the Alliance be extended. But before this happened, Europe was going to know years of distress and destruction.

REFERENCES
1. Western Section Minutes, March 23, 1920, p. 24.
2. Idem, p. 14.
3. Eastern Section Minutes, April 1, 1920, p. 2.
4. *The Quarterly Register*, vol. XI, no. 12, p. 270.
5. Idem, vol. XI, no. 14, p. 315.
6. Idem, p. 334.

7. Idem, pp. 344–346.
8. Idem, vol. XI, no. 13, p. 290.
9. Western Section Minutes, Feb. 16, 1921, p. 12.
10. Idem, p. 13.
11. Idem, p. 13.
12. Idem, p. 16.
13. Idem, p. 32.
14. Idem, p. 47.
15. Idem, p. 49.
16. *Proceedings 11th General Council*, p. 5.
17. Idem, p. 32.
18. Idem, p. 80.
19. Idem, p. 19.
20. Idem, p. 93.
21. Idem, p. 116.
22. Idem, p. 114.
23. Idem, pp. 118–119.
24. Idem, p. 179.
25. Idem, p. 191.
26. Idem, p. 345.
27. Idem, p. 308.
28. Idem, p. 321.
29. *Proceedings 11th General Council*, pp. 171–172.
30. Idem, p. 178.
31. Idem, p. 314.
32. Idem, p. 374.
33. *The Quarterly Register,* vol. XII, no. 4, p. 446.
34. Idem, vol. XII, no. 8, p. 535.
35. Idem, p. 537.
36. Idem, vol. XII, no. 9, p. 567.
37. Western Section Minutes, Feb. 14, 1923, p. 7.
38. Idem, p. 12.
39. Western Section Minutes, Feb. 8, 1922, p. 20.
40. Western Section Minutes, Feb. 14, 1923, p. 38.
41. *The Quarterly Register*, vol. XII, no. 12, p. 627.
42. Idem, p. 632.
43. Idem, p. 652.
44. Idem, p. 645 (under 3).
45. Idem, p. 634.
46. *The Quarterly Register*, vol. XII, no. 13, p. 667.
47. Western Section Minutes, Feb. 26, 1924, p. 24.
48. Western Section Minutes, Feb. 27, 1925, p. 11.
49. *Proceedings 12th General Council*, p. 40.

50. Idem, p. 102.
51. Idem, p. 145.
52. Idem, p. 385.
53. *The Quarterly Register*, vol. XIII, no. 4, p. 85.
54. Western Section Minutes, March 2, 1926, p. 14.
55. *The Quarterly Register*, vol. XIII, no. 8, p. 179.
56. Idem, vol. XIII, no. 10, pp. 231–232.
57. Idem, vol. XIII, no. 12, p. 295.
58. Idem, vol. XIV, no. 1, p. 11 et seq.

CHAPTER NINE

World Crisis and World War II

The great World Crisis which shattered so many countries on all continents started in 1929. This crisis prepared the ground for the development of totalitarian movements and was consequently responsible for World War II.

However, the storm had not yet broken when the delegates to the Thirteenth General Council met in Boston, U.S.A., from 19 to 26 June. The membership was once more almost totally Anglo-Saxon, only 13 delegates having come from the Continent of Europe, none from Asia and one from South Africa. But the problems were world-wide, and this is important.

One of the first acts of the Council was to send a Message to the 'Lutheran World Alliance'. The message says: 'The sons of Calvin, assembled at Boston . . . send to the sons of Luther best wishes for the success of the Union arrangements. They send brotherly greetings, convinced that the strengthening of one part of Protestantism will serve for the strengthening of Protestantism as a whole.'[1]

The Council rejoiced in the success of the Jerusalem Council of the International Missionary Council, 1928, where for the first time half of the delegates had come from the Younger Churches.

The delegates to the Boston Council were also concerned with social problems and felt that the Christian Churches ought to play a more positive role in the solution of these questions.

The Council heard Rev. Dr Lewis S. Mudge, Stated Clerk of the Presbyterian Church in the U.S.A., report on the Lausanne Conference of 'Faith and Order'. The report was a plea for a unity larger than the Reformed unity: 'Unity is necessary . . . a degree of unity far exceeding anything now in existence even among some of the members of our own family living in the same so-called Christian communities. Unity, that we may speak with a united voice for Christ.'[2]

The problem of unity compelled the Alliance to help its Churches to understand the essentials of their Faith more clearly and the subject was discussed at length at Boston.

The Council also decided to recommend that the member Churches hold a Reformed Churches' Day annually, if possible on the last Sunday in October. Finally, the Council passed a Resolution on Peace.

The Ninth Women's Conference, held during the 13th General Council, publicly declared: 'Everywhere it is admitted that, in the reorganization of the General Presbyterian Alliance now contemplated, the place of women in the scheme of work must be more distinctly recognized, and their range of interest not be limited to co-operation in Foreign Missions.'[3]

Professor Dr George W. Richards, of Lancaster Theological Seminary, who had been a leader in the Alliance for many years, was elected President of the Alliance and the Council came to a close.

*   *   *

1929 was also the year of the reunion of the Church of Scotland and of the United Free Church of Scotland. If it is difficult for us to agree with the Alliance General Secretary, who in his report to the Western Section saw in this union the greatest event of the year, there is no doubt that it was an important event and that it was greeted with joy by most Presbyterian leaders in Britain and in America.

In August of the same year, the Executive Committee of the Central Bureau, of which Dr Keller was the Director, convened a Conference of Protestant leaders in Basle to discuss the whole problem of Inter-Church Aid. The Conference, which was attended by many Presbyterian leaders and had the goodwill of the Alliance, decided that the work had to be continued and that the Bureau would from now on be known as 'the Central Bureau for Inter-Church Aid'; the decision was for five years and the Churches were asked not to slacken their efforts.

*   *   *

The crisis, which had started in the U.S.A. at the end of 1929 had not yet reached the Continent of Europe when the next Continental Group Conference met at Elberfeld, Germany, in 1930.

The delegates gathered there discussed how best they could increase the interest for the Alliance among the Continental Churches, and the General Secretary must have come back from Germany very happy, for he wrote to the Western Section, meeting in February 1931: 'Many of us returned from Germany with a powerful conviction that out of this great nation, which has nobly proved its mettle under trial and in a brave acceptance of hard situations, there might now once again come by God's appointment—even as happened 400 years ago—the revival of religion for which we long, and healing and peace for all the nations of mankind.'[4] Less than three years later Adolf Hitler became Chancellor of the Reich and Germany was on its way to becoming more nationalistic than ever!

*   *   *

Up to now Youth has seldom been mentioned in this book, and for a good reason. The fact is that the Alliance had rarely thought of Youth and of the place it should occupy in the Alliance. At the meeting of the Eastern Section, on 8 April 1931, Rev. W. T. Elmslie of Leeds, later General Secretary of the Presbyterian Church of England (who was to be killed during the war early in 1945, with most of the Staff of the Church, when a V2 bomb fell on the Church headquarters), referred to the widespread ignorance 'among the Younger people of the Churches concerning the achievements and potentialities of the Alliance' and suggested 'that small conferences of Young Presbyterians of different Churches might advantageously be organised in various centres both in Britain and overseas'.[5] Mr Elmslie did not rest until this was accepted, and the first Youth Conference took place in Liverpool in the early spring of 1933.

*   *   *

In 1931 the depression was beginning to be felt everywhere. Churches saw their incomes diminish and their work was menaced in many areas. But our Presbyterian leaders did not feel that this was a justification for relaxing their efforts on behalf of the Central Bureau for Inter-Church Aid. In his report to the Western Section meeting of 24 February 1931 the chairman of the Committee for Work on the Continent of Europe, Dr J. Ross Stevenson, said: 'If the Central Bureau closes the first year of its

"Five Year Program" without a deficit, it is due to the Presbyterian Churches.

'There can be no doubt as to the urgent need for further help to the Protestant Churches of Continental Europe . . . It must be remembered that the depression hits us after seven exceedingly prosperous years; over there, it comes on top of five years of destruction and another ten of most difficult readjustment.' The Section was especially concerned with the fate of the Mennonites of the Soviet Union, 200,000 in all, who had been 'crowded into cattle trains without food or water, and shipped off on the several days' journey to the swampy forest lands of northern Russia, there to be dumped, without food or equipment, miles away from a station, and left to shift for themselves. Half of them have succumbed'.[6]

And in 1932 the Western Section decided to send out of its own slender funds a sum of $4,000, with an additional $1,000 if possible, in answer to an urgent appeal from Dr Keller. The Eastern Section did not remain behind and at the meeting held on 4 November 1931 also decided to make a gift from its own funds to help launch APIDEP, the 'Loan Association for Inter-Church Aid', created by Swiss Evangelical bankers in association with Dr Keller's Central Bureau. A year later the Eastern Section decided to send a gift out of its funds to help Ukrainian Evangelicals.

Continental Conferences were very numerous at that time. After the 1930 Elberfeld Group Conference, another one was held in September 1931 at Mazamet, in the South of France. Though lack of accommodation limited the membership of the Conference to eighty persons, it was highly successful and helped make the Alliance known to French Reformed people.

In spite of these Conferences the Eastern Section remained very much a British—not to say a Scottish—affair, and it makes one smile when the Chairman of the 26 April 1933 meeting welcomed 'members who had come to the meeting from beyond Scotland'.[7] One has to remember that the Section included not only the whole of Europe, but also Asia, Africa and Australasia!

*　　*　　*

The Fourteenth General Council met in Belfast from 21 to 27 June 1933. The depression had hit the Churches of the Western World and Canada and the U.S.A. sent only 44 delegates. There were delegates from ten countries on the Continent of Europe; Asia, Africa and Australasia were represented, as well as the West Indies. For the first time there were many young people attending the Council as visitors; this was a real step forward in the right direction.

By this time Adolf Hitler had come to power and the Alliance Council showed great concern for the position of the Jews in Germany, although no one could foresee that Hitler was to establish a reign of terror all over Europe and that his policy would lead to the almost complete suppression of the Jewish population, not only of Germany, but of many other Continental countries.

The Council was glad to be informed that several prominent German Reformed Church leaders, amongst them the Swiss theologian Karl Barth, had published a 'Theological Declaration for the Form of the Church'. The delegates were given the full text of this declaration and so became acquainted with the problems facing the Church in Germany.

Dr Adolf Keller was present and made a strong appeal on behalf of the Central Bureau for Inter-Church Aid. The Council voted to give as much assistance as possible through its member Churches and to channel it through the Geneva office of Dr Keller.

The Council was also concerned with unity, and Professor W. A. Curtis, of Edinburgh, who was to be the new President of the Alliance, made a passionate plea for greater unity with the Lutherans. He said: 'I believe the time is at hand, foreshadowed by the recent Marburg commemoration of the historic colloquy between Luther and Zwingli, and hastened by the march of national events, when Lutheran and Reformed will be found co-operating with one another with hardly a trace of the old cleavage. Let us in this Alliance make ready to welcome and share in that rapprochement, with a lively regret that it has been so long delayed, and a profound sense of the momentous importance of the consequences which it portends. What a day would dawn for Europe, and for Christendom, if the Lutheran Churches of Scandinavia, Finland, the Baltic States, Germany, Poland, Austria, Hungary and France were at last to end their isolation and join hands with our more widely diffused Reformed Churches which are their internal or external neighbours . . .'[8] These words are at last becoming true; we can thank God that our fathers already worked for that unity.

*   *   *

The Council received a deputation from the International Union of Women's Missionary Societies of the Reformed and Presbyterian Churches. They presented a Memorial demanding that membership of the Council be opened to women. Churches having women elders should include them in their delegations; other Churches should appoint women corresponding members. The Council gave unanimous and cordial approval to the Memorial and transmitted it to the Sections 'for consideration'.

Youth also occupied a place in this Council. We have already seen that for the first time there were 'Youth Visitors' who had the status of corresponding members. Rev. W. T. Elmslie of Leeds, who had successfully organized the first Youth Conference in Liverpool in the spring of 1933, made an urgent plea to the Council in favour of Youth and of its participation in the work of the Council. The Youth Group of the Council suggested through Mr Elmslie that 'membership of the Council should be extended to Youth representatives of the Constituent Churches, in addition to the official delegates'.[9] It was proposed that this youth representation should not exceed 20 per cent of the membership of the Council. The Youth Group also asked the Youth Committees of both Sections of the Alliance to organize further International Youth Conferences.

The members of the Council manifested real interest in the proposal, but did not go further. No action was taken, as the Council felt that this would involve financial expenditure. This was certainly true, but one can only regret that the Council did not have the courage to take action and to involve Youth directly in the deliberations of the Councils. The delegates to Belfast showed a regrettable lack of vision, and it was not until after World War II that Youth began to take a more active part in the work of the Alliance.

*   *   *

Problems of the world were acute at the time of this Council. Rev. Dr John M'Naugher, on behalf of the Western Section, addressed the Council 'On the great problems facing the Church

c.s.—6

today'. He said: '. . . the utility of the Alliance of Reformed Churches has sometimes been sharply questioned in the West . . . They (the rank and file) were conscious . . . of their own great religious and moral problems . . . and many complained that the Alliance had not more frequently entered the world of activity with guidance regarding these. They had to answer this challenge or forfeit influence. The Alliance must intrude its voice in the sphere of practical affairs, and he felt the need of issuing a Manifesto.'[10]

A 'Manifesto and appeal on public questions in religion and morals' was then adopted by the Council. It has seven articles. On 'Christian Unity' the Manifesto says: 'The Alliance is in cordial sympathy with the world-wide aspirations and movements towards the reunion in Christendom and rejoices in their progress.' On 'Racial Relations' the Manifesto says: '. . . we protest against every form of slavery, oppression, exploitation, or spoliation . . . and we call for resolute efforts to redress social and racial wrongs . . .' On 'Industry and Business' the Manifesto says: 'We believe that the Christian Church has a peculiar responsibility for maintaining the dignity of human labour and securing for it a just reward.'[11]

A former Alliance President, Dr Charles Merle d'Aubigné, spoke on 'The Responsibilities of the Present-Day Church in Ecumenical Movements' and what he said shows a real ecumenical spirit: 'I believe that it would be necessary, for some at least of the Churches of our Order, to re-examine their position on some of the points which are raised and see whether by a more careful study of the affirmations of Scripture and of the teaching of the Reformers, we could not perchance come somewhat nearer to the position held by theologians of another school?'[12]

The Council decided to appoint a Standing Commission on Public Questions, which would have power to issue pronouncements on behalf of the Alliance between Councils; the Commission was to be made up of 15 members, from both Sections, together with the President, the General Secretary and the American Secretary.

The Council also extended cordial greetings to all Evangelical Churches and expressed the desire to have closer relations with them. Delegates voted that Continental Conferences should be held regularly midway between the General Councils and that steps should be taken to make fuller use of French and German at the General Councils, as was already the case at the Continental Conferences. It renewed its declaration of faithful support of the League of Nations and asked the member Churches not only to continue but to increase their work of Inter-Church Aid through the Central Bureau for Inter-Church Aid at Geneva.

The Council ended on a serious mood, but the delegates were far from realizing that the world was already on the path which was to lead to another terrible war.

*   *   *

Conditions in Germany were becoming more and more difficult for the Christian Church. In March 1934, the Alliance, under the signature of its President and General Secretary, sent a letter to Dr H. A. Hesse, Moderator of the Reformierter Bund. After reminding the German Reformed people that the Alliance had refrained from making pronouncements on the situation, the letter went on to assure our German brethren that they were constantly in the thoughts and prayers of Reformed Christians in other lands.

In July of the same year, some leaders of the Alliance had an interview with Bishop Heckel, of Berlin, head of the German Church External Affairs Office, who paid a warm tribute to the terms of the communication which had been sent in the name of the Alliance. From now on Germany was to be a constant preoccupation of our leaders.

If Germany gave cause for concern, there were happily still some bright spots in Europe. One was the developing Evangelical Movement in Polish Ukraine, and the Alliance, through its Churches, gave constant financial support to the Ukrainian Evangelicals. In 1934, Rev. W. T. Elmslie visited them on behalf of the Alliance and was greatly impressed by what he saw.

The Second Youth Conference of the Alliance was held in 1935; though 'International' in principle, it was mainly attended by British delegates and this is comprehensible, as the Conference took place from 26 to 30 April at Pitcorthie, Fife, Scotland. Young people at the time did not have much money and it was not easy for delegates from the Continent to undertake the journey to Scotland.

1935 also saw another Continental Group Conference. It took

place in Czechoslovakia, at Podebray and in Prague. The depressing situation in Germany does not seem to have influenced the delegates too much, for the General Secretary of the Alliance wrote in the November 1935 issue of *The Quarterly Register*: 'All our Conferences have been happy and worth-while, but none has been happier or more effective and stimulating than this one.'[13]

* * *

Christian leaders in all lands saw with grave concern that in 1936 the problem of non-Aryan refugees from Germany was becoming more and more serious. In the February 1936 issue of *The Quarterly Register* Dr Adolf Keller reported on the work the Central Bureau for Inter-Church Aid was doing and asked for the support of the Churches gathered in the Alliance.

But in 1936 Germany was not the only reason for concern. Civil war had broken out in Spain and the position of Evangelical Christians living in regions dominated by Franco's armies was becoming critical; the Alliance could not remain indifferent, though direct action was impossible.

Another country which continued to give serious preoccupations to the Alliance leaders was Romania, where the Hungarian-speaking Reformed Church complained of being deprived of the rights guaranteed by the Peace treaties. In September 1936, an Alliance Commission, composed of three persons, the Alliance Vice-President, the Convener of the Continental Committee of the Eastern Section and the General Secretary, spent several weeks there. It was mainly a visit of 'friendship and encouragement', for more could not be attempted. But the assurance that they were not forgotten by the Alliance was a real stimulus for the Reformed Church.

* * *

Since 1886 the Alliance had had a quarterly journal, *The Quarterly Register*, which helped to keep its large constituency informed of what the Alliance was doing. There was no desire to stop the publication of the quarterly, but a more explicit name was desired. Beginning with the February 1937 issue, *The Presbyterian Register* replaced the old *Quarterly Register*. 'This more definite name, we hope', wrote the Editor, 'may attract many others interested in the welfare of our Churches to peruse our magazine.'[14]

In a 'New Year's Survey' the Editor of *The Presbyterian Register*, Dr Hamilton, commented on the Ecumenical Movements and the Alliance: 'The emergence of the great ecumenical movements of our age, "Life and Work" and "Faith and Order", has revealed a gigantic, well-furnished effort to establish a new and active unity of the separated communions of Christendom and it may be mentioned that the great conferences of these two movements in Great Britain next autumn have somewhat seriously affected the availability of members in our various Churches for delegation to our Montreal Council. The greater magnitude and resources of these organisations may at times have tended to reduce the impressiveness of our Alliance; but surely their progress ought to make clearer than ever the necessity of a strong central witness to the solidarity of Presbyterianism.'[15]

There is no doubt that this shows little enthusiasm for the Ecumenical Movements of the time; it is certain that the General Secretary was not reflecting the thoughts of most Presbyterian leaders, both in Europe and in America. He failed to see that there was no competition between Confessional and Ecumenical Unity, but that they were complementary. The future was to show that the Ecumenical Movement needed strong confessional families, which could work in certain fields where it was difficult for the Ecumenical organization to do so.

In the same survey, the Editor noted 'the development among the Churches of the Continent of Europe—but also in the Churches of Britain and America—of a strong resurgence of what may, without disrespect or offence, be called Anti-liberalism . . .'[16] Dr Hamilton was of course referring to the growing influence of Karl Barth, the great Reformed theologian who had had to leave his teaching post at the University of Bonn (Germany) and was now Professor at the University of Basle, Switzerland. Professor Barth was more than an academic theologian, and the world was grateful to him for his leadership in the Church conflict in Germany. He was the first man to realize the nature of this conflict. In *The Presbyterian Register* of May 1937, the Editor wrote: 'Professor Karl Barth presents a stirring message to the Christians of the world. It is based on the thesis that "the Church conflict in Germany is significant for the whole world".'[17]

Meanwhile, the situation in Germany was becoming more difficult for the Confessing Church, and for our Reformed brethren in particular. In his report for the year 1936–37, sent in April 1937, the General Secretary wrote: 'The situation for the Evangelical Churches of Germany increasingly bespeaks our sympathy and aid . . . Germany will some day acknowledge that the brave stand of our brethren [Reformed, *Ed.*] has been an act of which all Germans have cause to be proud. But much must first be endured. The *Reformierte Kirchenzeitung* has been suppressed. The School at Elberfeld [Free Theological Academy, *Ed.*] has been closed by the Secret Police.'[18]

* * *

It was in such conditions that the Fifteenth General Council of the Alliance convened in Montreal, from 23 to 29 June 1937. Its theme was 'The Church in the Modern World'. Among the 'ex-officiis' members of the Council there was the new American Secretary Elect, Rev. Dr William B. Pugh, Stated Clerk of the Presbyterian Church in the U.S.A. In 1935 he replaced Rev. Dr Henry B. Master, who had filled the post of American Secretary with great distinction. Dr Pugh was to become American Secretary at the Montreal Council; and from then on until his lamented death in a car accident in September 1950, Dr Pugh was to be an outstanding figure in the Alliance and the principal instrument of the 1948 reorganization.

Delegations were smaller than at former Councils, especially from Churches outside the Western Hemisphere. The number of delegates from the Churches of the Eastern Section amounted to 44; 29 came from the British Isles, nine from the Continent of Europe and six from other Churches of the Section, Korea, China, South Africa, Ceylon and Peru.

One of the first acts of the Council was to recognize 'The International Union of Women's Missionary Societies of the Reformed Churches' as the official Women's Organization of the Alliance, and to decide that the Constituent Churches might, upon nomination of the Women's organizations of the Church, appoint a certain number of women corresponding members, who would attend the General Councils with the right to speak, but not to vote, unless they held places in the Council as ministers or elders.

The Council gave a great deal of time to the Continent of Europe. Dr Keller with his wide knowledge of the Continent and its problems was present and spoke on 'Three Present-Day Perils' which were menacing the Church: (a) extreme poverty which hampers the activity of the Church, (b) the State and (c) 'seduction through modern humanism, secularism and paganism'.[19]

On the ecumenical level the Council adopted a much more open attitude than the Alliance General Secretary, and cordial messages of greeting and goodwill were sent to the Conference on 'Life and Work' at Oxford and to the Conference on 'Faith and Order' at Edinburgh.

Human rights also had their place in the Council, not only with regard to the persecution of Jews in Germany, but also concerning the exploitation of the workers in industry. Rev. Dr E. E. Kresge of Lancaster, Pa., made a clear attack on the capitalist system as it had operated for too long: 'Animated by the profit motive, modern capitalism has, at those times when no social control was exercised over it, exploited its workers and the general public as mercilessly as the old orders of slavery and serfdom had done in their day . . .

'It is only in a co-operative industrial society that we can hope for the realization of human rights and the conservation of human values.'[20]

And Rev. F. D. Langlands, of Galashiels, Scotland, added a similar condemnation: 'In spite of the teaching of Jesus about human value, which is clear and unmistakable, His Church has often failed to bear witness for human value in the social relations of life . . . The Church has sometimes been the friend of reaction and the ally of tyranny.

'In every industrial country to-day there is a large section of the people compelled by their poverty to live under social conditions that hinder not only their physical health, but also their development as personalities of infinite value . . .

'The Church must inspire her members by word and action to witness against social conditions and a social environment which their consciences cannot approve.'[21]

The Council approved an important Manifesto, a 'Pronouncement on matters of Faith and Life'. This Manifesto had been prepared by the Commission on Public Pronouncements appointed by the Belfast Council in 1933. It contains eight articles.

The first article deals with 'The Church and Holy Scripture', and the Manifesto says: 'We believe that God is speaking through the Scriptures of the Old and New Testaments to the world in its sin and confusion . . .'

On 'The Church and Unity', the Manifesto speaks as follows: 'We believe in one Holy Catholic Church . . . as there is one Christ there can be only one Church.

'. . . we gladly acknowledge the duty laid upon us to promote, in accordance with the Word of God, unity both within and without our own Presbyterian Order and with Churches of other traditions and government.'

On 'The Church and its world-wide mission': '. . . By the world's distress the urgency of the missionary command is intensified . . .'

On 'Religious Freedom and the autonomy of the Church': 'The Reformed Churches have long been identified with re-sistance to oppression in Church and State . . . We therefore deplore, and make our protest against, the grievous restraints laid in our time upon the life and liberty of suffering Communions within the Church of Christ in various lands, Orthodox, or Roman Catholic, or Protestant . . .'

The Section on 'The Church and Social Life' is divided into several sub-sections. On 'Stewardship of Life and Property': '. . . The end of life is not to amass wealth or power but to serve and glorify God . . . We appeal for a wider and deeper realization of the Christian standard of stewardship.' On 'The Church and Social Order': '. . . The Church is summoned to direct the minds of her people towards the necessity for a re-ordained social life, in default of which distress is turning to bitterness and violence.' This section further deals with Temperance, Gambling and the Lord's Day.

Section VI deals with 'The Christian Church and Education' and reaffirms the 'profound interest and stake [of the Church, *Ed.*] in the education provided' by the State.

Section VII is concerned about 'The Church and the State' and affirms that 'The State exists not for its own ends, but for the promotion of the common good by the enactment and admin-istration of just laws . . .

'The State is called to serve the Church by the recognition of her distinctive character as a divinely ordered community, with distinctive rights and obligations.'

Section VIII deals with 'The Church and International Life'

and has two sub-sections: 'International Community and Co-operation': 'Confronted by aggressive nationalism, we condemn the view that nations are a law unto themselves, and are entitled to pursue what they interpret to be their own destiny without regard to the rights of others . . .' On 'The Church and War' the Manifesto proclaims that 'recourse to war by the nations of the world is a heinous evidence of the sin of man's heart and an offense to God and men. War can neither establish justice and security, nor reconcile enemies.'[22]

Naturally, Germany was constantly in the minds of the delegates to the Council, though no representative of the German Reformed people had been able to travel to Montreal, and the Council unanimously adopted a Resolution. Here is part of the text of this important message:

'The representatives of the Reformed Churches . . . view with profound and unabated concern the continuance of the deplorable crisis in the situation of their ecclesiastical brethren in Germany . . . They are agreed in making the following declaration:

'1. . . . we express our deep fraternal sympathy with our brethren in Germany . . .

'2. . . . we respectfully make appeal to the authorities of the German Reich to have regard for the inherent justice of the spiritual claims of our Confessional brethren . . .

'3. . . . Nevertheless we recognize that the conflict has assumed a form in which not only freedom of conscience and profession and the autonomy of the Church of Christ in matters purely spiritual are involved, but, above all, the security of certain essential doctrines which have long been sacred to our Communions.

'4. For us . . . the Word of God . . . is the only sovereign authority which the Church must receive, obey and proclaim . . . In all matters spiritual and theological the Church is responsible to her Lord alone . . .

'5. To the principles stated in the preceding paragraph the Reformed and Presbyterian Churches have continually adhered since the Reformation . . . and . . . they cannot do other than profess and maintain them in fidelity to their inheritance in the Word of God.'[23]

A new Commission on the Revision of the Constitution and

Rules of the Alliance was appointed and a new President was elected in the person of Rev. Dr Robert Laird, a minister of the United Church of Canada. The delegates voted that the next Council should be held, D.V., in Geneva, Switzerland, in 1941 . . . Little did they know that the next Council would not be held until 1948 and that in the meantime the world would go through a most terrible holocaust.

*   *   *

1937 was an important year from the Ecumenical point of view. We have already seen that both the 'Life and Work' and the 'Faith and Order' Movements met in Great Britain during the summer. In an article in the November 1937 issue of *The Presbyterian Register*, the General Secretary reports on these two Conferences. 'By the action of both the Conferences, a proposal to form a "World Council of Churches", uniting the interests of the two movements in a single representative body, is being submitted to the Churches of the world for their official approval. If the plan is consummated, it will mark a new stage in Christian history, for there will then come into being a world-wide council directly representing the great bodies of non-Roman Christianity and continuously functioning in co-operative tasks on their behalf.'

And Dr Hamilton ended with these remarks: 'The spiritual blessing of the Conferences is universally recognised . . . even the adversaries of the ecumenical movement admit that it exists and that we need it in the turmoil and pain of our time, and must collaborate to build that Church of faith which is going through her birth pangs in the persecution of Continental Christians.'[24]

*   *   *

If 1937 had been an important year from the Ecumenical point of view, 1938 was to be even more so. From 9 to 13 May an important meeting took place at Utrecht, when it was decided that a 'World Council of Churches (in process of formation)' should be created. The Alliance General Secretary had attended the meeting as the Alliance representative, and at a meeting of the Executive Committee of the Eastern Section on 16 May he reported that 'the WCC had not seen fit to give direct representation to the Presbyterian and kindred Alliances in its membership, but had made adjustments to secure provision of a number of places for minority Churches likely otherwise to be inadequately represented'.[25]

*   *   *

Alas, if 1938 was to be a great ecumenical year, it was also to see the prologue to the Second World War. Dr Adolf Keller, who had become one of the two Vice-Presidents of the Alliance at the Montreal Council, was in Vienna in March, and on the 15th he witnessed, as he reports in the May issue of *The Presbyterian Register* 'the marching of the German army . . . the entry of Herr Hitler and the indescribable jubilation of the population'.[26]

From Vienna, Dr Keller went to Berlin. He reports: 'Reinforced by a request from the General Presbyterian Alliance I took the opportunity to make an application to be allowed to visit Pastor Niemöller in the concentration camp. In the Ministry of Propaganda . . . the request seemed to be favourably considered . . . A direct application to the Secret State Police brought the announcement that the visit to Niemöller would not be permitted either now or in the future.'[27]

However war did not yet seem inevitable. In April 1938, a small conference of Youth leaders of the Eastern Section (mainly from British Churches) was to meet in Edinburgh 'to discover if we can make the Alliance and its ecumenical aim a greater force and reality among the younger generation to the mutual advantage of the Churches and the Alliance'.[28]

The meeting of the Eastern Section on 6 April 1938 cordially accepted the invitation of the Reformed Church of Hungary to hold the next Continental Conference in Budapest. The decision to hold the Conference was confirmed in November of the same year, in spite of recent events in Czechoslovakia, and it is only in April 1939, at the meeting of the Eastern Section on the 6th of the month, that it was 'reluctantly decided that the present unsettled condition of Europe now makes it imperative to postpone the International Conference'[29] planned for September of the same year.

1938 was the year of the Munich 'Agreement', which marked the first step in the elimination of Czechoslovakia as a Sovereign and Independent State. Though relief was felt by some that war had been postponed, many had the sad feeling that Munich had settled nothing and had imposed a grave injustice on Czechoslovakia. This was the feeling of the Alliance leaders, and in the November issue of *The Presbyterian Register*, the Editor wrote: 'In effect the agreement was made at the expense of Czecho-Slovakia, whose government had shown extraordinary patience and magnanimity throughout the crisis.'[30]

In the same issue Rev. Dr F. Zilka, of Prague, spoke for the Czech Christians: 'From our point of view . . . it is a mistake and a wrong conception to think that the Great Powers of the West have preserved us as a nation and state from a worse fate . . . It is a fearful mistake to lull the people into believing that by the sacrifice of Czechoslovakia peace has been assured . . .'[31] Dr Zilka was only too soon to be proved right.

*   *   *

The Civil War was still raging in Spain, and as the Republicans were losing ground, the situation of Spanish Protestants became increasingly difficult. The Alliance launched renewed appeals for support of these brethren through the Central Bureau for Inter-Church Aid.

*   *   *

In the field of what was still called 'Foreign Missions' the situation was also becoming more difficult. The report of the Foreign Missions Committee of the Western Section to the Section meeting of 23 February 1938 recorded the closing of missionary stations in Ethiopia, due to the conquest of that country by Mussolini. Speaking of Asia, the report continued: 'The Japanese policy of extending a totalitarian sway over all interests and relationships in Chosen [Korea, *Ed.*], Formosa and Manchuria threatens the complete suppression of the Christian education conducted by our Mission Boards.'[32] A year later the report of the same Committee reports on the invasion of China by Japanese troops and the consequent disruption of mission work in many areas. But the report makes special mention of the self-sacrificing devotion of missionaries and Chinese Christians.

*   *   *

Alliance leaders were anxious to make the Alliance more efficient. In the Eastern Section they had been considering the desirability of creating a British Churches' Sub-Section; instead, the Committee appointed to consider the proposal came to the unanimous conclusion that it was better to appoint a new British Churches' Committee of the Eastern Section. This Committee, which had as its object 'consultation on practical issues affecting British Constituent Churches'[33] would meet at least once a year. The Eastern Section meeting of 5 April 1939 (which was attended only by British delegates) voted the appointment of this Committee, under the chairmanship of Professor Roy D. Whitehorn, of Westminster College, Cambridge. This Committee, which still exists, was soon to prove its worth by developing united action among the Churches of the Reformed family in Great Britain.

*   *   *

The political and religious situation was becoming more and more difficult. But some of the men who knew the situation best, though pessimistic about the political future, were more optimistic with regard to the Christian Church. The May 1939 issue of *The Presbyterian Register* contains an article by Professor Dr Adolf Keller, entitled 'End and rebirth of Churches in Central Europe'. We read: 'In Russia . . . the end of an old Christian Church will be near . . . The Evangelical Church in Russia has been entirely wiped out. Of 200 Lutheran pastors, not a single one is still at work at the present time . . .'

After pointing out that what was coming to an end was a Church which had been bound to the State, a Church of wealth and power, a Church which knew better than Christ himself, the article went on: 'A new Church is born. It is yet an invisible Church with no known membership, with no structure or organization . . . It grows, we do not know how, in Russian villages, in the large woods, on the railway, a new spiritual Church of Christ which will get its form, its organization, its leadership, its theology later when such is God's will.

'A new Church is born also out of the Church struggle in Germany. Such an intrepid man like Niemöller is a Church builder although he sits in a concentration camp and is closely watched . . . his influence is spreading as an atmospheric power and kindling a new fire in the hearts of many young people.

'Where these two or three have this particular courage which is called faith by a better name, where they meet in the name of

Christ in private houses, in restaurants, on the market, on the railway, they build up a new Church of Christ.'[34]

*   *   *

Though the Budapest Conference planned for September 1939 had had to be abandoned, leaders of the Eastern Section were still anxious to establish as many bridges as possible between the Churches of the Section. It was decided that the Chairman of the Section, Rev. Dr J. Hutchison Cockburn, and the Convener of the Continental Committee, Rev. Professor G. D. Henderson, would visit Switzerland and the Netherlands respectively. As for the General Secretary, accompanied by the Moderator of the Presbyterian Church of England, Rev. J. M. Richardson, they were asked to attend the meeting of the Central Bureau for Inter-Church Aid, at Clarens, Switzerland, from 25 to 28 August, and then to proceed to the Synod of the Waldensian Church of Italy, from 2 to 7 September.

*   *   *

At dawn, on 1 September 1939, Hitler's troops invaded Poland and on the 3rd, Great Britain and France, bound by treaty with Poland, declared war on the Third Reich. The Second World War had begun.

In an article written by the General Secretary in the November issue of *The Presbyterian Register*, we have the first reaction of an Alliance leader: 'We urge our Churches to maintain as far as possible our work of evangelical solidarity, and to strengthen mutually their confidence that love is stronger than hatred.'[35]

On 6 October, the General Secretary had informed the member Churches of the Section, after consultation with the chairman, that 'the affairs of the Alliance should be remitted until further notice to a small *Emergency Committee* with powers'.[36] This Committee was to be entirely British, so that it could function normally.

The meeting of the Eastern Section of 1 November approved the letter sent by the General Secretary and appointed this Emergency Committee. It also decided to send a 'Message to all the Reformed Churches'. This Message was sent on 30 November. Let us quote a few sentences: 'It is not for us to assess the guilt of the nations, or any of them, in the long evil process that has now culminated in internecine strife. The event itself we contemplate with unfeigned grief; and we fear its effects upon the Cause which our Lord and Master committed as a sacred trust to all His disciples of every land and kindred, unless, by His Grace and an effort greater than mere human flesh and blood can achieve, the spirit of the discipleship . . . is preserved in purity and in the glorious hope of His victory and everlasting reign.

. . . . . .

'We pray all the brethren of our Christian family to whom this message shall come . . . to do everything within their power to knit our world-wide family in this time of darkness and distress; for Jesus' sake.'[37]

The Continental Committee had proposed that visits be made in the first months of 1940 to the Churches of France, Holland, Switzerland and Italy if the international situation permitted. The answers received were all very positive and it was decided to proceed with the arrangements. This was decided at a meeting of the Emergency Executive on 31 January 1940.

*   *   *

During World War I the Churches had been bitterly divided and the Spirit of Christ had been totally absent from many Church pronouncements. Where did the Churches stand in 1939?

In an article in *The Presbyterian Register* of November 1939, Dr Adolf Keller wrote: 'First: the Church is more conscious than in 1914 of the fundamental differences between Church and world . . .

'The second characteristic element in the present situation of the Church is the fact that a larger and deeper fellowship of the Churches has grown since 1914 . . . the Churches know to-day something of *the Church*—the Una Sancta—of the indestructible communion which cannot be divided even by war . . .

'The third characteristic element which differentiates the Church of to-day from that of 1914 is a deepening of the belief that human differences, and even ecclesiastical and theological differences, have not the final importance which was attributed to them in our former controversies . . . A Church inspired by this new spirit will be prepared to tackle the concrete task which God Himself lays on her. Such a Church cannot be divided even by war and will maintain relations as far as possible.'[38]

*   *   *

So far the war had not touched the Western Hemisphere, but the Western Section did not remain indifferent to the suffering of Christians in Europe. The May 1940 issue of *The Presbyterian Register* published a letter from the American Secretary, Dr W. B. Pugh, to the Alliance General Secretary. After thanking him for the messages of affection sent on behalf of the leaders of the Eastern Section, Dr Pugh went on: 'These messages call us to prayer for all our Christian brethren who everywhere are suffering the horrors of war, and for ourselves that we may make a humble and reverent offering of our will for the fulfilling of God's holy will in us . . .

'You will be interested to know that our Western Section is steadily taking a new interest and vigour. Assembled here at Rochester [for the Western Section meeting, *Ed.*] in numbers beyond our expectations, we are conscious of a deepening of our faith in God and of the spiritual reinforcement of our minds and wills . . .'[39]

*   *   *

In April 1940, two representatives of the Eastern Section, Professor G. D. Henderson and Rev. W. J. Baxter, both from Scotland, travelled by air to Holland and spent a busy fortnight there with the representatives of the Reformed Churches. Professor Henderson notes 'that it was a time of extreme tension in the Netherlands, but nothing could have exceeded the friendliness of the welcome offered to the delegates.'[40] A few weeks later Holland was invaded and the 'phoney war' came to an end.

Isolation was now complete for the Eastern Section of the Alliance, except with the Western world. The Chairman of the Section, Rev. Dr J. Hutchison Cockburn, was able to visit the Western Section early in 1942. But this was an exception. On the whole the Alliance became more and more a British affair, with its consequent limitations. The lack of contacts between the two Sections of the Alliance meant that inevitably each Section went its own way and that the world Alliance as such hardly existed.

On Christmas Day, 1940, Rev. Dr Robert Laird, the President of the Alliance, died after a long illness. His place was taken by the Vice-President, Rev. Dr George H. Donald, of Montreal, a minister of the Presbyterian Church in Canada.

Located in Edinburgh, the Alliance office did not have the opportunities which existed in London for contacts with Christians of other countries. The General Secretary, who had an able assistant in the person of Miss D. Neill, who had been in the service of the Alliance since 1925, decided to take up work outside the Alliance. In November 1941, he took up a post under 'The Huts and Canteens Committee' of the Church of Scotland, a post which he occupied until April 1942. Later, he undertook part-time work for his Church in order to relieve the burden on the finances of the Alliance. This could be understood, but it meant that the Alliance became very 'dormant' during the crucial years of the war, and this was deeply regretted by the brethren of the Western Section. It was to lead to real frictions before the reorganization of the Alliance in 1948.

*   *   *

The Western Section did not remain inactive. If the Canadian member Churches were involved in the war from the beginning, it is only in December 1941 that the American Churches were going to know the real meaning of this word. Help to Europe was one of the chief concerns of the Western Section, though the problem of the Younger Churches became a very urgent preoccupation after the Japanese attack on Pearl Harbor in December 1941.

Though war raged, Alliance leaders, like many other Christian leaders, were already thinking of the post-war period. At the meeting of the Emergency Executive Committee of the Eastern Section, on 1 November 1942, Rev. W. T. Elmslie spoke 'of a great number of young men in the nation anxious to give personal service in the work of post-war reconstruction'.[41] The General Secretary was instructed to communicate with Dr Pugh and Dr Cavert [of the Federal Council of Churches in America, *Ed.*] and others on this subject.

During all that time, the World Council of Churches was at work and became an increasingly great reality to many Churches and Christians. The Alliance was invited to appoint a delegate to the WCC Committee, and the meeting of the Emergency Committee of the Eastern Section, on 7 April 1943, appointed the General Secretary, Dr Hamilton, to be the Alliance representative on that Committee.

Meanwhile, there was no unanimity in the Presbyterian Churches of Britain regarding the development of the Ecumenical Movement. In an article published in the August 1943 issue of *The Presbyterian Register* and entitled 'The crucial Ecumenical difficulty', the Editor wrote: 'It seems to be difficult for many good people to understand that one may be a faithful recorder, yet not a partisan for or against any of the movements advertised. Our spokesman at the Scottish General Assemblies somewhat ruefully mentioned to us that the identical speech brought him from one group an accusation of "*crabbing* the ecumenical movement" and from another the accusation of "*boosting* the ecumenical movement". His endeavour, however, was merely to *report* a circumstance of great moment to several Churches . . . The point that presses on *our* office is just that the measure of Presbyterian unity we have reached has not been reached without cost and effort, and we should greatly desire that it might not be dissipated or destroyed in the process of the quest by this member or that for still wider unity independently of the others. We should greatly desire that into whatever wider unity the Church of Christ may be led by God to enter, our whole Presbyterian family may come as *one* and unbroken.'[42]

* * *

The same concern was expressed in the 1943–44 annual report of the Eastern Section to the member Churches. The report, signed by Rev. Dr J. Hutchison Cockburn and the General Secretary, says: 'The Alliance marks with prayerful interest the activities and ideals of the ecumenical movements of this age, in which leaders from many of its constituent Churches hold influential positions. We are confident of the value of the Presbyterian contribution, and our Western Section has given special attention to this subject during the past seven years . . . The Alliance by Constitution cannot, and would not, intrude in the autonomy of any of its Churches, but it must always confidentially hope that movement towards a wider-than-Presbyterian unity may be guided from Above towards such a sequence of events as may simultaneously strengthen, and not impair, the Presbyterian unity which we have striven to create and promote during the past seventy years . . . Nevertheless, the unity of Christ's Church stands as the goal of all the Churches, and we are happy that we have both direct and indirect representation on the Committee for European Reconstruction through which the new British Council of Churches hopes to aid the work of mercy and relief which Dr Keller and the Inter-Church Aid Relief Bureau at Geneva have sponsored and continue to guide.'[43]

There was soon to be a more direct link between the Ecumenical work of Reconstruction and the Alliance; early in 1945, Dr J. Hutchison Cockburn, Chairman of the Eastern Section, was appointed Director of the newly created Department of Reconstruction of the World Council of Churches.

We have already commented on the isolation of the Alliance office, located in Edinburgh. It was fortunate that at this time Professor Dr Adolf Keller (living in Geneva and one of the Vice-Presidents of the Alliance) was able to keep in touch with Reformed Churches in many countries on the European Continent. The April 1944 issue of *The Presbyterian Register* reproduces the text of a letter sent by Dr Keller to Dr Hamilton on 24 November 1943. Dr Keller writes: 'You have not heard for a long time from your Vice-President. You know how difficult it is to maintain correspondence in such a time as this. Nevertheless our spiritual relationship cannot be interrupted and I try to maintain fraternal relations with our Brethren on the Continent to whom I have transmitted Christian greetings and a stimulating Christian word from the large spiritual family to which they belong.'[44]

With the landing of Allied forces in France in June 1944, the isolation of Great Britain quickly came to an end. The 1 November 1944 meeting of the Emergency Executive Committee of the Eastern Section felt 'that the time is near when efforts to resume communications with leaders in liberated countries, etc., should be made, and it was urged that regular liaison with the Committees of the World and British Councils of Churches on Reconstruction should be effected.'[45]

Soon the atrocious war was over, first in Europe and then in Asia. But the aftermath remained and there was terrific destruction and suffering everywhere. The work of Christian Reconstruction went on, and the Alliance gave its full support to the great Ecumenical enterprise in the field of Inter-Church Aid. The Central Bureau of Inter-Church Aid, so ably led for years by Dr Adolf Keller, became merged with the new Department of Reconstruction of the WCC and the Churches of the Reformed family naturally used the new channel put at their disposal.

What was to be the role of the Alliance and of other Confessional Organizations in this new situation? The leaders of the Western Section, even more than those of the Eastern Section, who had been directly involved in the war, had thought about this problem. The American Secretary, Dr Pugh, who was an ardent supporter of the Ecumenical Movement, was no less enthusiastic in his support of the Confessional family which the Alliance represented. In the Report of the Western Section for the year 1945 we read: 'The Western Section rejoices in the Ecumenical Movement . . . and we pledge our loyalty and support to this uniting bond of the Protestant Churches.

'At the same time we are confirmed in our judgment that the Alliance has a definite service to render the Protestant cause, and we register our purpose to enlarge and strengthen the bonds already existing, which unite the Churches of the Reformed Faith in the fellowship of the Alliance.

'The time is opportune for placing the purpose and program of the Alliance on a firmer, surer foundation, to the end that the distinctive doctrinal standards that unite the constituent Churches of the Alliance may strengthen and advance the Protestant Christian Church in all parts of the world.'[46]

In order to make this strengthening of the Alliance effective, Dr Pugh was asked by the Western Section to undertake an extensive tour on the European Continent. Dr Pugh arrived in Britain early in January 1947, and on 9 January, a Special meeting of the Eastern Section was convened in Edinburgh to meet Dr Pugh, who explained fully the position taken by the Western Section: Ecumenical involvement and strengthening of the Alliance. He reminded his hearers that both he and President Dr John A. Mackay of Princeton, were on the American Committee of the WCC, but that they agreed on the need for strengthening Presbyterian solidarity.

A few days later, Dr Pugh, accompanied by the Alliance General Secretary and by Rev. Dr Alex King, Convener of the Eastern Section's Continental Committee, left by air for Amsterdam. They visited the Netherlands, Belgium, Czechoslovakia, Switzerland and France. They also wanted to go to Hungary and Austria, but could not obtain the necessary permits.

In the annual report of the Eastern Section sent in April 1947,

Dr Hamilton wrote: 'Wherever our commissioners went in their travels they were reassured by the evident acceptance by all our brethren of our argument and plea that the wider ecumenical movement can have stability and success only if each family of Churches adhering to it maintains and strengthens its own cohesion and solidarity . . . Because of this, we all feel a need for increasing the activity of the Alliance, travel and inter-church visitation among its constituent members, and we have noted this while at the same time recognizing that such a programme as we might imagine and devise would require increases of equipment, staff and finance, which in the present world-circumstances would be hard to contrive.'[47]

As a first step towards the strengthening of the Alliance it was decided that the Geneva Council, originally planned for 1941, should take place from 11 to 18 August 1948, just prior to the First Assembly of the World Council of Churches. It was decided that it should be a smaller Council than hitherto, but everybody realized that this was to be an important meeting and an important date in the life of the Alliance.

In his annual report published in April 1948, the General Secretary referred to the 'Future of the Alliance in the new Ecumenical age' and wrote: 'Our Presbyterian organ has always had far too limited organisation, staff and financial resources for the work that needs to be done. It has but one salaried officer, with a single assistant. It alone of the larger communions is without any travelling and interpreting official resident in Geneva or other European centre supported by corps of workers . . . These weighty matters must inevitably come under the Council's consideration.'[48]

And so we move toward the Sixteenth General Council in Geneva, which was indeed to prove decisive in the life of the Alliance. This we shall see in Part Two of this volume.

REFERENCES

1. *Proceedings 13th General Council*, p. 108.
2. Idem, p. 263.
3. Idem, p. 317.
4. Western Section Minutes, Feb. 24, 1931, p. 4.
5. Eastern Section Minutes, April 8, 1931, p. 3.

6. Western Section Minutes, Feb. 24, 1931, p. 21.
7. Eastern Section Minutes, April 26, 1933, p. 2.
8. *Proceedings 14th General Council*, p. 177.
9. Idem, p. 229.
10. Idem, p. 233.
11. Idem, p. 236 et seq.
12. Idem, p. 292.
13. *The Quarterly Register*, vol. XVI, no. 8, p. 221.
14. Idem, vol. XVII, no. 1, p. 2.
15. Idem, vol. XVII, no. 1, p. 11.
16. Idem, vol. XVII, no. 1, p. 12.
17. Idem, vol. XVII, no. 1, p. 39.
18. WARC Archives Geneva, WPA/EA2.
19. *Proceedings 15th General Council*, pp. 121–122.
20. Idem, pp. 171–176.
21. Idem, pp. 171 and 181.
22. Idem, pp. 219–225.
23. Idem, p. 252.
24. *The Presbyterian Register*, vol. XVII, no. 4, p. 107 et seq.
25. Executive Committee Eastern Section Minutes, May 16, 1938, p. 6.
26. *The Presbyterian Register*, vol. XVII, no. 6, p. 160.
27. Idem, p. 162.
28. Western Section Minutes, Feb. 23, 1938, p. 6.
29. Eastern Section Minutes, April 5, 1939, p. 3.
30. *The Presbyterian Register*, vol. XVII, no. 8, p. 216.
31. Idem, p. 221.
32. Western Section Minutes, Feb. 23, 1938, p. 19.
33. Eastern Section Minutes, April 5, 1939, p. 2.
34. *The Presbyterian Register*, vol. XVII, no. 10, p. 305.
35. Idem, vol. XVII, no. 12, p. 345.
36. Eastern Section Minutes, Nov. 1, 1939, Annex to p. 1.
37. Eastern Section, Appendix to Nov. 1, 1939, Minutes.
38. *The Presbyterian Register*, vol. XVII, no. 12, p. 348.
39. Idem, vol. XVII, no. 14, p. 408.
40. Idem, vol. XVII, no. 15, p. 418.
41. Minutes Emergency Executive, Eastern Section, Nov. 4, 1942, p. 6.
42. *The Presbyterian Register,* vol. XVIII, no. 4, p. 119.
43. WARC Archives Geneva, WPA/EA2.
44. *The Presbyterian Register*, vol. XVIII, no. 6, p. 198.
45. Minutes Emergency Executive Eastern Section, Nov. 1, 1944, p. 3.
46. 1946 Minutes, General Assembly Presbyterian Church in the U.S.A., part I, pp. 323–324.
47. WARC Archives Geneva, WPA/EA2.
48. WARC Archives Geneva, WPA/EA2.

PART II
1948–1975

CHAPTER TEN

A New Beginning

The Sixteenth General Council of the World Alliance of Reformed Churches which convened in Geneva on 11 August 1948 was different from the preceding Councils in many respects. It was the first time that an Alliance Council took place on the continent of Europe. Of the fifteen General Councils held between 1877 and 1937, eight took place in Great Britain, five in the U.S.A. and two in Canada. There had been some continental Conferences, but the Alliance as such had never gathered on the continent of Europe.

Naturally, the continental Churches took an active part in the Council. Seventeen Churches from fifteen different countries were represented by 54 delegates. The delegates of the Reformed Church of Romania and of the Reformed Church of Yugoslavia were absent only because they could not get the necessary visas to travel to Geneva.

If Europe was well represented and if the delegations from Great Britain and North America were very large, other parts of the world had far too few delegates at Geneva. Australasia had nine and Asia seven, but of the six Asian Churches represented, only three were members of the Alliance. South Africa had sent two delegates, from two different Churches, and the Egyptian 'delegate' was in fact the pastor of the Swiss Church in Cairo. Latin America had one delegate, sent by the Presbyterian Church of Brazil.

A second innovation was the decision to divide the members of the Council into six Study groups, each group presenting a report to the plenary session.

The six groups studied the following subjects:

I.   The Historical Confessions and the Present Witness of the Church

II. Freedom and Justice in the Light of the Bible
III. Presbyterianism and the Present Ecumenical Situation
IV. The Forms of Reformed Worship
V. What is Fundamental in Church Order?
VI. The Church in the Modern World (Theme of Montreal 1937)

Whereas the first fifteen Councils had used only English as their official language, it was decided that English, French and German should now be the official languages of the Conference. Papers were delivered in these three languages and summary translations were handed out to those delegates who could not understand the language of the speaker. Simultaneous translation was not yet used in Geneva, but interpreters were present in the study groups, so that real discussions could take place.

More important still: many of the delegates gathered at Geneva were 'new men', many of them young men, who saw no opposition between confessional loyalty and devotion to the ecumenical ideal. This was going to have important consequences for the future as these men were due to take an increasingly active part in the life and work of the Alliance.

The Council, which met only a few days before the first Assembly of the (still in formation) World Council of Churches, adopted a message for transmission to the Amsterdam Assembly of the WCC. Part of the message reads as follows:

'The Sixteenth Council of the Alliance of the Reformed Churches holding the Presbyterian System, now meeting at Geneva, sends warm greetings to the First Meeting of the World Council of Churches in Amsterdam . . .

'Its [the Alliance, *Ed.*] constituent Churches welcome to the Lord's Supper those who are members of any branch of the Holy Catholic Church, and recognize as valid ordinations carried out with prayer, according to the established order of every such branch.

'In the confident hope that the World Council will, by the grace of God, succeed in establishing a wider co-ordination and co-operation, to which the varied families of the one Church of Christ will bring their own contributions, the Council thankfully welcomes the Amsterdam meeting, and earnestly prays for a blessing on its labours.'[1]

The ecumenical note was emphasized again by two Alliance leaders who spoke on 'Presbyterianism and the Present Ecumenical Situation'. They were the Very Rev. Dr J. Hutchison Cockburn, Director of the Department of Reconstruction of the WCC, and President Dr John A. Mackay, of Princeton Theological Seminary, who for the next eleven years was to play such an outstanding role in the life of the Alliance. No wonder that the Geneva Council unanimously adopted the report of Study Group III (The Reformed Churches and the Present Ecumenical Situation), which says: 'With profound thankfulness to God for what He has done hitherto in and through the Reformed Church of the world . . . the World Alliance . . . welcomes as a manifestation of the Spirit and will of Jesus Christ . . . the prospective formation of a World Council of Churches.

'. . . we would earnestly recommend to all constituent members of the Alliance . . . that they give serious and prayerful consideration to applying for membership in the World Council, towards the maintenance and extension of the world-wide fellowship and witness of the Church.'[2]

It was at the Geneva Council that the Alliance of Reformed Churches adopted a certain line concerning its attitude towards the World Council of Churches. This has been faithfully adhered to ever since.

The 'Cold War' was as yet unknown, but tensions were already increasing between the 'socialist' nations of Eastern Europe and the nations of the West. Christians were not spared these tensions and this was apparent at the Geneva Council, especially in the Study Group on 'Freedom and Justice in the Light of the Bible'. There were two reports. The majority report said amongst other things:

'4. It is fully agreed that a Christian man and Church must always protest against and finally say "no" to any power which completely disregards the rights of men to freedom and responsibility of action . . .

'5. It is finally agreed that Christians ought to work against such concentration of power . . . which however beneficial and for whatever good aims of social justice, have the possibility of open or hidden threat to take away any man's freedom to live as a child of God redeemed by Jesus Christ.'[3]

A second report was submitted by Professor Dr Josef Hromadka, of Prague, who was to become a Vice-President of the Alliance at the end of the Council. Here are some extracts from this report:

'1. The present crisis of our civilization has shaken the foundations of all institutions that had . . . been established as a safeguard of freedom and rights . . . We are standing in many ways on the ruins of the old order.

'3. The Church . . . penitently admits that all political systems established by Christians have been corrupted by selfishness, greed, and the will to power . . .

'4. The Church is obliged to respect any state authority as long as it . . . acknowledges a form of righteousness, respects the sacredness of man's responsible personality, and gives the Church the freedom to carry on her mission in the world . . .'[4]

Valuable reports were also presented by the other Study Groups. Group IV, on 'The Forms of Reformed Worship', submitted seven theses which were due to be transmitted to the Alliance Liturgical Commission (which unfortunately was never formed). Here are two of these theses:

'IV. A series of historical accidents . . . having in the course of centuries deformed the Reformed Liturgy, the necessity for its restoration is recognised everywhere today in the Presbyterian world.

'V. This restoration should not consist in "enrichments" dictated by psychological motives, but, on the one hand, in a purification in line with the original intention of the Reformers, and, on the other hand, in a recovery of evangelical elements found in other traditions and accidentally lost by ours.'[5]

The ecumenical movement compelled the delegates to the Geneva Council to state more clearly the Reformed point of view on 'What is fundamental in Church Order'. This was done by Study Group V, and it is interesting to read some of their conclusions:

'III. Jesus Christ, the Head and Ruler of the Church, has ordained the office of the ministry of the Word and Sacraments . . .

'At the same time we recognize that all believers are prophets, priests and kings, and that the manifestations of the Spirit are not confined to the office of the ministry of Word and Sacraments. Prophecy or charismatic gifts are to find a place in the corporate life of the Church.

'IV. Further it is our finding that in so far as the ministry of Presbyters and of Bishops is concerned, the New Testament teaches the parity of these offices in the ministry of the Word and Sacraments. Therefore, in the light of this fact, the faith and polity of the Reformed and Presbyterian Church has no place for a sacerdotal episcopacy.

'Nevertheless, it is increasingly evident that the requirements of the order, unity and peace of the Church may demand, in certain national situations, the setting apart of chosen Presbyters to act as *Pastors pastorum*, but without independent authority.

'Furthermore, it is our judgment that in cases where it would contribute to the greater effectiveness of the Church as the servant of Christ and open the way towards wider unity in the body of Christ, the several member Churches of the Alliance, as occasion requires, may take steps to provide for a constitutional episcopacy.'[6]

* * *

If we have entitled this chapter 'A new beginning' it is not because of the excellent reports presented to the Geneva Council by its study groups. It is because a complete reorganization of the Alliance took place in Geneva. In his Preface to the *Proceedings of the 16th General Council*, the Editor, Rev. Dr W. H. Hamilton, General Secretary, wrote: 'No reader of the following record of the Sixteenth Council is likely to feel that the Council failed to make a bold and drastic effort to galvanize and expand the activity of the Alliance and to consolidate its organization, as the General Secretary had urged for fifteen years and the Western Section no less eagerly for a shorter period . . .'[7]

Here are the facts. The Executive Commission of the Eastern Section, in its report to the General Council, had made proposals concerning the future organization. These proposals demanded an increased budget, in order to allow the General Secretariat in Edinburgh to expand its activities, but made no suggestion for a fundamental reorganization of the Alliance. The Western Section wanted a great deal more and at its meeting in February 1948 adopted proposals which were transmitted to the Edinburgh office in July only. On arrival in Geneva, seven members from each Section had met informally and endeavoured to reach an agreed finding. On Monday afternoon, 16 August (the last day but one of the Council) the 'Committee on the re-organization' of the Alliance submitted its report. In view of its importance, we do not hesitate to quote large extracts:

'PREAMBLE

'Whereas in view of the tragic possibilities of the world situation, and the urgent necessity to mobilise the resources of the Presbyterian world for the assistance of the Continental Churches and the defence of the Reformed Faith in Europe, and in view of the expansion of the Ecumenical Movement, and the immediate call to the Alliance to play a worthy part in the activities of the World Council of Churches, it has become essential to reconstruct and expand the secretariat of the Alliance, it is hereby resolved that:

'1. An office of the Alliance be established in Geneva.

'2. Section Five of the Rules [rc. General Secretary, *Ed.*] be entirely repealed, and that the post of General Secretary as therein defined be discontinued as from a date to be determined by the Executive Committee hereinafter named.

'3. An Executive Secretary be appointed to reside in Geneva and from this centre direct and co-ordinate the work of the Alliance . . .

'4. In view of his years of dedicated services, his deep and informed devotion to the ideals of the Alliance, and his practical experience gained through a period of over twenty-one years, Dr Hamilton shall be asked to continue as a secretary of the Alliance with the title of Associate Secretary . . .

'7. Rules I. and II. regarding "The Executive Commission" be wholly repealed, and an Executive Committee be formed, consisting of fifteen members representative of the entire Alliance, together with the President of the Alliance . . . The Executive shall hold office until the next Council . . . this Council shall appoint the persons to constitute the Executive Committee . . .

'8. The matter of revising the Constitution and Rules of the Alliance shall be remitted to the Executive Committee . . .

'9. The functions of the Executive Committee shall be in the main those which have hitherto been exercised by the Executive Commission . . . In the immediate case of finding and appointing of an Executive Secretary and in the supervision of his work, said Executive shall act with the authority of the Alliance.'[8]

These proposals were very drastic indeed, for they brought to an end the activities of Dr Hamilton as General Secretary of the Alliance and made Edinburgh a small 'appendix' of the office to be created in Geneva. We can fully understand that the General Secretary was shaken by these proposals, though he reacted with real dignity. Many delegates also felt unhappy for Dr Hamilton, but they realized that it was essential for the Alliance to make a completely new start, and therefore the proposals made by the Western Section, on the initiative of Dr William B. Pugh, the energetic American Secretary, were finally accepted by the whole Council.

Before coming to an end the Council voted that a World Conference of Reformed and Presbyterian Youth be held on the continent of Europe in August 1949. The President and the Secretary of the Women's Branch of the Alliance were received by the Council, and the Secretary, Miss Lavery of Belfast, addressed the Council. Mr W. H. Mill, an Edinburgh layman who had been the Hon. Treasurer of the Alliance since 1927, and Miss Dora Neill, who had held the post of Assistant Secretary with great distinction since 1925, were warmly thanked for their devoted services.

The Very Rev. Dr Edward J. Hagan, of the Church of Scotland, in Edinburgh, was elected President of the Alliance. The two Vice-Presidents were Rev. Professor Dr Josef Hromadka, of the Evangelical Church of Czech Brethren, in Prague, and Rev. Dr Edgar J. Romig, of the Reformed Church in America, in New York.

The Council ended on 17 August, just in time for many of the delegates to travel to the First Assembly of the World Council of Churches in Amsterdam.

*   *   *

The Geneva Council had voted that an Executive Secretary be elected, to direct the work of the Alliance from Geneva. The Executive Committee was charged with finding the new secretary. A 'Committee of Four' immediately set to work. During the Amsterdam Assembly, Rev. Marcel Pradervand, a minister of the Reformed Church in the Canton de Vaud (Switzerland), who had been for ten years Minister of the Swiss Church in London before coming to the World Council of Churches to work as Secretary for Latin Europe in the Department of Reconstruction, early in 1948, was approached by some of the Alliance leaders. He was hesitant to accept the post of Executive Secretary, as he did not wish to take the place of Dr Hamilton. However he was made to understand that the decisions of the Geneva Council regarding the reorganization of the Alliance were final and that Dr Hamilton would not be asked to continue as General Secretary of the Alliance. Further discussions took place, and on 25 October 1948, Rev. M. Pradervand was appointed as Executive Secretary of the Alliance, with headquarters in Geneva. His duties were to start on 1 January 1949, for a period of five years; the World Council agreed to release him for his new task.

Immediately an important question arose: Where in Geneva should the Alliance offices be located? Some Presbyterians were anxious to see the offices established in the Calvin Auditorium (which was later to be restored by the Alliance); but the new Executive Secretary felt that there was no sense in moving the Alliance Office to Geneva unless it were located on the campus of the World Council of Churches at 17 Route de Malagnou so that close contacts could be maintained with the WCC. This was accepted by the Alliance leaders. And so, in January 1949, the Alliance began its activities in one of the wooden barracks erected by the WCC next to its General Secretariat. The Alliance was not the first organization to work on this campus. The Lutheran World Federation, with its growing staff, was already there.

This was indeed a new beginning, and if the Continental Churches were happy at the move, some representatives of the Presbyterian Churches of Great Britain had misgivings. It is only fair however to say that from the very beginning the new Executive Secretary found the most loyal support on the part of most British leaders and soon developed warm friendships with many of them.

The Geneva Council wanted the Alliance to develop its activities in many directions. But the only decision taken so far was to move the Alliance office from Edinburgh to Geneva. The new Executive Secretary had only a young secretary to help him in his work. Shortly afterwards Dr Hamilton decided to leave the service of the Alliance to take a parish in Scotland.

The finances of the Alliance were extremely modest. In 1949, only one Church on the Continent contributed to the budget of the Alliance, the Federation of the Protestant Churches of Switzerland, a country which had not been directly affected by the war. The budget voted by the Geneva Council for the work of the Alliance amounted to $9,000 for the year 1949 and it was not increased in 1950. This was expected to pay the Executive Secretary and his assistant, the office rent and office expenses, and the travels of the Executive Secretary. Surprisingly, the Geneva Secretariat managed on the sum allocated!

The Geneva Council had adopted the reorganization of the Alliance 'in view . . . of the urgent necessity to mobilise the resources of the Presbyterian world for the assistance of the Continental Churches' (see reference 5).

The new Executive Secretary, who had worked in the Department of Reconstruction of the WCC for one year, was well aware of the problems of these Churches, and especially of the minority Churches, whose situation was extremely difficult. He immediately set to work to see that the larger Churches of the Reformed family gave special consideration to these Churches in their giving programmes. But he was fully aware that there was no need for the Alliance to organize a special 'Reformed Inter-Church Aid'. The administration of the World Council was available to all Churches and the Executive Secretary worked in full harmony with the Department of Reconstruction of the WCC which soon became the Department of Inter-Church Aid and Service to Refugees.

Another urgent task for the Alliance was to try to re-establish direct contacts with the Reformed Churches of Eastern Europe, now situated behind what was commonly called 'The Iron Curtain'. It is therefore not surprising that the first visit of the new Secretary to a member Church was to Czechoslovakia, early in March 1949. Thanks to the help of Professor Hromadka, he was able to receive the necessary visa and paid a week's visit to the Evangelical Church of Czech Brethren and to the Reformed Church of Slovakia. Eastern Slovakia was still a battlefield, with terrible destruction left on all sides by the retreating armies of the Third Reich, but one was struck by the determination and the courage of Church leaders and Church people alike. There were of course many problems in the Churches of Czechoslovakia, as

C.S.—7

the country had become a communist country in 1948. But this first journey to a People's Republic convinced the Secretary that Christian witness was possible there as in other countries, and that the Christian Church was not bound to any regime. This did not mean that the task for the Christian Church there was easy, and the Executive Secretary could feel the tension under which most of the Czechoslovak brethren had to live.

*   *   *

Readers of the first part of this book will remember that on more than one occasion we indicated that the Alliance was in fact, not a world organization, but two organizations, the 'Western' and the 'Eastern' Sections, each following their own way and not always concurring in what was to be their aims and objectives. The Geneva Council happily put an end to this situation, as the Sections now worked under the authority of a World Executive Committee.

But it was urgent for the new Executive Secretary, located in Geneva, to make personal contacts with the member Churches in North America. The American Secretary of the Alliance, Rev. Dr William B. Pugh, who had contributed more than any other person to the reorganization of 1948, immediately invited Mr Pradervand to come to North America and to visit the General Assemblies of the member Churches there. And so, in May 1949, the Executive Secretary left Geneva for a five-week visit to the Churches of the U.S.A. and Canada. Dr Pugh had prepared a full programme for the representative of the Alliance, and he was able to address the General Assemblies of the Presbyterian Church in the U.S.A., the Presbyterian Church in the U.S., the United Presbyterian Church of North America, the Reformed Church in America and the Presbyterian Church in Canada. The United Church of Canada did not hold its General Council at that time, but the Secretary of the Alliance was able to have useful discussions with the leaders of that Church.

In the course of this trip the Executive Secretary was awarded a D.D. by Maryville College, Maryville, Tenn., whose President, Rev. Dr Ralph W. Lloyd, was soon to play a major role in the Alliance, first as American Secretary and then as President.

Dr Pradervand was struck by the fact that the Church leaders of North America were fully aware that they had to work both for the 'family' of Reformed Churches and for the larger unity which the WCC was trying to achieve. They saw no opposition between the two, and this was made especially clear by President Dr John A. Mackay, of Princeton Seminary, who had become a member of the Executive Committee of the Alliance. Dr Mackay was fully engaged in ecumenical work; he was a member of the Central Committee of the WCC as well as President of the International Missionary Council and had a longing for unity. But he was also fully devoted to the cause of the Alliance and was later to inspire its policy for several years, before becoming its President in 1954.

Unfortunately, the European attitude was different. While some Church leaders were still anxious to give full support to the Alliance, many others had the feeling that the creation of the World Council of Churches made confessional organizations superfluous, and it was not always easy for the Executive Secretary to convince them of the need for taking the Alliance seriously and giving it the support it needed. Happily the situation soon changed and the larger Churches of the Continent of Europe stood solidly behind the Alliance; they had been convinced that the Alliance wanted to remain a modest organization and had no desire to imitate other world organizations which, by the size of their programme, could become a danger to the Ecumenical Movement.

*   *   *

The first meeting of the new Executive Committee took place at Westminster College, Cambridge, England, from 4 to 6 July 1949. It was chaired by the President, Dr E. J. Hagan, and its first task was to ratify the action of the 'Committee of Four' in appointing Dr M. Pradervand as Executive Secretary of the Alliance.

The problem of Inter-Church Aid was discussed, as many of the minority Churches of the Reformed family needed urgent help and it was decided that, without setting up an organization of its own, the Alliance should see that these needs be met within the larger ecumenical programme.

It was decided that the contacts between the Churches of the Alliance should be developed and that studies in common should be undertaken. The Ecumenical issue was naturally discussed, and the Minutes of the meeting note that: 'There was unanimity of thought among the members present . . . It was felt that while we want to be true to our Reformed and Presbyterian convictions, we are glad to be in the larger body of the World Council of Churches. We want to take our full part in the building of the "Una Sancta".'[9]

The 'Younger Churches' were becoming more numerous and it was easy to see that they were called to play an ever-increasing role in the life of the Church Universal. It was therefore natural that the Executive Committee discussed the relation of the Alliance to these Churches. President John A. Mackay, who, as Chairman of the Board of Foreign Missions of the Presbyterian Church in the U.S.A., had an intimate knowledge of the problem, took a leading part in the discussion. He expressed the hope that the Alliance would never develop narrow Presbyterianism, for, added Dr Mackay: 'If a certain trend in the confessional missionary Movement develops, it will break the Ecumenical Movement. It would tend to crystallize for the future the ecclesiastical traditions of the past. That would be a tragedy.'[10]

Several of the members of the Executive Committee were also members of the Central Committee of the World Council of Churches; they left Cambridge for Chichester, where the Central Committee convened almost immediately. The Executive Secretary was also there as fraternal delegate of the Alliance.

In August of the same year a World Conference of Reformed and Presbyterian Youth took place at Montpellier, in the South of France. About ninety delegates, coming from several continents, were present. The Conference, which had been organized by Rev. W. S. Robertson, of Hull, England, one of the youngest delegates to the Geneva Council, was chaired by Rev. D. H. C. Read, then Chaplain at the University of Edinburgh. French and German were used as well as English and there was real enthusiasm among the young people present. They asked for a greater place to be given to Youth in the Alliance and they decided to hold another Conference in 1951.

* * *

During his first year of office the Executive Secretary visited several European Churches. An important contact was the visit to the 'Reformierter Bund' of Germany and to the Evangelical Reformed Church of N.W. Germany. The Reformed Christians felt neglected, as many Reformed and Presbyterian visitors seemed completely unaware that there were Reformed Christians in Germany; consequently, their needs were overlooked. This was happily to change, though the situation of our people, who had suffered so greatly during the war, was not to improve immediately.

*   *   *

At Cambridge the Executive Committee of the Alliance had decided that a meeting of the 'Eastern Section' should be held in 1950 and that the conference should take place on the Continent. Thanks to the kindness and generosity of the Reformed Church of Alsace and Lorraine, and especially of its President, Pasteur Charles Bartholmé, representatives of twenty European (British and Continental) Churches from twelve countries gathered at Strasbourg from 24 to 28 August. Most delegates were given hospitality in homes of members of the Church; this was important in view of the financial limitations of the Alliance and of the poverty of many of the Churches represented. If there were no delegates from Churches outside Europe belonging to the Eastern Section, the Churches of Czechoslovakia and of Hungary were able to send representatives, and this was important for the conference.

Two subjects were studied: 'Reformed Ecclesiology and Ecumenical problems' and 'The ministry of the Church in the world'. The President of the Alliance, though already in poor health, was able to chair the Conference with great distinction; once more, German and French were used as well as English.

At Strasbourg, Bishops A. Bereczky and J. Peter, of the Reformed Church of Hungary, invited the Executive Secretary to visit their Church; they made the necessary arrangements with the Hungarian authorities and in October Dr Pradervand was able to spend two and a half weeks in the People's Republic of Hungary, visiting the four districts of the Church, the Reformed Colleges and Theological Seminaries, preaching in local congregations and meeting representatives of the State Office for Church Affairs. This visit resulted in increased co-operation between the Alliance and the great Reformed Church of Hungary.

In September 1950 the Alliance suffered a very serious loss. The devoted American Secretary of the Alliance, Rev. Dr William Barrow Pugh, Stated Clerk of the Presbyterian Church in the

U.S.A., was killed in a motor accident. We have already said that he was the main artisan of the Alliance reorganization in 1948. He had previously visited the Churches of the Continent of Europe and it was he who had the vision of what the Alliance could and should do for them. From then onward he worked incessantly to make the Alliance a useful instrument in the service of the Reformed Churches. His untimely death was a serious blow for the Alliance.

At about the same time, Miss Fehr, the young secretary who had worked for Dr Pradervand, first at the WCC then in the Alliance office, left Geneva to get married. The Executive Secretary was fortunate in securing the services of Miss Paulette Piguet, a member of the Swiss Reformed Church, well versed in theology and a remarkable linguist. She started working for the Alliance in September 1950 and soon proved to be much more than a secretary. In the long absences of Dr Pradervand in years to come, she was able to act very responsibly in the interests of our organization. This was recognized by the Executive Committee; on its recommendation the Princeton General Council, in 1954, elected her an Executive with the title of 'Assistant Secretary' and later of 'Associate Secretary'.

*   *   *

The financial limitations imposed on the Alliance did not make it possible for the Executive Committee to meet every year; it was decided at Cambridge that the next meeting of the Executive Committee should take place in 1951. As the Central Committee of the WCC convened at Rolle, near Geneva, at the end of July 1951, it was decided that our own Executive should also meet in Switzerland, in order to prevent unnecessary travel expenses. The meeting took place at the 'Missionshaus' in Basle (Missionary Center of the Basle Mission) from 13 to 15 August. The Alliance President, Dr E. J. Hagan, was unable to be present owing to a serious illness, and the two Vice-Presidents were also prevented from attending. It was therefore decided that the different sessions should be chaired by several members of the Executive.

One of the first actions of the Executive was to confirm the appointment of Rev. Dr Ralph W. Lloyd, President of Maryville College, Tenn., U.S.A., as American Secretary. Dr Lloyd, who had attended the Geneva Council in 1948, had an intimate knowledge of the problems of the Alliance, and it is to him more than to any other man that the Alliance owes the increased support it soon received from the Churches of the Western Section. Until 1959 Dr Lloyd was to fulfil this honorary but very heavy post with great distinction before becoming President of the Alliance.

The Executive Secretary was able to inform the Executive Committee that the Presbyterian Church of the Gold Coast (now Ghana) and the United Church of Christ in the Philippines, which had been invited by the Cambridge meeting of the Executive to join the Alliance, had responded favourably and were now members of the Alliance. The application made by the Presbyterian Church of Formosa was unanimously approved. The Executive Committee also asked the Alliance Secretary, who was due to undertake an extensive visit of the Churches of the Reformed family in Latin America 'to convey the cordial greetings of the Executive Committee and express its desire for closer fraternal relations with them . . .'.[11]

The Committee also gave serious consideration to drafts submitted by the two Sections concerning the revision of the Constitution and Rules of the Alliance. A Committee of the Executive for the revision of the Constitution was then formed under the chairmanship of Dr R. W. Lloyd, who had prepared the Western Section draft. His legal mind was to be most useful in preparing the final text of the new Constitution.

The Geneva Council had decided that the next General Council should take place in 1953. But as the WCC had decided to postpone its Second Assembly from 1953 to 1954, it was decided to do the same and to hold the General Council in the U.S.A., prior to the Assembly of the WCC. No final decision about the location was taken at Basle, but the Executive decided to give serious consideration to the invitation brought by President Mackay that the Council should be held at Princeton Theological Seminary.

The main object of the Executive Committee's meeting in Basle was the definition of the role of the Alliance in relation to the Ecumenical Movement. Dr John A. Mackay played a decisive role in defining this relationship. He had prepared a draft statement which, with minor corrections, was unanimously adopted by the Executive Committee and became the historic 'Basle Statement' on 'The World Presbyterian Alliance in the Present

Ecumenical Situation'. This statement was received with gratitude by leaders of the World Council of Churches, as it clarified the position of the Alliance in the new situation created by the founding of the WCC. We do not hesitate to quote extracts from this important declaration:

'. . . it is the true nature of Presbyterianism never to be merely an end in itself, but to serve the Church Universal of Jesus Christ, the Church which is His Body.

'. . . There are Presbyterians today who are both more Presbyterian and less Presbyterian than ever before. They are *more* Presbyterian because they believe that in their religious heritage there are treasures of thought and life which are important for the Church Universal. They are *less* Presbyterian than ever before because they recognize that what God has said and done through the medium of other Christian Communions is also needed to enrich the Church Universal. They believe, therefore, that it is the highest glory of the Reformed tradition to maintain the vision and viewpoint of the Church Universal, seeking continually its welfare and unity, in accordance with the mind of Jesus Christ, the Head of the Church, and through the power of the Holy Spirit who indwells the Church.

. . . . . .

'In the judgment of the Committee, Presbyterians in the world of today have a very special task. They are charged by God to see to it that the resurgence of denominationalism, which is manifest around the globe, shall not become sectarian, but shall remain ecumenical in character. If the great world denominations, the Reformed Churches among them, pursue denominational pre-eminence and make their great world bodies ends in themselves, they will betray Jesus Christ. But if they desire, and succeed in their desire, to make denominational emphasis an enrichment of the common evangelical heritage, they will, by so doing, fulfil the designs of the one Head of the Church and be true organs of the Holy Spirit. Let Presbyterians be in the best sense ecumenically minded Presbyterians. Grasped afresh by Jesus Christ Himself, let us dedicate ourselves to propagate the one Holy Faith throughout the world and to seek the unity of the one Church of Jesus Christ.'[12]

*   *   *

As already mentioned in the report on the Basle meeting of the Executive Committee, Dr Pradervand undertook a journey to Latin America from October to December 1951, in the course of which he visited the Presbyterian Churches of Mexico, Guatemala, Colombia, the Evangelical Church of Peru, the Presbyterian Church of Chile, the Reformed group in Argentina and the Waldensian Church of Uruguay, the Presbyterian Church and the Independent Presbyterian Church of Brazil, as well as the Hungarian-speaking Christian-Reformed Church of that land; his final stop was with the Presbyterian Church of Venezuela. Owing to the very limited budget of the Alliance, this trip would not have been possible but for the financial assistance of the Board of Foreign Missions of the Presbyterian Church in the U.S.A., which was concerned at the spreading of Dr Carl McIntire's anti-ecumenical ideas among many of the Presbyterians of Latin America, and hoped that a visit by the Executive Secretary of the Alliance, a European, would help bring these Churches into closer contact with the world family of Reformed Churches. This was happily the case. In 1951, only the Presbyterian Church of Mexico was really a member of the Alliance. The Presbyterian Church of Brazil, which was considered to be one of the member Churches, had never applied for admission. But within the next few years nearly all the Latin American Churches joined the Alliance.

In 1952, the Executive Secretary of the Alliance undertook another two-month journey to Africa; he visited Egypt and the Synod of the Nile in this country; after a further stop in Kenya (in the middle of the Mau-Mau emergency) in order to establish contact with the Presbyterian Church of that land, he spent six weeks in South Africa, visiting at the same time Basutoland (now Lesotho) and Mozambique. In the Republic of South Africa, the Executive Secretary visited the Dutch Reformed Churches of the Cape, Transvaal, the Orange Free State and Natal, the Presbyterian Church of South Africa, the Bantu Presbyterian Church, the Swiss Mission of North Transvaal (now the Tsonga Presbyterian Church), the Ned. Hervormde Kerk van Afrika and the Gereformeerde Kerk. In all his contacts, the Alliance representative made it clear that unity of Faith was greater than the differences in colour and that the Christian Church could never accept racial separation between Christians. He was struck by the fact that if the government defended its policy of *apartheid* and

was supported by many Reformed Christians there were courageous men and women in the country who were willing to suffer
in order to proclaim that racial separation cannot be justified in
the light of the Christian Gospel. May those who make wholesale
judgments on South Africa never forget this. May they also realize
that among the Afrikaans Christians there are many men and
women wholly devoted to Jesus Christ, who try to serve Him
faithfully, even if they differ from us on this important question.

*　　*　　*

During his first years as Executive Secretary of the Alliance,
Dr Pradervand paid many visits to European Churches, both in
Great Britain and on the Continent. He attended many Synods
and General Assemblies and was able to explain the position of
the Alliance within the larger ecumenical set-up of the day.

Unfortunately, relations with the Churches of Eastern Europe
did not develop as rapidly as the Alliance had hoped. Though the
Executive Secretary had been able to visit Czechoslovakia in 1949
and Hungary in 1950, visits to the Reformed Church of Poland
and to the Reformed Church of Romania proved impossible for
several years. It was only in 1956 that the necessary visas to visit
these countries were granted. Between 1950 and 1954, it became
impossible to visit our member Churches in Czechoslovakia and
in Hungary. Yugoslavia, which had more or less broken away
from the Socialist camp, was in a different position, and in 1953
the Executive Secretary was able to pay an extensive visit to the
Reformed Church of that country, as well as having useful talks
with State representatives.

It is important to say, however, that though visits proved
difficult or even impossible, correspondence between the member
Churches in Eastern Europe and the Alliance Secretariat were
very frequent and cordial; as a result, the Churches of these
countries fully realized that they belonged to a fellowship where
political problems played no part and where unity of faith was
the only important consideration.

*　　*　　*

In the first part of this volume mention was constantly made
of the problem of religious freedom and of the Alliance's activity

on behalf of persecuted minorities. So far, no mention has been made of this problem in the second part of this book. This does not mean that religious freedom was now complete or that the Alliance had no more interest in it.

Already at the end of 1948, the new President of the Alliance, Dr E. J. Hagan, had to intervene on behalf of Rev. Dr G. A. Hadjiantoniou, then Moderator of the Greek Evangelical Church, who had been arrested in Greece for distributing evangelical literature. Dr Hagan, on behalf of the Alliance, asked the British Foreign Office to help in securing the release of Dr Hadjiantoniou. The British Government intervened, and the Moderator of the Greek Evangelical Church was liberated after a few weeks in prison. However this was unfortunately not the end of the difficulties of the small but active Greek Evangelical Church, although both the great Greek Orthodox Church and the small Greek Evangelical Church belonged to the World Council of Churches.

More serious still was the problem of the Evangelical minority in Colombia, South America. In the course of his visit to this country, in November 1951, Dr Pradervand was forced to realize that the Evangelical minority, including the Presbyterians, were denied the most elementary religious rights, and that some of them were even being violently persecuted. The Roman Catholic Church, which had not yet been through the cleansing experience of Vatican II, had too often little understanding for religious freedom, and in 1948, Father Cavalli, a Jesuit, had written in the Italian Catholic Review *Civiltà Cattolica*: 'The Catholic Church, being convinced, by reason of her divine prerogatives, that she is the one true Church, claims for herself alone the right to freedom, for this right may only be possessed by truth, and never by error . . . The Catholic Church would be betraying her mission if she were to proclaim either in theory or in practice, that error can have the same rights as truth . . .'[13]

This the Alliance could not accept and between 1951 and 1954 we fought incessantly to secure the rights of religious minorities in that country. It is good to be able to report that the situation has now completely changed and that collaboration between Roman Catholics and Evangelical Christians has developed in many areas.

*   *   *

The Netherlands warmly welcomed several Alliance meetings in 1953. All these meetings were held at Woudschoten, near Zeist.

First the Executive Committee met from 14 to 17 August. The Alliance President was still seriously ill and the chair was taken by one of the Vice-Presidents, Rev. Dr Edgar F. Romig of New York. Much time was given to the preparation for the 17th General Council; it was decided that it would take place at Princeton Theological Seminary, Princeton, N.J., U.S.A. from 27 July to 5 August 1954. A great deal of preparatory work had already been done by the Committee on Preparations and especially by its active Chairman, Rev. Dr Ralph W. Lloyd. The Theme, 'The Witness of the Reformed Churches in the World Today', was approved and it was decided that there would be five Study Commissions to work on the sub-themes of the Council.

The Executive Committee, after hearing one of its members, Rev. Max Dominicé, of Geneva, unanimously approved to recommend to the Princeton Council that the Alliance undertake the restoration of the Calvin Auditorium (Knox Chapel), one of the high places of the Calvinist Reformation in Geneva.

The meeting of the Executive Committee was followed by a meeting of the Eastern Section from 20 to 24 August; it was devoted to the study of the problem of the ministry. Though the Moderator of the Presbyterian Church of Korea was present, the 'Eastern Section' was in fact European, and delegates to Woudschoten heard with real joy that the proposed new Constitution, which was to be submitted to the Princeton Council, replaced the 'Eastern Section' by a 'European Area'; geographically this was much more realistic, as it was not possible for Churches of Asia and Africa to attend 'regional' meetings in Europe!

The organization of further Areas was to be left to the Churches of the different continents. If, in spite of many attempts, new areas (apart from the N. American and the European) have as yet not been organized, this is mainly due to financial considerations. It is regrettable, but inevitable, as the Alliance has intentionally remained a 'small' organization and does not want to make excessive appeals for funds to its member Churches.

During the same months, Woudschoten housed for twelve

days the Third World Conference of Reformed and Presbyterian Youth. The theme was 'Renewal by Christ' and there were lively discussions among the delegates from all over the world.

REFERENCES

1. *Proceedings 16th General Council*, p. 91.
2. Idem, p. 209.
3. Idem, p. 206.
4. Idem, p. 206.
5. Idem, p. 213.
6. Idem, p. 215.
7. Idem, Preface, p. 5.
8. Idem, p. 181.
9. Minutes 1949 Executive Committee, p. 10.
10. Idem, p. 11.
11. Minutes 1951 Executive Committee, p. 9.
12. Idem, Appendix IV, pp. 2–3.
13. *Presbyterian World*, vol. XXI, no. 5, p. 195.

CHAPTER ELEVEN

The Princeton Council and the Growth of the Alliance

We have already mentioned that the 1948 Geneva Council marked the beginning of a new era in the history of the Alliance. For the first time there was now a world Executive Committee which could speak and act responsibly on behalf of the Alliance. This Executive had given a great deal of time to the preparation of the 17th General Council, both at its 1951 and 1953 meetings. It had carefully chosen the theme and sub-themes of the Council and though there were only two people in the Geneva office (with a part-time assistant in the last months before the Council) it had been decided to send a study booklet to all the delegates before the Council. This booklet was prepared by the then Secretary of the British Churches' Committee of the Alliance, Rev. W. S. Robertson; it was then translated into French and German, as the three languages were now the official languages of the Alliance.

In 1954, however, the Alliance was not yet a 'world' organization in the full sense of the word. Among the delegates to the Princeton Council, the British and North American representatives were still the large majority. Only eleven Churches from the Continent of Europe were represented; two were not present because of the refusal of the American State Department to grant the necessary visas; several Churches from Eastern Europe could not secure the necessary exit permits for the delegates; the cold war was still a reality in many ways.

Four African Churches were represented at Princeton; six Asian Churches had been able to send delegates and there was a full representation from the Churches of Australasia; six Churches from Latin America and the Caribbean had sent delegates. It is interesting to note that, for the first time, there were women delegates apart from 'Women Corresponding Members'. But their number was still very limited as the Constitution demanded that delegates be either ministers or elders. The number of Churches who had women elders in 1954 was still very small. Fortunately the new Constitution adopted by the 17th General Council allowed 'ministers and *members*' to be delegates to the Alliance Councils; the alteration of one word was to open the door to a much larger number of women at the next General Council.

If the Alliance was not yet representative of all the Reformed Churches of the world, progress had already been made between 1948 and 1954 and in his report to the members of the Council the General Secretary was able to show that of the thirteen Churches admitted by the Executive Committee since 1949, three came from Africa, three from Asia, two from the U.S.A., four from Latin America and only one from Europe. Other Churches from Latin America and Asia, which had not yet been admitted into the Alliance, were represented by fraternal delegates; the Council admitted into membership the Ronga-Tsonga Church of Portuguese East Africa, thus bringing the membership of the Alliance to 66 Churches.

The President of the Alliance since the Geneva Council, the Very Rev. Dr E. J. Hagan, from Edinburgh, was prevented by ill-health from being present, and the sessions of the Princeton Council were chaired by the two Vice-Presidents, Rev. Dr Edgar F. Romig of New York, and Professor Dr Josef Hromadka, of Prague.

The theme of the Council was 'The Witness of the Reformed Churches in the World Today' and President Dr John A. Mackay, of Princeton, delivered the Opening Address, which made a deep impression on the delegates.

A big step forward had been made in order to facilitate the work of the Council; simultaneous translation equipment had been installed in the Hall where the plenary sessions were to be held, so that delegates who did not know English were able to partake fully in the Council. This was to be improved in later Councils, where simultaneous translation was available in the section discussions as well.

There were five sub-themes:

I. The Reformed Churches and the Ecumenical Movement

II. The Outreach of the Church
III. The Several Ministries in the Church
IV. The Church's Freedom and Responsibility
V. The Renewal of the Church's Inner Life

The Sections were able to spend many hours discussing the sub-themes which were proposed to them, before bringing their reports to the plenary sessions. These were then discussed and revised before being approved by the Council and commended to the Churches for study and appropriate action.

Limitation of space does not allow for long quotations. We cannot however refrain from quoting in full a paragraph of the report of the Section on 'The Reformed Churches and the Ecumenical Movement' as it clearly states the Reformed position on the problem of intercommunion and was received with gratitude by many member Churches of the Alliance. It reads as follows:

'As Reformed and Presbyterian Churches we bear witness to our fellow Christians that we recognize the ministry, sacraments, and membership of all Churches which, according to the Bible, confess Jesus Christ as Lord and Saviour. We invite and gladly welcome the members of all such Churches to the Table of our common Lord. The Church has received the sacrament of the Holy Communion from Christ and He communicates Himself in it to the believer. The Table of the Lord is His, not ours. We believe that we dare not refuse the sacrament to any baptized person who loves and confesses Jesus Christ as Lord and Saviour. It is our strong conviction that unwillingness, particularly at this time, to practise such intercommunion gravely impedes the cause of unity and lends an air of unreality to much of our talk about it. We cannot proclaim the Gospel of reconciliation without demonstrating at the Table of the Lord that we are reconciled to one another. Therefore, we would welcome face to face talks with our fellow Christians in other Churches looking towards the time when all sincere Christians will be welcome around a common Table.'[1]

The whole Council was very ecumenical, as the reports show. The General Secretary of the World Council of Churches, Rev. Dr W. A. Visser't Hooft, who had been a member of the

Alliance Executive since 1948, delivered an address on the World Council of Churches. The Council also adopted a resolution on Inter-Church Aid, proposed by Rev. Dr Eugene C. Blake, who was to become one of the leaders of the Alliance before succeeding Dr Visser't Hooft as General Secretary of the WCC in 1966. The resolution reads as follows:

'The World Presbyterian Alliance is not organised for the administration of Inter-Church Aid, and does not propose so to organise, because of the conviction of many of our Churches that the giving and receiving of Aid has ecumenical implications beyond our Reformed family.

'It is our natural concern, however, that in the ecumenical administration and allocation of aid to Churches, the Presbyterian and Reformed Churches should continue to have full and fair attention given to their desires and needs . . .'[2]

This did not prevent the Council from giving full attention to the problem of religious freedom. The Greek Evangelical Church was still facing difficulties and the Council felt compelled to adopt a resolution which expressed admirably the position of the Reformed Churches on the problem of religious freedom:

'We are compelled by our loyalty to the truth in Jesus Christ, as we understand it, and by our loyalty to our brethren of the Reformed Faith in Greece, to state our conviction that it is God's will that every Church of Christ should be allowed freedom by State and Church:

'Freely and publicly to worship God according to the Scriptures after their own practices; and

'By word and act freely to proclaim the Gospel of Jesus Christ to all men everywhere, so long as that proclamation is a true and responsible witness about other communions, and that truth is ever spoken in love.'[3]

The Alliance was well aware that the existence and the development of world confessional organizations was not without dangers for the ecumenical movement; and the Council, on the recommendation of Study Section I, adopted the following resolution:

'1. Whereas the ecumenical concern is a primary obligation of all Churches; and whereas the present development of world confessional organisations raises a number of serious problems which ought to be examined in common as befits brethren in Christ, so as not to hinder the sound development of Christianity:

'The 17th General Council therefore resolves to remit to the Executive Committee of the Alliance the consideration of the best ways and means of furthering such consultations, and the taking of any action.'[4] The initiator of the resolution was Dr John A. Mackay, who was to play a major role as President of the Alliance, in bringing the different world organizations together for consultation.

We have already seen (p. 188) that the Executive Committee, in 1953, had responded favourably to a suggestion that the Calvin Auditorium in Geneva be restored by the Churches of the Reformed family, under the auspices of the Alliance. The Princeton Council had named a 'Special Committee on the Calvin Auditorium'. The Committee was chaired by a man of great enthusiasm and devotion to the Reformed cause, Rev. Dr H. R. Anderson, of Chicago. The Council, after hearing Dr Anderson's report, approved the restoration of the Auditorium and an agreement between the Alliance and the National Protestant Church of Geneva. Soon, the Committee was going to start its work of collecting funds, and within a few years (1957–1959) the restoration of the building where Calvin had taught theology for several years and where John Knox had been the minister of the 'English' congregation of Geneva was to be achieved with the assistance of Reformed and Presbyterian Churches all over the world.

A new Constitution and By-Laws for the Alliance were adopted. We have already noted that it allowed 'members' of the Church (instead of 'elders') to become delegates to the Alliance Councils. This was important. Another important decision was to create a 'Department of Women's Work', which replaced the former 'Women's International Union'. It meant that for the first time women were called to be full partners in the work of the Alliance. One can regret that this decision came so late, yet at the same time be thankful that this step was taken at Princeton.

The Executive Secretary was re-elected until the end of the next General Council, but the title of Executive Secretary was abandoned and Dr Pradervand became General Secretary. Miss Paulette Piguet, who had served the Alliance with much intelligence and devotion since 1950, was made Assistant Secretary.

The Council also recommended to the Executive Committee the appointment of a Theological Commission. In fact, two Commissions were to be created, one by each organized Area, before a Theological Department was instituted at the 18th General Council in 1959.

A new Executive Committee was elected with Dr John A. Mackay as President. Dr Mackay was to help the Alliance become a world-wide organization; at the same time he played a very active role in the ecumenical movement. For the first time three women were on the Committee: the Chairman of the Department of Women's Work and two of the fifteen elected members.

The Council voted an increased budget for the Alliance, but it was still very modest and only amounted to just over $23,000. In view of the increased responsibilities of the Alliance, this was a minimum.

The Princeton Council had been attended by many 'Youth corresponding members', who published a statement expressing their desire to play a larger role in the life of the Alliance.

A Message was adopted by the Council, for transmission to the member Churches of the Alliance. Here are a few lines of this message:

'The sharpest challenge to us who have certain faith in the crucified, risen and victorious Christ is to live and teach that faith (that men may see in Christ the only real hope for mankind, the one effectual remedy for all their fears) and so to witness that no one shall be turned away from the Christian hope by our default. For any hope but that which is in Him will finally succumb before life's limitations and tragedies, or break on the rock of God's eternal justice.

'We beg you, therefore, to heed God's Living Word as it comes to you through the Scriptures.

'Claim the whole world for Jesus Christ

'Seek to close the divided Christian ranks

'Love all men, even your enemies, knowing that they too are called to become children of God's family. Strive to break down racial barriers, to promote understanding between classes and people, to provide an opportunity for every man to enjoy his share of God's bounty and to earn a livelihood for himself and his family.

'Work with those who are seeking to promote peace and righteousness among nations, recognizing that unrest will continue and that there will be no immunity against irretrievable disaster until the new powers that have been put at our disposal through scientific discovery and technological advance have been made available for human welfare instead of human destruction.
. . . . . .

'Pray without ceasing.

'Whatever befalls, remember that ancient word: "Have I not commanded you? Be strong and of good courage: be not frightened, neither be dismayed, for the Lord your God is with you wherever you go".'[5]

A report on the Princeton General Council would be incomplete if no mention were made of the decision to appoint a Commission on Ordination, to formulate afresh the Reformed doctrine on this important subject. The Executive Committee elected Professor John A. Barkley, of Belfast, as chairman of the commission of nine.

Finally on the enthusiastic proposal of Dr James I. McCord, then Dean of Austin Theological Seminary, in Texas, and member of the new Executive Committee of the Alliance, the Council decided to appoint a Committee to publish the as yet unpublished sermons of Calvin; Dr McCord was made chairman of the Committee and he worked unceasingly on this important project for many years.

The Alliance now had as President Dr John A. Mackay, who was to make a real impact on the life of our organization. Already at the end of January 1955, Dr Mackay published a 'Letter to the Reformed Family of Churches' in *The Presbyterian World*. Here are some extracts from this letter:

'. . . Members of Reformed Churches are involved today in unhappy racial tensions in South Africa and in the United States. Others maintain a robust evangelical witness in Communist countries . . . Still others play a dominant part in evangelical communities in Spain and Colombia where Fascist tyranny has persecuted, and continues to oppress, the Protestant minority . . .

'Even more striking is the part being played by members of the Reformed Churches in the Ecumenical Movement of our time . . . Presbyterians today play a crucial role in the two basic issues of the ecumenical effort; to carry the Gospel into all the world, and to pursue the world-wide unity of all Christ's followers . . .

'The health of the Body of Christ is fulfilled only when all the members, acting in perfect unison, obey the missionary mandate of the Head. Christians have no right to regard themselves as ecumenical unless they are prepared to do two things: first to carry the Gospel into all the world, and secondly, to do this together. For us who belong to the Reformed tradition the mission of the Church and the unity of the Church are inseparably bound together . . .'[6]

The world was living the time of the 'cold war', not only in Europe, but also in the Far East. The United States of America had refused to recognize the People's Republic of China, and there was much tension between the two nations. Dr Mackay, who had from 1949 onward spoken in favour of the recognition of Communist China, delivered an address at the 1955 North American Area Council of the Alliance, which took place at Ottawa from 15 to 17 February. In the course of his address, Dr Mackay dealt with the situation in the Far East. He said: 'When persons or peoples are estranged from one another, there is no substitute for direct dialog between them. Dialog is the way in which God deals with men. He is willing to "reason" with the worst men. He does not demand that man qualify for direct conversations with Him. God condescends to listen patiently to what the most reprehensive people have to say.

'Monolog is insufficient in human affairs. If discussion is to be fruitful, a quarrel settled, men must not merely talk *at* one another or *about* one another; they must talk *to* one another. They must meet face to face . . .

'The restoration of world order demands the rediscovery of forgiveness . . .

'. . . No problem of so-called co-existence today is more terrible than the problem which emerged in the 16th century between Roman Catholics and Protestant Calvinists. Yet, gradually it became possible for both to live in the same world.'[7]

In view of later developments in the Far East, one can only regret that the voice of the President of the Alliance was not heard earlier. It might have saved many lives and prevented much suffering.

At Princeton it had been decided that the Executive Committee of the Alliance would now meet every year, as it was otherwise impossible to supervise and direct the growing work entrusted to the Alliance.

The 1955 meeting of the Executive Committee took place at Crêt-Bérard, a retreat centre of the Reformed Church of the Canton de Vaud, in Switzerland, from 18 to 21 July.

Naturally, the problem of ecumenical relations played an important part in the deliberations of the Committee. In his report to the Executive, the General Secretary had spoken of the relationship of the Alliance with other World Confessional Families: 'There are some confessional groups to whom we feel more closely related than to others. None are closer to us than the Lutheran family of Churches. It has been my constant concern to develop friendly relations with these Churches, in spite of the strong confessional spirit of some of our Lutheran brethren. I am glad to report that following private conversations which took place last year at Evanston between representatives of our two confessional groups, the "Faith and Order" Division of the WCC has arranged for a consultation to be held at Davos [during the meeting of the Central Committee of the WCC, *Ed.*] between Reformed and Lutheran "Faith and Order" representatives. Our representatives ought to know that we shall follow their work with real interest and hope. The Alliance is not an end in itself; our aim is to be of service to the whole Church of Jesus Christ.'[8]

The Committee further accepted a motion presented by Dr E. C. Blake, which reads as follows: 'That the President be asked to consult some officers of the WCC and some officers of the Lutheran World Federation to see if on a private basis conversations might be arranged on matters of mutual concern to Lutherans and member Churches of the Alliance.'[9] This was to be the beginning of discussions which have since then developed remarkably, both in Europe and in North America, as readers of this book will see in the coming chapters.

The Executive Committee admitted another Church, the Independent Presbyterian Church of Brazil, into the membership of the Alliance. At the same time we heard with regret of the withdrawal of the Free Church of Scotland, which could not agree with our ecumenical openness. This was all the more regrettable because the Alliance President originally came from that Church and had a brother who was a minister of the Free Church of Scotland.

The Executive Committee of the Alliance, in 1949, had decided that the Alliance should not set up its own organization for Inter-Church Aid, but that they should use the channels of the World Council of Churches. At the same time, the Committee had made it clear that the Alliance was deeply interested in the problem of Inter-Church Aid, and especially in helping the weaker Churches of the Reformed family to receive the assistance which they needed.

This action had been confirmed by subsequent Executive Committees, as well as by the Princeton General Council. Consequently, the General Secretary had been in contact with the giving agencies of the larger Churches in Europe and in America and he had been assured that the weaker Churches would receive the help which was still indispensible for their needs. The 1955 Executive asked the General Secretary to continue working along this line.

The Alliance quarterly had been renamed *The Presbyterian World* in 1949. The General Secretary was not too happy about the title. He had the feeling that it was time to emphasize the word *Reformed*, which was much more important than the term *Presbyterian*, which only referred to the form of Church government, whilst the word 'Reformed' indicated the substance of the faith of the Churches gathered in the Alliance. But as the Churches of the Anglo-Saxon world almost exclusively used the term 'Presbyterian' it was not easy to abandon it, as far as the Alliance was concerned. At the 1955 meeting of the Executive, President James E. Wagner, of the Evangelical and Reformed Church of the U.S.A. (now part of the United Church of Christ) reminded his colleagues in the Alliance Executive that his Church came from Europe and that the use of the word 'Presbyterian' was foreign to them. It was therefore decided at Dr Wagner's suggestion that, from 1956 onwards, the Alliance quarterly should be renamed *The Reformed and Presbyterian World*, a title which was kept until the end of 1970; it was then decided that the quarterly should be renamed *The Reformed World*.

The Executive was also concerned to see that the quarterly had a circulation which was hardly over 2,000. It decided to invite Churches to subscribe to the quarterly for all their ministers.

Before the end of the year, the Presbyterian Church of New Zealand, through its Presbyterian Bookroom, decided to take bulk subscriptions for all the ministers of the Church. The following year, the largest Church of the Alliance, the United Presbyterian Church in the U.S.A., did the same and the circulation of the quarterly rose to 12,000. This made it possible for the Alliance to be better known than previously.

From the beginning, the General Secretary, elected in 1948, was anxious to make the Alliance a real world organization and to bring into its fellowship Churches from all Continents. He had already visited the Churches of Latin America in 1951 and in 1952 some of the Churches of Africa. He had planned to visit Churches of the Reformed family in Australasia and Asia in 1953; but the large amount of work entailed by the coming General Council of Princeton compelled him to postpone this visit. The visit finally took place in 1955 and lasted 2½ months. This was the first time that the Alliance Secretary visited the Churches of New Zealand and Australia and he was very warmly received everywhere; six weeks were spent in these two countries and valuable contacts were established with leaders of the Churches there.

Travelling northwards he then spent over two weeks in Indonesia. In this great land, where the Reformed Churches were very strong, the Alliance had as yet not one member. The Indonesian Churches believed that by belonging to the Alliance, they would be unable to fulfil their ecumenical obligations, which were a first priority. We were able to explain that this would not be the case. The fact that Dr Mackay, a great ecumenical leader, was President of the Alliance, was the best evidence of this. After reflection one Indonesian Church joined the Alliance; soon others were to follow, and at present the Alliance has more member Churches in Indonesia (twenty) than in any other country of the world! The Alliance is backing the efforts of our Indonesian brethren to form one great Protestant Church in their country and it is clear that membership in the Alliance has not made the Churches of the Reformed family in Indonesia more 'confessional' in the narrow sense of the word.

*   *   *

In his report to the member Churches for the year 1956, the General Secretary wrote: 'The year 1956 began with signs of an easing of the international situation and with the hope of peaceful co-existence. It has unfortunately ended less happily. The tragic story of Hungary and the Middle East has shown how precariously the peace of the world is held, and how easily the passions of man can be rekindled.'[10]

The 1955 Executive Committee had expressed the hope that the 1956 meeting could take place in Czechoslovakia. In the course of a visit to Czechoslovakia, prior to the 1955 meeting of the Executive, Dr Pradervand had been able to discuss the matter with Government representatives and they had shown themselves sympathetic. And so it was decided to hold the meeting in Prague, from 7 to 11 August, immediately after the meeting of the Central Committee of the World Council of Churches in Hungary.

This meeting was remarkable from more than one point of view. For the first time, the Executive of the Alliance was able to meet in a People's Democracy; it looked as if the old misunderstandings between Communist Governments and Christian Churches had been overcome. There is no doubt that Professor Hromadka, Vice-President of the Alliance, was instrumental in bridging the gap, as far as the Alliance was concerned.

One other remarkable feature of this Executive was the fact that for the first time a direct contact was re-established with the Reformed Church of Romania and the Reformed Church of Poland; two fraternal delegates from Romania and one from Poland assisted at this meeting.

And, last but not least, a great public service took place in the historic Chapel of Bethlehem, where Jan Hus had proclaimed the Reformation message and where no Protestant service had been held since 1620. The Bethlehem Chapel, which had been restored by the Government and was a national monument, was kindly put at the disposal of the Alliance by the Czechoslovak Government. Nearly 3,000 people attended this great service at which the President of the Alliance, Dr John A. Mackay, was the preacher. It was truly a great and moving occasion.

But the Committee did not only attend a public service of worship. It did a great deal of work, as the present report will show.

We have already noted that the President of the Alliance was very concerned about the resurgence of confessionalism; the

Basle Statement of 1951 had clearly indicated that he did not wish the Alliance to work for confessional ends and the Princeton documents expressed the same point of view.

At the Prague meeting, Dr Mackay presented to the Executive a statement on 'The Confessional Resurgence and the Ecumenical Movement with special reference to the role and development of the World Alliance of Reformed Churches.'

The statement was warmly received by the members of the Executive Committee, as it expressed with great clarity the Reformed point of view. Dr Mackay then proposed the following motion:

'The Executive Committee of the World Alliance of Reformed Churches expresses the hope that in the near future an informal gathering can be arranged between representatives of the several world confessional bodies in the Protestant family of Churches. The object of this meeting would be to provide an opportunity for the representatives of each Confession to interpret to their brethren of the other Confessions the nature, objectives and development of the group to which they belong.

'The Committee accordingly requests the officers of the Alliance to consult with the officers of other confessions with a view to a small informal gathering being convened for the purpose above indicated.'[11]

The officers, and especially the President, set to work, and the first meeting of representatives of the different families took place at Yale, U.S.A., in July 1957, during the meeting of the Central Committee of the WCC. This was to be the beginning of a new era in the relations between the Confessional Families, and we are grateful that, thanks to its President, the Alliance could play a pioneering role in this field.

The two Areas of the Alliance had now formed a Theological Commission and the chairmen of these Commissions, both members of the Executive Committee, Professor Laszlo Pap, of Budapest, Hungary, and Dean James I. McCord, of Austin, Texas, were able to indicate that the first meeting would be held shortly.

It was felt however that the creation of these two commissions was not sufficient and that the theological work of the Alliance demanded the presence in the Alliance offices of a man who could devote all his time to this work. The Executive Committee therefore voted to create a new post on the Alliance staff, the post of Theological Secretary. It was not however until the end of 1957 that the Theological Secretary could begin his work.

The Committee heard with great interest of the work done by the Committee for the Restoration of the Calvin Auditorium and of the sums already received or promised. It was therefore decided that the restoration work should start in 1957 and be finished in 1959 for the Calvin Jubilee.

We have mentioned above the steps taken by the Executive Committee in order to bring the World Confessional Families together in an informal discussion. The General Secretary felt that apart from these general conversations the Alliance should engage in bilateral conversations. In his report to the Executive, after having expressed his gratification at the talks already in progress between the Lutheran World Federation and the World Alliance of Reformed Churches, under the auspices of 'Faith and Order' he said: 'With regard to the International Congregational Council, as more and more Churches of our two confessional families are now engaged in discussion with a view to union, it becomes imperative for us to ask ourselves if we should not undertake conversations on the world level to examine the future relations of our own Alliance to the ICC.'[12]

Both organizations agreed with the suggestion and soon set to work. This was facilitated by the fact that both the World Alliance of Reformed Churches and the International Congregational Council belonged to the Reformed family. We shall devote a whole chapter to the International Congregational Council and to the development of relations between the two organizations, development which culminated in 1970 in the coming together of the 'Alliance of the Reformed Churches throughout the World holding the Presbyterian Order' and the 'International Congregational Council' in the new 'World Alliance of Reformed Churches (Presbyterian and Congregational)'.

*   *   *

Soon after the Prague meeting of the Executive Committee there was a Council of the European Area, which took place at Emden, N.W. Germany, from 16 to 21 August. This was the time of the *détente* between East and West, and the Churches of Hungary, Czechoslovakia, Romania, Poland and Yugoslavia were all represented. Only the three member Churches in the Soviet Union (the Reformed Church of Carpatho-Ukraine, the Reformed Church of Lithuania and the Reformed Church of Latvia) were not present.

The Council, which was chaired by the Chairman of the Area, Rev. Dr Max Dominicé, of Geneva, studied 'The Problem of Worship in the Reformed Churches'; simultaneous translation was available and excellent work was done at Emden. On the Sunday evening, a great public meeting was held in the ruins of the 'Grosse Kirche' (Great Church) of Emden; one of the speakers that evening was Bishop Janos Peter, of Debrecen, who was later to become the Foreign Minister of Hungary. He was at the time Bishop of the largest District of the Hungarian Reformed Church, and Vice-Chairman of the European Area.

The Council elected a new Chairman of the Area, Rev. Dr Alex King, of Edinburgh, who had already been for years a trusted adviser and friend of the General Secretary and who had contributed more than any other man to help overcome the misunderstandings which existed in some Scottish circles after the 1948 reorganization of the Alliance.

In October of the same year the General Secretary was able to undertake his long-delayed visit to the Churches of Romania and Poland. When he arrived in Romania, on 18 October, everything seemed perfect; on his way to Bucharest he made a short stop at Budapest airport, where he discussed with Professor Pap problems related to the theological work of the Alliance. It was a beautiful autumn day and everything was quiet. In Bucharest, he was most cordially received by the President of the State Office for Church Affairs, and the representative of the Romanian Government had real understanding for the desire of the Alliance to develop the contacts between the Reformed Church of Romania and the Alliance member Churches in the West.

Alas, within a few days, everything changed. On 23 October the 'Hungarian Revolution' started and the efforts made by many to bring a closer and more cordial co-operation between East and West came to an end.

The General Secretary was now cut off from the West, as air communications between Romania and Switzerland went over Budapest, but eventually he was able to leave for Prague and from there take a plane to Warsaw. Poland had just had its peaceful 'revolution'. Gomulka had taken over and the people felt jubilant at the change which had taken place; news of what was happening in Hungary did not reach us there, and there was a real feeling of hope.

As far as the Reformed Church was concerned, it was facing difficult financial problems. It was only a remnant of the pre-war Reformed Church and its Church building in Warsaw had suffered greatly during the war; it had not yet been fully restored, but the Government showed understanding for this small Church and the Alliance was able to secure funds from member Churches in the west for the full restoration of the building as well as for assisting the Church in other ways.

It was only on arrival in Switzerland on 30 October that we realized the extent of what had happened in Hungary. Soon afterwards, the intervention of Russian troops brought a large number of refugees to the West. Much help was given to the refugees, but many people in the West forgot that most of the Hungarians had remained in their country and that their economic situation was extremely difficult. Dr Pradervand urged the Reformed Churches to put money aside for helping our brethren in Hungary. Some Churches, especially the Presbyterian Church in Ireland, heard his appeal and put substantial sums at the disposal of the Alliance for food parcels to be sent to a large number of Reformed families during the winter of 1956–57.

Christian organizations with headquarters in the West have been accused of having helped or encouraged the Hungarian revolution of 1956. As far as the Alliance is concerned—and we are sure that it is also the case for other organizations—nothing is further from the truth. Our only concern was and always has been to help the Reformed Churches, wherever they are, to give a faithful witness and to be constantly renewed by the Word of God and the Holy Spirit. We have always believed that Christians could live under any regime and that it was not the Alliance's responsibility to concern itself with the form of government under which our member Churches have to live. We know that if there are difficulties in the East, there are difficulties of a different nature in other parts of the world. It is certain that the pressure under which some of our brethren there had to live has made them more mature and more devoted to the Christian cause than ever before.

For the Alliance, the year 1956 saw a further development. We have already mentioned that the circulation of the Alliance quarterly increased to over 12,000, thanks to bulk subscriptions from several Churches. This meant that the financial position of the journal was now excellent. As a result, it was possible for the Alliance to engage an Associate Editor for *The Reformed and Presbyterian World*. The Church of Scotland had decided to send a minister to Geneva to take charge of its congregation there, but the financial burden was heavy and the Church of Scotland was happy to make an arrangement with the Alliance: its minister was to devote half of his time to his pastoral duties and the other half to the Alliance as Associate Editor of the quarterly. Rev. Niall D. Watson arrived in Geneva in September 1956 and his presence in the Alliance offices was very beneficial. Mr Watson immediately took a real interest in the affairs of the Alliance and was for several years a very much appreciated colleague. Unfortunately, the growing work of his congregation later compelled him to give up his position as Associate Editor.

*   *   *

The 1957 meeting of the Executive Committee of the Alliance took place at Stony Point, N.Y., U.S.A., from 8 to 13 August, after the meeting of the Central Committee of the WCC at Yale. It was at Yale that the first informal meeting of representatives of World Confessional Families had been held and Dr Mackay was able to report on this first meeting. But the Alliance Executive wanted to do more and it adopted a statement, which we reproduce:

'The Executive Committee receives with gratitude the report of its chairman that, pursuant to a recommendation adopted at Prague a year ago, he was able to bring about an informal conference of responsible representatives of the seven world-wide confessional groups . . .

'The Executive Committee believes that the confrontation thus initiated should be followed up and therefore encourages and authorizes the President of the Alliance to secure a further conference at which both the chairmen or presidents and the executive secretaries of the confessional groups should be present. It is suggested that in the light of the present meeting in New Haven the meeting might be held at the next meeting of the Central Committee of the World Council of Churches . . .

'Such a conference as is here proposed should engage in frank and friendly discussion of the place of confessionalism in the ecumenical movement; the contribution which resurgent confessionalism can make to the enrichment of that movement; and the points at which, if any, confessionalism becomes a threat to that growing oneness in Christ which the ecumenical movement seeks; and ways in which the commitment of the Churches to the ecumenical movement presupposes some restraint on the consciousness and practice of mission on the part of the confessional groups with reference to each other . . .'[13]

In view of the importance that these meetings of representatives of World Confessional Families were to take, it is good to know that the Alliance played a leading role in their development. There is no doubt that these meetings, which soon became annual, helped to clear the atmosphere between the WCC and these organizations and that they made it possible for the World Confessional Families to play a more active and positive role in the whole ecumenical situation of our time.

The Executive Committee had to deal with many other problems. One was the race question. Two of our member Churches in South Africa, the Dutch Reformed Churches in Transvaal and in the Orange Free State, had sent representatives to the Executive meeting and there was a frank discussion on the race problem. The Executive Committee decided to send a letter to the Synods of these two Churches, which reads as follows:

'We appreciate your taking the initiative in sending to us the report of the ad hoc commission for race relations of your Church. We have begun to examine it with great interest and care. We have noted with special appreciation the following paragraph: (C. 6, p. 13)

"To an increasing degree the Christian Church is becoming aware of the danger of acquiescing in race relations which may perhaps not be in accordance with the Word of God. Therefore the Dutch Reformed Church is also listening afresh to what the Word of God has to say to us on the above-mentioned matter with respect to the present situation."

'As you listen afresh to the Word of God, we trust you will not feel it amiss for other Churches in our confessional family to comment upon the Biblical and the theological position which is developed in the report . . . The true glory of our heritage from John Calvin has been the willingness, sometimes at great cost, to act boldly as the conscience of the community and nation in simple obedience to the Word of God.'[14]

*   *   *

The 1956 Executive had decided to appoint a Theological Secretary; the Executive at Stony Point was able to welcome the secretary designate, Rev. Lewis S. Mudge, Jr, son of a former Stated Clerk of the Presbyterian Church in the U.S.A. Mr (later Dr) Mudge was to begin his work in October 1957 and remain in the service of the Alliance until the summer of 1962. He developed the theological work of the Alliance in several directions and started *The Bulletin of the Department of Theology* which appeared quarterly in three editions: a printed edition in English and mimeographed editions in French and German. Thanks to these two mimeographed editions, theologians of the Continent of Europe were able to take a more active part in the theological thinking and work of the Alliance. This was a most welcome development.

The Executive Committee also gave a great deal of thought to the 1959 General Council. It was decided that it should be held in Campinas (this was later changed to São Paulo), Brazil, from 27 July to 6 August 1959 and that the general theme should be 'The Servant Image of the Church'. The theme was chosen on the recommendation of the President, Dr John A. Mackay who felt that it was time for the Alliance to emphasize the fact that the Church, which was made up of disciples of Jesus Christ, was here to serve and not to triumph; this seemed especially important in view of the triumphalist attitude of the Roman Catholic Church in Latin America at that time.

The chairman of the Committee on the publication of Calvin's unpublished sermons, Dr James I. McCord, was able to report good progress. This was in no small measure due to work of Dr McCord himself; he had been able to secure funds to make possible the publication of the first volumes.

Dr McCord, who was also chairman of the 'Committee on the

translation into Portuguese of Calvin's Institutes', could also report progress here. Unfortunately, the man who was chosen to do the translation, Dr Maurer of São Paulo, became seriously ill and died soon afterwards, and the whole enterprise was seriously delayed.

More Churches were admitted into the Alliance and it is interesting to note that practically all the new members of the Alliance were 'Younger Churches'. The aim of the Alliance to be a genuine world organization was now being realized and soon the Younger Churches were to be more numerous in the Alliance than the Churches of Europe and America.

*   *   *

In 1958, the Alliance was preparing for the 18th General Council, which was to take place in 1959 in São Paulo, Brazil. The theme was finally worded: 'The Servant Lord and His Servant People' and the new Theological Secretary of the Alliance prepared a Study Booklet which was translated into French, German and Portuguese and widely distributed among the member Churches. Plans to ensure a good participation of as many Churches as possible were made by the Executive at its Edinburgh meeting; apart from a 'travel pool', which meant that the Churches of North America were in fact subsidizing the journey of delegates from other continents, a special fund for helping weaker and poorer Churches was created and this was to prove important in making possible a better world representation at São Paulo.

In 1958 the Alliance was also concerned with the proper celebrations of the 1959 and 1960 Jubilees. What were these Jubilees? In his annual report for the year 1958, the General Secretary wrote: 'It is in 1959 that the Reformed Church of France celebrates the 400th anniversary of the Church's first National Synod; and the same year the National Protestant Church of Geneva celebrates the 400th anniversary of the foundation of Calvin's Academy, later to become the University of Geneva. In 1960 the Church of Scotland and with her a great many Presbyterian Churches of the English-speaking world, celebrate the fourth centenary of the Scottish Reformation.

'In the spring of 1958 it was felt by some members of the Executive Committee that the Alliance could well play a part in these anniversaries in showing their relevance to our own

C.S.—8

world today. Thus the Alliance undertook the sponsorship of a
30 minute film *For God's Glory*, devoted to the work of John
Calvin and to the Churches which spring from the Geneva
Reformation.

'Later, the Executive Committee decided to appoint a Secretary
for the Jubilee Celebrations. The Rev. James E. Andrews, a
minister of the Presbyterian Church in the U.S., was their
choice.'[15] Mr Andrews immediately started to work in Geneva,
in July 1958, with great enthusiasm, and it is thanks to his
untiring work that Reformed Churches all over the world were
provided with a leaflet which allowed them all to take part in the
Day of Prayer which was to be celebrated by all our member
Churches on 31 May 1959.

The 1958 Executive heard a report of Professor Barkley, of
Belfast, chairman of the Commission on Ordination. It was
decided that the full report of the Commission, which stated the
Reformed point of view with great clarity, should be submitted
to the São Paulo Council for information.

Ecumenical relations were again discussed by the Executive.
The Committee voted to begin conversations with the International Congregational Council. As we deal with this subject in
a special chapter, we say no more at this stage.

The Executive was informed that a small Committee of representatives of the Reformed Church of France had asked the
General Secretary to join them in order to help former Roman
Catholic priests who had left their Church and wished to give a
Christian witness in a Protestant Church. It was made clear that
this was done in an ecumenical spirit. The Committee refrained
from attracting priests; but in cases where there was a genuine
desire to leave the Church of Rome and to witness in another
Church, the Committee was trying to help. This action was
approved by the Committee. The work has been going on for
years, without any publicity, and through this group some men,
who might otherwise have been lost to the Christian cause, again
became ministers of the Gospel or active members of an
Evangelical Church.

Finally, in view of the coming Reformed Jubilees, the Executive
Committee appointed a Committee: 'to draft a Statement from
the Alliance to our fellow Christians, to be released to the public
on June 1, 1959, and later to be presented for adoption by the

Eighteenth General Council. The Statement will be an expression of our concern, after 400 years, for the truths recovered in the Reformation; an expression of our dedication to the renewal, unity and mission of the Church; a declaration that, apart from our brothers in other branches of the Church Catholic, the Reformed and Presbyterian Churches cannot fulfil their obedience to the Lord Jesus Christ; an invitation to our brothers in all the Churches to join with us in renewed dedication to the service of our common Lord; and a reaffirmation of our readiness to follow with them, under the Word of God, the leading of the Spirit into whatever new and active form of life, relationship, order and witness that He may bring.'[16]

Dr E. C. Blake was made chairman of this Committee, which included Reformed leaders from all over the world.

REFERENCES

1. *Proceedings 17th General Council*, p. 75.
2. Idem, p. 36.
3. Idem, p. 29.
4. Idem, p. 37.
5. Idem, p. 72.
6. *Presbyterian World*, vol. XXII, no. 1, pp. 1–3.
7. Idem, no. 2, p. 54.
8. Minutes of the 1955 Executive Committee, App. I, p. 4.
9. Idem, p. 11.
10. Report of the General Secretary for 1956, p. 1.
11. Minutes of the 1956 Executive Committee, p. 6.
12. Idem, App. II, p. 4.
13. Minutes of the 1957 Executive Committee, p. 20.
14. Idem, App. XXIV, p. 1.
15. Report of the General Secretary for 1958, p. 2.
16. Minutes of the 1958 Executive Committee, p. 16.

CHAPTER TWELVE

Towards the WARC–ICC Unity

The history of the International Congregational Council has already been written and readers of this book should consult the following publications:

1. *International Congregationalism* by Albert Peel and Douglas Horton. Published by Independent Press Ltd, London, 1949.
2. *Congregationalism—Plus* by Norman Goodall. Published for the ICC by Independent Press Ltd, London, 1953.
   This booklet of 53 pages explains what Congregationalism stands for.
3. *A Review of World Congregationalism 1953–1957*. Edited by Ralph F. G. Calder. Published by the ICC, London.
   This 48-page booklet gives a survey of the member Churches of the ICC as well as a two-page report on the recent activities of the ICC.

As these publications can be consulted in many libraries, it is not our intention to give a detailed account of the life of the ICC. However, we feel that a few indications about the world family of Congregationalists will not be out of place here, as the member Churches of the former ICC are almost all, since 1970, part of 'The World Alliance of Reformed Churches (Presbyterian and Congregational)'.

'As early as 1874, in the American *Congregational Quarterly*, Dr Hastings Ross had written on "An Ecumenical Council of Congregational Churches" and copies of this article were widely circulated in many countries. Dexter [an American Congregational leader, *Ed.*] and Hannay [Secretary of the Congregational Union of England and Wales, *Ed.*] discussed the subject at the Triennal Council of the Churches of the U.S.A. in 1880, and four years later the Union of Ontario and Quebec invited the Union of England to convene an international Council if the project seemed possible. They replied that they judged such a Council would be a great service, and recommended that correspondence be opened with Congregational Churches throughout the world, including the mission fields . . .

'The arrangements for the Council were made by the English Union in consultation with the National Council of the United States. An Assembly of 300 delegates was agreed upon, equally divided between England, America, and the rest of the world—Wales, Scotland and Ireland apparently being deemed part of "the rest".'[1]

The First Council met in London from 13 to 18 July 1891. This meeting helped delegates from small Unions to realize that they belonged to a world-wide fellowship, and this was not without significance. The Council decided that there should be other such Councils, but the International Congregational Council remained for many decades a loosely structured organization. Here is the list of the following Councils:

> Second Council, Boston, Mass., 20–29 September, 1899
> Third Council, Edinburgh, 30 June–9 July, 1908
> Fourth Council, Boston, 29 June–6 July, 1920
> Fifth Council, Bournemouth, England, 1–8 July, 1930.

'In July 1947 an International Committee met in Bournemouth, England, at which it was decided to hold the next Council at Wellesley College, Massachusetts, in June 1949, to set up an International Office in London, and to invite Dr Sidney M. Berry, the acting Moderator of the Council and the Secretary of the congregational Union of England and Wales, to be the first Secretary.'[2]

Dr Sidney M. Berry became the first 'Minister and Secretary' of the ICC, a post similar to the one of 'General Secretary' in other world confessional organizations. He held this post with distinction until 1955 when he was succeeded on 1 January, 1956, by Rev. Ralph F. G. Calder, then Secretary of the Colonial Missionary Society, in London.

The Sixth International Congregational Council was held at Wellesley College, Wellesley, Mass., U.S.A., from 17 to 24 June 1948, and this was by far the most important Council yet organized by the ICC. A Constitution was adopted and signed by representatives of all Continents. Dr Sidney M. Berry, who was the

Moderator of the Council, was elected to the post of Minister and Secretary, as we have just indicated. An Executive Committee was elected and a Budget adopted by the Council. From now on the International Congregational Council became a well organized world confessional family, and this was very important. Dr Douglas Horton, a well known American Congregational leader, was elected Moderator until the end of the next Council. (For more details, consult *Proceedings of the Sixth International Congregational Council*, published jointly by Pilgrim Press, Boston and Chicago, and Independent Press, London, 1949.)

The Seventh International Congregational Council was held at St Andrews University, Scotland, from 20 to 29 June 1953. For the first time, the Council had a theme, 'Congregational Churchmanship'. A new Executive Committee was elected and Rev. Dr S. Maurice Watts, of London, became the new Moderator of the ICC. (See *Proceedings of the Seventh International Congregational Council*, Pilgrim and Independent Presses, 1953.)

The Eighth Assembly of the International Congregational Council was held five years later, from 2 to 10 July 1958, at Hertford, Conn., U.S.A. The theme of the Assembly was 'God speaks to our world'. A considerably amended form of Constitution was adopted. The Council dealt with the question of their relationship with the World Alliance of Reformed Churches, as we shall see in the next few pages. Rev. Dr Russell H. Stafford was elected Moderator. (See *Proceedings of the Eighth Assembly of the International Congregational Council*, Independent Press, London, 1958.)

The Ninth Assembly of the International Congregational Council took place at Rotterdam, Netherlands, from 4 to 12 July 1962. The theme of the Assembly was 'Essentials of Faith'. The World Alliance of Reformed Churches was represented by three fraternal delegates. Rev. Dr Norman Goodall, of London, who had already played a major role in the life of the ICC, was elected Moderator. (See *Proceedings of the Ninth International Congregational Council*, Independent Press, London, 1962.)

The last ordinary Council of the ICC was the Tenth Assembly, which took place at Swansea, South Wales, from 7 to 11 July 1966. The theme was indicative of the direction now taken by the ICC: 'A Reformed Church in a New Age. Reformed Faith and Congregational Churchmanship in an Ecumenical Era'. The closer ties existing with the World Alliance of Reformed Churches were indicated by the fact that the Alliance General Secretary was one of the three fraternal delegates of the WARC. Important decisions regarding the future of WARC–ICC relations were taken. Dr Norman Goodall, the retiring Moderator, was made Chairman of the Executive Committee and Assistant Secretary; Rev. Ralph F. G. Calder continued as 'Minister and Secretary' of the Council. A new Moderator was elected in the person of a distinguished American Congregational layman, Dr Ashby E. Bladen, who was to lead the ICC into the union with the 'Alliance of the Reformed Churches throughout the world holding the Presbyterian Order'. (See *Proceedings of the Tenth International Congregational Council*, Independent Press, London, 1966.)

*   *   *

In Chapter 11 of this volume we have already indicated that in his report to the 1956 meeting of the WARC Executive, the General Secretary had written: 'With regard to the International Congregational Council, as more and more Churches of our two confessional families are now engaged in discussions with a view to union, it becomes imperative for us to ask ourselves if we should not undertake conversations on the world level to examine the future relations of our Alliance to the ICC.'[3]

Dr Pradervand had been thinking about this problem for many months. He felt that as Presbyterian and Congregational Churches could unite in many countries there was no reason why the World Families of these two branches of the Reformation should not eventually become merged into one organization. That it took fourteen years for this merger to be consummated will not surprise readers of this book; they know that Churches and Church organizations move very slowly. But the main thing is that it happened.

It must be emphasized that, from the beginning, the desire for closer co-operation was shared by leaders of the two organizations. Before 1956 there had already been many letters exchanged between the Alliance office and leaders of the ICC. In 1955, Dr Pradervand sent to Dr S. Maurice Watts, then Moderator of the ICC, the volume of *Proceedings of the 17th General Council* held at Princeton in 1954. On 22 September of the same year, Dr Watts wrote to the Alliance General Secretary:

'I have been thrilled in reading this report, and especially, if I may say so, by the great speech of Dr Mackay. When I had finished I asked myself "Where do the Congregational Churches differ from this?" or "Where does this differ from our Congregational witness?" Is there not some preliminary approach desirable between these two bodies?'[4]

A close friendship had developed between the General Secretaries of the two organizations, which naturally helped for mutual understanding.

In 1957, the new Theological Secretary of the WARC wrote an official letter to the Minister and Secretary of the ICC suggesting talks on a world level between the two world organizations. This was done at the request of the Alliance General Secretary and with the full approval of the Executive Committee. At the 1958 Assembly of the ICC, at Hertford, Rev. Ralph F. G. Calder referred to this in his report to the Assembly. It was then voted 'that this Assembly hears with pleasure of the invitation from the Executive Committee of the World Alliance of Reformed Churches to hold a conference to discuss the theological agreements and community of outlook between the member Churches of the two Confessional bodies. It asks its officers to accept this invitation and to share its findings with the Constituent Member Churches of the Council'.[5]

In August of the same year, the Executive Committee of the WARC, meeting in Edinburgh, heard with interest and pleasure of the decision taken by the Assembly of the ICC. 'The Committee believes that such discussions are appropriate and full of promise because many member Churches of the Alliance, like many in the International Congregational Council, cherish a common heritage deriving from the Westminster Confession of Faith. Moreover, there have been a number of recent instances in which Churches belonging to both Confessional groups have found common ground to a marked degree.

'The Committee is convinced that, at the outset of such conversations, those taking part should not be pre-occupied with questions of polity reflected in the participating bodies, but should carry on conversations within the wider context of the witness and mission in the light of the Reformed Faith held by them in common.'[6] The leadership of Dr John A. Mackay, Alliance

President, can be felt in the hope expressed by the Executive on the nature of those bilateral conversations.

It was at Mansfield College, Oxford, that the first meeting took place on 8–9 January 1959. There were three representatives on each side, including the General Secretaries of the two organizations. A 'Preliminary Statement of Accord Drafted at Mansfield College' was presented to the 18th General Council of the Alliance and later to the ICC. It ends: 'We are convinced that fuller expression of this unity would result from common practical and theological work undertaken to carry forward the life of the Reformed tradition in which we stand.

'We therefore recommend to our respective confessional groups that they should begin a joint investigation of these questions, which should consider both the richness of the diversity within these groups and the nature of the unity which binds us together, as well as ways and means by which these realities can be faithfully expressed in thought and action.'[7]

The Council received this statement with pleasure and voted the continuance of the conversations between the WARC and the ICC.

It was not long until the next meeting was held. On 1–2 August 1960 a meeting of representatives of the two organizations took place at Sèvres, near Paris, when further progress was made in the understanding between the two world families. The meeting, which was attended by officers of both organizations, voted several recommendations, which were subsequently approved by the Executive Committees of the WARC and ICC. Here are the last two of these recommendations:

'3. That the Executives of the ICC and of the Alliance be asked to consider the possibility of appointing a joint committee or commission to work on the Reformed doctrine of the Church in the light of the common history of Congregationalists and Presbyterians, their differences both real and supposed, and their common ecumenical experience and responsibility.

'4. That the Executives of the ICC and the Alliance be asked to consider the advisability of inviting visitors from each group to attend Area meetings, meetings of theological commissions or committees, etc. in order to foster understanding and co-operation.'[8]

The Ninth Assembly of the ICC in Rotterdam, July 1962, showed that real progress had already been achieved in the relations between the WARC and ICC. Three fraternal delegates from the Alliance attended the Rotterdam Assembly, and the Assistant Secretary of the ICC [Rev. Glynmor John, M.A., *Ed.*] was able to report that he had been invited to participate in studies undertaken by the Alliance. The Assembly warmly accepted the following resolution: 'That this Assembly of the ICC hears with gratitude of the relationship already established with the WARC and the Joint Studies which have been initiated. It gives its unqualified approval to the continuance of such studies in the furtherance of mutual understanding between the Council and the Alliance . . .'[9]

A month later, the Alliance Executive, meeting in Ibadan, Nigeria, heard with joy of the decisions taken at Rotterdam and voted for developing contacts with the ICC.

Things moved a step further in 1964. Three fraternal delegates of the ICC attended the Frankfurt Council of the Alliance. One of them, Rev. Ralph F. G. Calder, Minister and Secretary of the ICC, referred in his address to the Council to a resolution recently voted by the Executive Committee of the ICC which reads as follows: 'That this meeting of the ICC expresses to the WARC its pleasure in being engaged with the Alliance in common study and consultation, and now invites the Alliance to take with it the further step of establishing a *joint committee* to explore all possible forms of future relationship between the two bodies.'[10]

The Alliance President, Dr Ralph W. Lloyd, then read the recommendation of the WARC Executive, as follows: 'The Executive Committee of the WARC recommends to the General Council that the invitation of the Executive Committee of the ICC be accepted. It is further recommended that the General Council propose to the ICC that there should be up to five members from each group on the Joint Committee.'[11]

The two recommendations were unanimously approved by the Council.

From now on things moved rapidly. In his report for the year 1965, the Alliance General Secretary wrote: 'Significant steps toward a closer relationship between the ICC and the WARC were taken in 1965. A Joint Committee . . . has been constituted . . . The Committee met in two sections in July 1965: one met at

Princeton (USA), the other in London. As a result of these meetings proposals have been made to the Executive Committees, which they will study in 1966. We hope that immediately after the meeting of the two Executives it will be possible to make concrete proposals to the member Churches of the ICC and WARC with a view to uniting the two organizations.'[12]

The International Congregational Council was to act first. Its Tenth and last Assembly took place at Swansea from 4 to 12 July 1966. The Executive Committee reported that it had received from the Joint Committee a Report, a Statement of Principles and Proposals. It strongly recommended that these documents be sent to the ICC member-Churches as recommended by the Joint Committee. After a discussion, in which the Alliance representatives took part, 'it was agreed without dissent that the Assembly should strongly commend the Proposals to the Member Churches'.[13]

It was not long before the WARC acted in a similar way. The 1966 meeting of the Executive Committee took place at Strasbourg, France, from 28 July to 2 August. The ICC was well represented; its Moderator, Dr Bladen, was there as alternate for a member from the United Church of Christ, while Rev. Ralph F. G. Calder, Minister and Secretary, and Dr Norman Goodall, Chairman of the ICC Executive, were present as guests.

After discussion, the Executive voted unanimously: 'that the Principles, the Proposals and the Constitution be sent to the member churches along with a covering letter indicating that the Proposals come with the hearty endorsement of the Executive Committee and requesting that appropriate action be taken.'[14]

Because of their importance, we do not hesitate to quote in full from the Principles those that are given under sections 8 to 12.

'8. It is our principle in relation to the World Council of Churches to do nothing separately which can be done in cooperation, and to enter as fully as facilities allow into its program, especially in the area of studies. We do not wish to administer Inter-Church Aid or other similar funds, but prefer to support the aid programs of the World Council of Churches, providing special counsel on the situation of minority Churches.

'9. Historically, the prominent traditions of our Churches have arisen over a wide field of reform and mission during and since the time of the Reformation. Some reside within largely Eastern Orthodox areas.

For the most part, however, our Churches exist in contrast and dialogue with Rome. This situation ceased to be predominantly "Western" with the modern missionary movement, and is now world-wide. We now recognize no purely "Western" Church, no strictly "Western" traditions, but only a great complex of histories and problems in which the life of every Church more and more interpenetrates the life of all the others. In our time, we have come to see even within the very lineaments of so-called secular history that in Christ there is no East or West, no North or South. This situation has intensified a typical diversification among the Reformed Churches which extends from Reformation times. The classic *Reformed* part of the 16th century Reformation in Europe goes back not only to Geneva, but also to Strasbourg, Zürich, Heidelberg, Debrecen, the Hague, Edinburgh, and many other towns, great and small. Many Reformed congregations were founded by refugees, and this has continued to be true throughout the intervening centuries. There were then, and have continued to be, admixtures of the *Reformed* line with that of the Reformation's "left wing" from 16th century Strasbourg on. Some Congregational churchmen feel closer at many points to the Baptists or to the Disciples of Christ than to the Presbyterian or Reformed Churches in their area, and some within the latter Churches, including many "evangelicals", do too.

'In view of all this history of criss-crossing, everchanging relations, it is not strange to find, therefore, that in some areas Congregationalists have been more firmly Reformed in faith or Presbyterian in polity than those who held to those two names, and vice versa. This is, if anything, even more true of the contemporary period, which has seen great mobility in belief and practice among our Churches. We can regard ourselves, taken together, as in large part Reformed, not because of any single historic norm of either faith or order but because our internal histories have overlapped to such a great extent, beginning with our common point of departure in the Reformation, and indeed have come to such a culminating point of common life in our time. The name also indicates the priority we give to matters of faith, while also suggesting the great stress we lay upon the integrally related task of forming and re-forming the Church's order.

'10. We believe that in Jesus Christ, God, the Creator of all that is, the Father of mankind, and the covenant Lord of Israel, has reconciled the world to himself and that by the continuing presence and power of his Spirit he has especially entrusted the ministry of reconciliation to the fellowship of Christ's people, the Church. We seek to find the supreme authority for belief and practice in God himself, speaking ever afresh by his Spirit in and through the Scriptures, telling us of his being and purpose as it was revealed in Jesus of Nazareth, the world's only Saviour. As world families of Churches, we do not claim to contribute any "special doctrines" to the rest of the Church. Out of the experience of our own histories, we do, however, at this time tend to lay emphasis upon the ministry of the whole people of God, upon the diversity of gifts which are to be shared within the one fellowship of faith, upon the responsibility of the Churches to provide that God's Word shall be preached and that the sacraments of baptism and the Lord's Supper shall become a vital force in every congregation, and upon the task of letting our common worship and witness penetrate into the whole present life of humanity. We also lay emphasis upon the primacy of fellowship within the whole order and service of the Church, upon the participation of the whole people together in the government and ministry of the Church, upon the sovereignty of God over the whole society of man, and upon God's call upon the Church to attest that sovereignty before the State and within all the structures of society, not only in the interest of its own liberty but also on behalf of that responsible freedom God wills for all men. Such emphases do not stand for the whole of our faith or even for the substance of our program, but rather spotlight the meeting-place of our several traditions at this time. They point to the fact that it is in the testimony of faith, above all, that we come together. They express our desire that all questions of Church order or program should be determined by the Gospel of Christ.

'11. Neither body requires a strictly defined confessional position of its members. Although the Alliance's Constitution has spoken since 1875 of agreement in principle to a "consensus" of the Reformed confessions, no consensus has ever been officially stated by the Alliance in all its history. Nor is membership based on a supposed consensus, except in the most general sense. Confessional documents are also used in a variety of ways by its present member Churches. For some of these, a confessional statement is part of the constitution, and subscription may be required of ministers and officers; for others it is not, nor is subscription required. Most of the Churches in both bodies have at some point in their history adopted a confessional statement as an official standard secondary to Scripture, to be used as a guide in matters of faith and practice. In the present, brief constitution of the International Congregational Council, currently under revision by order of the 9th Assembly, the world body welcomes united Churches which maintain "the principles of Congregational Churchmanship" and Churches "Congregational in outlook and polity", as well as national or regional unions of Congregational Churches. The aims of both bodies are not to uphold an historic confessional outlook or polity, but to serve within the ecumenical movement as a whole by providing a place where Churches of like traditions may examine these traditions together and exercise their common witness to the Gospel. In this respect, what they have to grow out of may require their togetherness even more than what positive traditions they share in common.

'12. No institutional form of the Church either covers the whole field where Christ expects the Church to serve and to be joined to him in ministry or stands as the sole locus of authority for the Church's common faith, whether congregation or presbytery, diocese or denomination, union or council. The locality of the Church is where Christ is carrying out his ministry in and for the sake of the world. Hence the need for the continued re-formation of the institutional form of the Church in order that it may more fully reflect and express this omnipresent activity of its Lord.

'(a) An important consequence of this view is our conviction that oversight (*episkope*) within the Church is basically a corporate task. Thus we lay stress upon the freedom and responsibility of congregations, upon government by covenant and constitution, and upon the conciliar process at all levels of the Church's life. By faith and practice, our Churches tend to deny that any individual minister or representative may in his own person assume sole ministry or authority in any matter fundamental to the Church's life, either by succession or by appointment. They also tend to emphasize that the gifts which God bestows on individuals in his service are also part of that ministry which belongs to the whole people of God.

'(b) In this view, therefore, the whole people accepts corporate responsibility for authorizing and sustaining whatever ministries are required by their mission. Indispensable among these ministries, precisely because it stands for the equipping of the whole people in their faith, worship and service, is the special ministry of Word and sacraments, with the responsibility of leadership and pastoral care which the faithful exercise of such a task requires.

'(c) Within the contemporary situation, it has become easier for us to see that the mission of every "local" Christian community is defined first of all by Christ's ministry to the whole world, and that only then, and within the scope of this larger, universal ministry, do they receive their own peculiar irreplaceable tasks. The local congregation is the primary and indispensable form of the Church not simply because it has a place where people are listening together for the Word of God and are celebrating the sacraments, but because and insofar as it is gathered under the call of Christ to engage in Christ's mission to the world.

'(d) Finally, this view means, for us, that the Church in all its present forms must continually seek new means for ordering its common life. Nowhere is the locality of the Church simply given. It must be also found, in obedience to the call of Christ.'

The Proposals read as follows:

'In mutual obedience to our common Lord, in repentance for past failures and offenses, and in witness to our common faith, we make the following proposals "in the name of the Lord Jesus, giving thanks to God the Father through Him". In doing so, we recognize that we are all under constant need of renewal and reformation by the Holy Spirit, and acknowledge that what we here propose can only be in partial fulfilment of God's will for the whole of Christ's Church in this world'.

'*Be it RESOLVED:*

'(1) that the two organizations now known as the International Congregational Council and the Alliance of Reformed Churches throughout the World holding the Presbyterian Order shall unite;

'(2) that we take this step not only in order to carry out the major aims for which we have existed separately, but above all in order to seek how we may better serve the whole of Christ's Church; this we should seek to do by examining together the traditions of faith and practice within that Reformed family to which, in various ways, we all belong, by supporting one another as we move within the tremendous scope of mission to which Christ is calling all his people in our time, and by working together for the unity of all men in Christ, but especially for the unity of all who call upon the name of the Lord;

'(3) that in entering upon this common way, we together affirm our faith in Jesus Christ and covenant to share according to such common purpose as we shall discover in the tasks he lays upon the Church in our time, asking to order our common life by his grace alone;

'(4) that the name of the new organization shall be: The World Alliance of Reformed Churches; but that, in order to draw attention to our heritage and position as one family within the Church catholic incorporating the traditions of Congregational, Presbyterian, Reformed and United Churches, under appropriate circumstances a fuller official name may also be used: The World Alliance of Reformed Churches (Presbyterian and Congregational).

'*The Executive Committees hereby request:*

'(1) that the member Churches of the two bodies register approval or disapproval of the proposals above stated for their union into one body, and report their decisions by June 30, 1968, so that, should it be the will of two thirds of these Churches, according to the rules of their

respective constitutions, plans may be made for holding a uniting
Council in 1970;

'(2) that the member Churches receive, at the same time, a draft
constitution for information and comment (also to be received by
June 30, 1968, at the latest) with a view to possible revision, under the
direction of the two Executive Committees, should approval of union
be established; the Executive Committees of the two bodies having the
power to draft such amendments to their existing constitutions as will
provide a new constitution for presentation at the uniting Council
(one-year notice being required for Alliance member Churches and
six-month notice for ICC member Churches.)'[15]

* * *

In the two organized Areas of the WARC, things had also been
moving. ICC representatives were taking an active part in the life
of the Theological Commissions and were invited to attend the
meetings of Area Councils. They were consulted on many
subjects which were on the agenda of the Alliance, and a great
unity already existed between the two organizations.

During the 1967 meeting of the WARC Executive, which was
held at Toronto, there was a short Joint meeting of the two
Executives, the ICC being represented by the Moderator and the
Minister and Secretary, who attended the WARC Executive as
fraternal delegates. At that Joint Session, the Theme and Place of
the Uniting Council were discussed. The Joint Committee further
decided, at the request of the WARC General Secretary, to give
power to a small group in attendance at Uppsala [Fourth Assembly
of the WCC, July 1968, *Ed.*] to sit as an Executive.

The two Executives decided that, from 1 January 1968, *The
Reformed and Presbyterian World* would become a joint publication
of the two bodies.

It was also decided to establish a Committee on structure, to be
responsible for proposals as to structure, staffing, by-laws of the
uniting body, and its budget after 1970; three persons on each
side, plus a convener, were to be chosen by the two Presidents in
consultation.

Another Committee, on publications, was also to be established,
to examine the future requirements as to publications and information, as from the beginning of 1971. The Presidents were
also to choose the two members from each body and the convener.

The Minister and Secretary of the ICC, Rev. Ralph F. G. Calder, decided in 1967 to leave his post to undertake new responsibilities. The WARC Executive Committee, at its Toronto meeting, expressed its gratitude to Mr Calder for the part he had played in helping to bring together the two organizations. The ICC decided that Dr Norman Goodall, Chairman of the Executive Committee and Assistant Secretary to Mr Calder, should be the Acting Minister and Secretary of the ICC for the time being.

In 1968 the Secretary for Information of the WARC, Rev. Lewis L. Wilkins, Jr, a minister of the Presbyterian Church in the U.S., who had held this post since 1965, returned to his country to occupy the post of secretary of church relations to the Board of Christian Education of the Presbyterian Church in the U.S.

As a successor had to be found for this post it seemed best to use this opportunity to bring the two world families more closely together without waiting for the merger due to take place in 1970. With the full approval of the WARC officers the General Secretary suggested to the ICC officers that they propose a Congregational minister to fill the post of Information Secretary. This was gladly accepted by the ICC, and, in the spring of 1968, Rev. Fred A. Kaan, a Dutchman who had done part of his studies in England and had become a minister of the Congregational Church of England and Wales, was appointed to the post, as from 1 September 1968. The ICC officers asked Mr Kaan to become at the same time Minister and Secretary of the ICC. The two organizations decided that Mr Kaan should give 20 per cent of his time to the ICC and 80 per cent to the Information Secretariat of the WARC; the ICC offices, which had up till then been in London, were transferred to Geneva, and so it was that part of the Alliance offices became the headquarters of the ICC.

During the year 1968, co-operation between the two organizations was constant; in fact, they already seemed to be but one family. Though the meeting of the WARC Executive Committee, at Cluj, Romania, at the end of June, was not a 'Joint Committee', it was attended by the Moderator, the Chairman of the Executive Committee and the newly elected Minister and Secretary of the ICC. The ICC representatives took a full part in the deliberations and the decisions of the WARC Executive.

Immediately after the meeting of the WARC Executive Committee, the Joint Committee on Structure met in Vienna and prepared the Draft of a Constitution and By-Laws for the new organization.

A few days later, on 13 July, members of both Executives met at Uppsala, during the Assembly of the WCC. They were informed that the proposal to unite the two organizations had been accepted by over two-thirds of the member Churches of the ICC and of the WARC and that the merger therefore became operative.

On 22–23 July, a Joint Theological Consultation took place at Stockholm. It drafted a Message on 'The Significance of the Reformed Position in an Ecumenical Age'; this message was later revised and approved by the 1969 Joint Executive Committee before being sent to the Churches. The Consultation did excellent preparatory work on the theme of the Uniting Council, 'God reconciles and makes free' and on the four sub-themes. Complete unity was achieved, and when there were differences of opinion, they were not between WARC and ICC representatives, but between individuals. It was clear that all the people present at Stockholm were 'Reformed' and that the polity of their Churches was hardly considered.

1969 was the last year before the merger of the WARC and ICC. Member Churches of both organizations were informed of the result of the postal ballot on union and were invited to attend the Uniting Council of 1970 in Nairobi. As already noted above, the Joint Executive Committee, which met at Beirut, Lebanon, from 1–6 August, adopted a 'Message' to be sent to the member Churches. Here are some paragraphs of this message:

'Both the WARC and the ICC are composed of Churches whose historic origins lie mainly in the Reformation. This means that both bodies live in common reliance upon the Word of God as revealed through the Scriptures of the Old and New Testaments; they share common affirmations concerning the Lordship of Jesus Christ and the nature of the Church as a fellowship of the Spirit through which Christ is carrying his ministry in and for the sake of the world.

'While these affirmations have from time to time found expression in formal statements of faith or confessions, neither organization has been founded upon a confessional basis and neither is content to be known primarily as a world confessional organization. They regard themselves rather as families of

Churches deeply akin in spirit and purpose. More especially, they would wish the term *Reformed* always to be understood and accepted in the sense of *semper reformanda.*

'There is no *fixed* body of "Reformed heritage" which the Alliance would narrowly foster as its defined and unique contribution to the life and work of the whole Church of Jesus Christ. We acknowledge the temptation of rigidity in respect to creed and polity, but the theological principle of *semper reformanda* requires us to resist closed confessional and ecclesiastical systems. So we would at this time in our history resist the temptation, and stress rather certain theological accents which over the centuries have given to the Reformed Churches their distinctive character.

'The Reformed Churches and their theology testify to the dynamic sovereignty of the living God . . . We proclaim Jesus Christ as King of all kings. We acknowledge that his coming Kingdom has already broken into the structures of our history and now urges us to active deeds of gratitude and obedience.

'In the light of this biblical vision, the Reformed Churches and theology emphasize the social dimension of Christian faith . . . The Church *and* the society are the field of the creative gratitude and obedience of the believer. *Ecclesia et societas semper reformandae!*

'The Reformed Churches of the Presbyterian and Congregational families emphasize the fraternal character of their church order. There is only one Master of the Church and his people are all brothers and sisters . . . While recognizing fully the need for committed leadership, we are here affirming that all members of the Church, according to their gifts, have their essential part to play in the structure of the Reformed Churches, and that authority in the Churches finally belongs only to the Head of the Church. The "Priesthood of all believers" is a basic insight and inspiration in the life and organization of the Church as a *communio viatorum.*

. . . . . .

'In serving the Lord Jesus Christ, we in the Churches of the Reformed family are moved by his Spirit to be a community of service for the world. We hold that this service centres in the proclamation of the Gospel and requires both the ministries of compassion and responsible participation in the public life of our time.

'Therefore, we seek a style of involvement in the world which bears the marks of obedience to Jesus Christ and of openness towards men without distinction of sex, race, or nation. We believe that God is at work in contemporary history, and we acknowledge that he calls us in faith to change our cherished ways and institutions for the sake of greater obedience and more fruitful service.

'As the new WARC comes into being, currents of rapid, world-wide social, economic, and political change are running with unprecedented swiftness. The outcome is in the balance. How shall we face such a time?

'Let us live in the confidence that the Living God who has brought us to such a time can empower us to discern and carry forward those forms of faithful service which he requires for the renewal of the Church and the healing of the nations! Let us, in company with all our brethren in the Church catholic, pray for the gift of obedience and live and work in the hope of the Kingdom.'[16]

This is a long quotation, but it helps to understand the spirit in which leaders of both organizations were entering into union. There was no desire to form a stronger 'Reformed' bloc, but the desire to fulfil more faithfully the responsibilities entrusted to the Reformed Churches by the Lord of the Church.

*　　*　　*

We have already noted that both organizations were working practically as one. An example will best illustrate this. Since 1968, there had been informal contacts between the Secretariat for Promoting Christian Unity of the Vatican and the World Alliance of Reformed Churches, with a view to starting an official dialogue. The decision to answer the approaches made by the Vatican positively was taken by the 1969 Joint Executive. Earlier in the year, when representatives of the Vatican and of the WARC had held a consultation in the Netherlands to discuss the problem, the ICC was represented.

1970 saw the final act of Union. On Thursday, 20 August, representatives of the WARC and of the ICC gathered in Taifa Hall, University College, Nairobi, Kenya. There were short formal meetings of 'The 11th Assembly of the International Congregational Council' and of 'The 20th General Council of the

Alliance of the Reformed Churches throughout the world holding the Presbyterian Order'. Both organizations voted unanimously to merge into 'The World Alliance of Reformed Churches (Presbyterian and Congregational)'. The members of the Council then marched in procession to St. Andrew's Presbyterian Church to join in a Service of Word and Sacrament to give thanks for the merger of the two Families. After the sermon, preached by the General Secretary of the World Council of Churches, Dr Eugene C. Blake, the delegates joined in an act of Covenant in these terms:

'WE, THE REPRESENTATIVES OF REFORMED, PRESBYTERIAN AND CONGREGATIONAL CHURCHES IN ALL THE CORNERS OF THE EARTH, HOLDING THE WORD OF GOD GIVEN IN THE BIBLE TO BE THE ULTIMATE AUTHORITY IN MATTERS OF FAITH AND LIFE, ACKNOWLEDGING JESUS CHRIST AS THE HEAD OF THE CHURCH, AND
REJOICING IN OUR FELLOWSHIP WITH THE WHOLE CHURCH, COVENANT TOGETHER
TO SEEK IN ALL THINGS THE MIND OF CHRIST,
TO MAKE COMMON WITNESS TO HIS GOSPEL,
TO SERVE HIS PURPOSE IN ALL THE WORLD,
AND,
IN ORDER TO BE BETTER EQUIPPED
FOR THE TASKS HE LAYS UPON US,
TO FORM FROM THIS DAY
THE NEW WORLD ALLIANCE OF REFORMED CHURCHES.

LORD KEEP US FAITHFUL TO YOURSELF
AND TO OUR FELLOWMEN. AMEN.'[17]

It is in that spirit that the delegates to the Uniting Council began their work. We pray that it be in the same spirit that the Alliance formed at Nairobi will continue giving its witness.

REFERENCES
1. *International Congregationalism*, by Albert Peel and Douglas Horton, pp. 9–11.
2. Op. cit., p. 61.
3. Minutes of the 1956 WARC Executive Committee, App. 11, p. 4.

4. WARC Archives, Geneva, Correspondence with ICC.
5. *Proceedings 8th Assembly of the ICC*, p. 21.
6. Minutes of the 1958 WARC Executive Committee, p. 18.
7. *Proceedings 18th General Council*, p. 194.
8. Minutes of the 1960 WARC Executive Committee, p. 107.
9. *Proceedings 9th ICC*, p. 19.
10. *Proceedings 19th General Council (WARC)*, p. 40.
11. Idem, p. 40.
12. Report of the WARC General Secretary for 1965, p. 1.
13. *Proceedings 10th ICC*, p. 21.
14. Minutes of the 1966 WARC Executive Committee, p. 7.
15. Idem, App. 5b, p. 72 and 5c, p. 77.
16. Minutes of the 1969 Joint Executive Committee, App. 1, p. 23.
17. *Proceedings of the Uniting General Council*, p. 11.

CHAPTER THIRTEEN

The 1959 Jubilee, São Paulo and After

As indicated in a previous chapter, 1959 was a Jubilee year for the Reformed Church of France which celebrated the 400th anniversary of its first National Synod and also for the people of Geneva who celebrated the 400th anniversary of the founding of Calvin's Academy.

The Alliance was closely associated with these Jubilees. Its representatives first took part in the celebrations of the National Synod of the Reformed Church of France which started on 27 May in Paris. Immediately afterwards the Geneva celebrations began. On Sunday, 31 May, solemn services were held in all the churches of Geneva and these were followed by a mass meeting of the Reformed people of the city. In other parts of the world, Reformed Churches were marking the anniversary by following an order of service prepared by the Alliance and translated into many languages.

In Geneva, the next day was even more important for the Alliance, as the dedication of the newly restored Calvin Auditorium took place on Monday, 1 June. The man who more than anyone else had made the restoration possible, Rev. Dr Harrison Ray Anderson of Chicago, was present and took a leading part in the ceremony in the crowded Auditorium, together with Rev. Dr Max Dominicé, whose enthusiasm and untiring devotion to Genevese history and spiritual things helped this long cherished plan to materialize.

A convention had been signed between the National Protestant Church of Geneva and the World Alliance of Reformed Churches. The Alliance undertook the full responsibility of the Auditorium for fifty years; at the same time, it became the only organization to decide on its use.

Should the Alliance offices be moved to the newly restored building? On the floor above the sanctuary there was enough space to do this. But the same question as Dr Pradervand had had to face in 1948 again came up for discussion before the Executive Committee: having moved the Alliance headquarters to Geneva, was it worthwhile if the offices were not on the campus of the World Council of Churches? After some discussion, and with the full approval of the General Secretary, it was decided that the Alliance offices should remain with the WCC at the Route de Malagnou; later these offices were to be moved to the new Ecumenical Centre at the Route de Ferney, where they still are today.

This did not mean that the restored Auditorium was not to be used extensively. We are glad to say that the Church of Scotland, the Netherlands Reformed Church and the Waldensian Church of Italy decided that their Geneva congregations should worship there. For a time, the congregation of the Spanish Evangelical Church also worshipped there. But the only hour when the Auditorium could be put at its disposal was not very convenient, and the congregation had to move to another church.

The restored Auditorium is still fully used, especially by the Scottish congregation, who regularly organize their coffee hour, crèche and Sunday School on the first floor. Visitors from all over the world come on weekdays to see this historic building. By this restoration, accomplished with the help of Churches from all over the world, some very poor and very far from Geneva, the Alliance has shown that the Reformed people of all continents were conscious of their debt to Calvin and to the City of Geneva.

*   *   *

The manifestations organized for the Reformed Jubilee did not mean that the Alliance was living in the past. On the contrary. The main preoccupations of the Alliance staff, in the spring of 1959, were the preparations for the forthcoming Eighteenth General Council of the Alliance, which took place in São Paulo from 27 July to 6 August 1959. This was an historic meeting in more senses than one. For the first time, the Alliance dared to move out from North America and Europe, where it had strong Churches and where the organization of a Council was therefore made easy. In Latin America, there were many Presbyterian Churches, but they were young and most of them small. It is true that the Presbyterian Church of Brazil and the Independent Presbyterian Church were growing fast and that they had great enthusiasm. This was felt by the Alliance leaders, who found men and women of great devotion, ready to give their time and their money in order to facilitate the physical arrangements of the Council. Without these fine Christian people, it would not have been possible to hold a Council in São Paulo.

Latin America, however, was not a 'Presbyterian' land and the majority of its people knew very little about the Reformation. If the Presbyterian Church of Brazil celebrated the centennial of its existence in 1959 and if the Rio de Janeiro celebrations of this centennial, which were held immediately after the Council, were honoured by a visit of the President of the country, the fact remains that in going to Brazil, the Alliance was really breaking new ground. Many delegates from other continents took advantage of this fact to visit other Churches of that continent, and there is no doubt that the Council helped to strengthen the ties between the Presbyterian Churches of Latin America and Churches of the Reformed family on other continents.

The theme of the Council was also revolutionary. 'The Servant Lord and his Servant People' had been chosen by the Executive Committee on the strong recommendation of its President, Dr John A. Mackay. In his Foreword to the *Volume of Proceedings* of the Council, Dr Mackay says: 'The most important circumstance by which the Brazil meeting of the World Alliance will be remembered will undoubtedly be its theme . . .

'Today when the Christian Church and secular institutions tend to glory in what they have and what they are, it is imperative that all people be made to see that neither they nor their creations can have any future in God's world unless they be willing, one and all, to "take the form of a servant".'[1]

The world character of the Alliance was indicated by the geographical position of the Churches which had been admitted since Princeton. They were thirteen in all; one only came from Europe and two from North America; three came from Africa, two from Latin America and five from Asia. The Council admitted two more Asian Churches into our fellowship thus bringing the membership of the Alliance to 78.

The membership of the Council was also more world-wide than before. Nine African Churches were represented at São Paulo;

there were eleven from Latin America, though three of them were not yet fully independent and belonged to the Alliance through their mother Church; eleven Churches from Asia had sent delegates to the Council. Churches of Australasia, Europe and America were fully represented.

The Council at São Paulo had four official languages, as it was felt that it would be wrong to hold a Council in Brazil without having Portuguese as one of the languages of the Council. In fact, there was a fifth language which was often used: Spanish. It is in Spanish—which most Brazilians understand—that the President of the Alliance, Dr Mackay, preached his sermon at the opening service, held in the first Independent Presbyterian Church of São Paulo.

The multiplicity of languages put a heavy burden on the Alliance. But we were fortunate—as at all the other Councils since Princeton—to find a team of devoted Christian linguists, pastors, missionaries and laymen and women, who gave their services without a salary, so as to contribute to the success of the Council; and as was the case at Princeton already, they were led by the man who was to become the General Secretary of the Alliance in 1970, Rev. Edmond Perret. Mr Perret was to fulfil this function again at Frankfurt (1964) and at Nairobi (1970), when he had already been called to be Dr Pradervand's successor.

The Council, which had been prepared with great care by an Alliance Committee under the chairmanship of Rev. Dr Ralph W. Lloyd, North American Secretary of the Alliance, and a Brazilian Committee on Hospitality, headed by Rev. Dr Benjamin Moraes, of Rio de Janeiro, was marred by two deaths. A few days before the opening of the Council the devoted General Secretary of the Brazilian Committee on Hospitality, Mr Waldemar G. Xavier, died accidentally; and during the Council, one of the delegates, Rev. Dr Charles T. Leber, Executive Secretary of the Commission on Ecumenical Mission and Relations of the United Presbyterian Church in the U.S.A., died of a heart attack. The death of Dr Leber, who was loved and trusted by all delegates of the Younger Churches, and who had done so much to make the Alliance a world family where all Churches, Young and Old, stood on an equal footing, was a great blow to the Council and was felt as a personal loss by many, including the Alliance General Secretary.

The Council divided into four sections, to study the sub-themes, which were as follows:

I.   The Service of Theology
II. The Service of the Church
III. The Service of the Christian
IV. The Service of the State

After days of intensive work, the Sections presented their reports to the Council. They were discussed, revised and finally adopted for transmission to the Churches. Here are a few quotations from these reports.

On 'The Service of Theology' the Section had this to say: 'In the light of the theme of the 18th General Council . . . we see the service of theology to be grounded in the service of our Lord "who . . . emptied himself, taking the form of a servant".

'It follows that the theology of the Church cannot in its own right and by its own wisdom, power or authority, determinate its task, formulate its theme or project its objectives. Rather, it springs forth out of an encounter in which God, as Father, seeks and meets us in His Son, Jesus Christ.'[2]

In view of later 'wild' developments of a certain theology, it is not without importance to know what the Reformed Churches, gathered at São Paulo, had to say to theologians of the whole world.

The report on 'The Service of the Church' reads as follows: 'It is the Servant Lord who calls a new people into existence, a people who are, at one and the same time, recipients of his service and his servant people in the world . . . The primary response of God's Servant People is worship . . . But any true response to this service of Jesus Christ must lead to service in and to the world. This unity of "worship" and "service" is strikingly evident in the New Testament in which worship always implies service and service is seen as the praise of God.'[3]

The report of the Section on 'The Service of the Christian' says things which are especially important, in view of the present development of the movement of renewal through the power of the Holy Spirit.

'3. It is significant that, all over the world, Christians of all races and all nations are . . . becoming vital Christians through the power of the Holy Spirit. This has happened as they have ceased

paying lip service to the basic truths of the Christian faith, have
taken them seriously and then have found that they are compelling.

'4. Some of these truths are:

'a. That God is the Lord Omnipotent and the King of kings . . .
God rules over all, even in this twentieth century, even in this
atomic age . . .
'b. That Jesus Christ, the Servant Lord, *was* born, *did* live, *was*
crucified, dead and buried, *did* rise again in order that men
through him might attain eternal life . . .
'c. That as he promised, through the Holy Spirit, His power
remodels and redirects my life bringing triumph where there was
defeat and power where there was weakness.
'd. That these facts demand a positive response from me . . .

'9. The heart of the service of the Christian is that, as with the
Servant Lord so his servant people, everything that a man is or
has, paradoxically, is not his but a gift from God to be used in his
service and that each of us is now, and will finally be called upon
to give an account of how he has used these gifts.

'27. We realize to the full that to subject oneself to God's
Spirit leads to no easy life. That there will be difficulties and
defeats is sure and that there will be suffering certain. This is one
reason why worship, Bible study and meditation are necessities
for each day. As we abide in Christ his Spirit will change us and
we will grow in grace. We will begin to live that more abundant
life as Jesus promised. Those around us will become aware and
seek to share it with us. Thus the world around us will be changed
by the presence in it of those who are, as Jesus says, the salt of
the earth and the light of the world.'[4]

The Section on 'The Service of the State' after having proclaimed
again that all power belongs to Jesus Christ and that the States
are never sovereign, goes on:

'In the light of all this and we pray, by the Holy Spirit, we dare
to address the Churches and our fellow Christians in all the varied
circumstances of their many lands and States.

'These things we say to the Churches:

'1. Your most important service to the State is to raise up
citizens of unselfish loyalty and intelligent commitment to the
common good who are the greatest need of every State.

'4. As a Church you have the duty to speak to the State in behalf of justice, freedom and mercy for all men of every race and situation . . .

'6. As a Church you have also the duty to hearten, to assist spiritually, and to pray for all those who because of sincere Christian conscience resist the State and are in danger, persecution . . .

'And these warnings we give to the Churches:

'1. Never confuse or identify the Church with any established regime . . .

'3. Never use the power, or prestige of your Church, to win from the State benefits for your own Church which would damage the interests of others.

'And to the members of the Churches we say this:

'1. Be very courageous to serve the Lord Christ as a member of his body and as a citizen of your State despite whatever danger or persecution you may encounter.

'2. . . . Be ever careful not to confuse your personal, family, class, racial, national or Church's interests with the will of God.

'4. In all your service to the State remember the poor and the underprivileged, the outcast, the prisoner, and the weak, for it is in serving them that you can serve Christ.'[5]

With regard to the internal affairs of the Alliance, the Council took a number of important actions. It decided to create a Department of Theology, as it was felt that this would help develop the theological work of the Alliance, which was ably led by the Theological Secretary, Rev. Lewis S. Mudge, Jr. Dr James I. McCord, who had just been appointed to succeed Dr John A. Mackay as President of Princeton Theological Seminary, was made chairman of the Department, and for over ten years he gave continual and remarkable leadership.

The Council also created a Department of Finance, and elected as Chairman Rev. Dr Glenn W. Moore, who was already chairman of the Permanent Committee on Finance and who had looked after the interests of the Alliance with great care for several years; he continued to do so until 1964.

The Council adopted a Statement on 'The Alliance and other world Confessional Bodies' which says:

'1. The 18th General Council re-affirms the position taken by the 17th General Council at Princeton that it should develop its program and give its witness within the framework of the ecumenical movement, seeking to strengthen and enrich the latter, being even willing to subordinate its own interests in order that there may increase the realization of oneness in Christ in which historic loyalties may find their fulfilment.'[6] The statement further confirmed the decision taken by the Executive Committee in 1956 to seek consultations with other confessional groups. Special mention was made of the ICC–WARC conversations; but as we have devoted the preceding chapter to this problem, we say no more here.

The General Secretary and the Assistant Secretary were re-elected to their respective posts until the next General Council, and a new Executive Committee elected. Its President, who also became President of the Alliance, was Rev. Dr Ralph W. Lloyd, President of Maryville College, Tennessee, U.S.A. Dr Lloyd had served the Alliance with distinction since 1951, when he became North American Secretary. He had been the chairman of the Committee on Preparations for the São Paulo Council and had given considerable assistance to the General Secretary for many months; his election to the post of President was a sign of gratitude and confidence on the part of the Council. In the years between São Paulo and Frankfurt (the delegates gathered at São Paulo had accepted the invitation of the 'Reformierter Bund' of Germany to hold the 19th General Council at Frankfurt/M.) Dr Lloyd was going to devote a great deal of his time—especially after his retirement as President of Maryville College—to the Alliance.

There is no doubt, however, that the retirement of President Mackay was deeply felt. One could not forget the remarkable leadership he had given to our organization and the courage he had shown on more than one occasion. What Dr Eugene Carson Blake wrote about Dr Mackay on the occasion of his retirement from the Presidency of Princeton Theological Seminary (June 1959) sums up what many Reformed Christians from all countries felt when he relinquished the Presidency of the Alliance. Here are some sentences from Dr Blake's article: 'It has been a great era in the life of our Church. Working out in numerous directions from the pivot post of the Presidency of its oldest and largest Theological Seminary, John Mackay has influenced the whole

Church by its leadership in thought and activity more than any other man of his time. If the United Presbyterian Church is stronger, more mature in its faith, more ecumenical in its vision, more respected in the nation, and more influential in the world family of Churches, it is in no small measure due to John Mackay.'[7]

Before leaving Brazil, many of the delegates to the São Paulo Council were able to take part in the Centennial celebrations organized by the Presbyterian Church of Brazil in Rio de Janeiro. This was the crowning of a great Council, and many people still remember the happy days they spent in the beautiful city of Rio in the fellowship of their Brazilian brethren.

※　　※　　※

If, for the Alliance, 1959 was in many ways a Latin American year, 1960 was to be an African year. The six new member Churches admitted during that year all came from Africa. In his report to the member Churches for the year 1960 the General Secretary wrote: 'The fact that the World Presbyterian Alliance has now 19 member Churches in Africa, that 11 of them are in South Africa, and that these Churches belong to all racial groups of that country lays upon us certain responsibilities, particularly in the area of inter-racial understanding. Last April, the Administrative Committee of the European Area sent a letter to Member Churches in South Africa, expressing concern at the situation that had developed there. Later, the Executive Committee, after a long and full discussion of the racial problem, sent a further message to these Churches. The text of this message has not been published, but it may be said that several of the South African member Churches have not remained indifferent to its contents.'[8]

One can add that apart from correspondence between the Executive Committee and the South African member Churches, there was an exchange of correspondence between the General Secretary and one of our member Churches in the Republic of South Africa. The General Secretary reaffirmed the Christian principle that there can be no separation in the Church of Jesus Christ between people of different races, and that membership in any one Church should be opened to people of all races.

Why did the Alliance give no publicity to the action of its General Secretary and of its Executive Committee? Simply because we believed—and still believe—that publicity can be harmful, and that discussion between Christians can be more fruitful if it takes place between brethren, without the intervention of the general public. But the position of the Alliance was clear and has not changed since 1960. The letter sent by the Executive Committee under the signatures of the President and the General Secretary confirms this:

'While we recognize that many good and Christian things have been done and continue to be done by our predominantly white Churches in South Africa for the black African people . . . nevertheless we must confess that some of the positions taken by Reformed and Presbyterian Christians in South Africa appear to us to be clearly contrary to the Word of God and lacking in understanding of the legitimate aspirations of the black African people.

'We do not believe that anything but evil can come from any man blaming the present African drive for equality, participation in government, and for a place of human dignity as creatures of God, on agitators, or Communist influence, or upon secular revolutionary concepts. We are sure that Jesus Christ is speaking to us all in this revolutionary age. We fear that white citizens of South Africa, both Christians and non-Christians, will have to pay for the injustices, economic exploitation, prejudices, and indignities suffered by their black brethren. Indeed we tremble for all our nations "when we reflect that God is just".

'Dear brethren can you not pray together, talk together, seek with all your heart for that miracle from God that alone can lead you and us out of the horror and death that our sin has brought nigh unto us?

'We do not write this letter in a spirit of self-righteousness; we pray that God will enable you to believe that it is in Jesus Christ and for His sake that we must address you . . . Continue in our fellowship. Believe us that we shall continue to cherish all the bonds that bind us with you in common faith, common joy and common sin and common suffering.'[9]

We have mentioned the 1960 meeting of the Executive Committee. We should add that it took place in Geneva and that the sessions were held on the upper floor of the restored Calvin

Auditorium. Amongst other things, the Committee discussed how it could make the Alliance relevant to the Churches of the Reformed family in Africa. It was felt that a consultation would be the best way to do this. But because of the distances on that continent, it was decided that the Conference should be 'regional'. This Conference was to be held in 1962, and we shall refer to it in the coming pages.

The General Secretary reported on the coming Celebrations of the 400th anniversary of the Scottish Reformation. The Alliance had prepared a 'Form of Prayer' to be used by Member Churches on Sunday, 9 October, as an Act of Thanksgiving. The General Secretary was appointed as the official delegate from the Alliance at the Special Meeting of the General Assembly of the Church of Scotland, in October. All the Reformed Churches had been invited to Edinburgh and many of them, from Europe and from other continents, were present.

The Theological Secretary, as well as the Department of Theology, reported on their increasing work. But as we are dealing with the theological work of the Alliance in the next chapter, we say no more at this point.

The General Treasurer of the Alliance, Mr Georges Lombard, was able to give to the Committee the final accounts for the restoration of the Calvin Auditorium. A total of about Sw.Fr. 845,000 had been received by the Alliance; as the restoration had cost about Sw.Fr. 700,000, there was still some money available to ensure the maintenance of the building, for which the Alliance had now taken full responsibility. Soon, some of that money was to be used for providing an organ, though a very large contribution was received for that purpose from Dr Anderson's Church, Fourth Presbyterian Church in Chicago.

While we speak of accounts, let us mention that the Alliance was still running on a very modest budget. The accounts for the year 1959, presented by the General Treasurer, indicated that the total expenditure for the year had been just over Sw.Fr. 113,000 (the U.S. Dollar was then worth Sw.Fr. 4.28) and that there remained a small surplus.

It may not be out of place to mention here that Mr Georges Lombard, a Genevese banker, who had accepted to become General Treasurer of the Alliance as from 1 January 1949, when the Alliance Headquarters were moved to Geneva, filled this honorary post with great distinction until the end of 1970; during all these years, he worked constantly in the interests of our organization, and we owe him a great debt of gratitude.

We have already seen in the last chapter that conversations had begun between the Alliance and the International Congregational Council. But the Alliance leaders were not concerned only with Congregationalists. In his report for the year 1960, the General Secretary wrote: 'It also seems natural that we should seek to establish closer relations with our Lutheran brethren. For the Lutheran and Reformed Churches are the two main branches of the Protestant Reformation. This was clearly seen by the North American Area when it decided to approach the leaders of the Lutheran Churches in North America, and to propose conversations on those problems which today still divide Lutheran and Reformed Christians.'[10]

The problem of peace continued to be one of the preoccupations of the Alliance. The General Secretary believed that it was the duty of our organization to work incessantly to establish better relations between East and West, and he was fully backed by the Executive Committee. This is the reason why Dr Pradervand attended (as an observer) the great Conference organized in Prague, in September 1960, by the Christian Peace Conference, which was at the time chaired by Professor Josef Hromadka, initiator of the organization. The Prague Conference was attended by many Christians from the Churches of Eastern Europe, and it was possible for the Alliance Secretary to establish new and valuable contacts.

*   *   *

1961 was a year of great activity. The North American Area Council took place early in the year. Though these Councils are held every year and no mention is made of them usually in this book, it must be emphasized that they have been and still are very important for the life of the Alliance. They have helped the Churches of the Reformed family in North America to know each other better and to work together in many fields. They have also helped the Churches of the Reformed family to have a better understanding of the problems and tasks of the Alliance, and this is the reason why the Churches of the North American Area have given increased financial support to the work of the Alliance.

Without this support, it would have been difficult, not to say impossible, for the Alliance to fulfil its obligations.

In Europe, the European Area Council was held in Zurich, Switzerland, from 24 to 29 August. The theme of the Council was 'The Service of the Christian in Europe today'. The Council was really representative of the Churches of Europe, though once more member Churches in the Soviet Union could not send delegates. Rev. Pierre Bourguet, President of the Reformed Church of France, was elected chairman of the Area. He replaced Rev. Dr Alex. King of Edinburgh, who had been chairman since 1956 and had served the Alliance with competence and devotion.

Earlier in August the Executive Committee of the Alliance met in Oegstgeest, Netherlands. The growing 'world' character of our organization was emphasized once more; the five Churches admitted to membership came from Asia, Africa and Latin America.

The President announced that he would be able to undertake a long presidential visitation of our member Churches, and this without any financial responsibility for the Alliance. Dr Lloyd undertook this journey soon afterwards. He attended the European Area Council and then went to Eastern Europe. From there he went to Africa. After attending the Third Assembly of the World Council of Churches Dr Lloyd went to visit several Churches of Asia; he then paid extensive visits to our member Churches in Australasia before returning to the U.S.A. in June 1962. He was accompanied by Mrs Lloyd who established contacts with several Women's Organizations of member Churches.

The main event of 1961 was the Third Assembly of the World Council of Churches in New Delhi, from 19 November to 5 December, which the Alliance General Secretary attended as a fraternal delegate. The World Confessional Organizations came up for considerable criticism and the Assembly invited these organizations to join in a study of the relationship which should exist between them and the WCC and also between them and the Younger Churches.

The Alliance felt untouched by these criticisms, as it had constantly advocated a policy of restraint on the part of World Confessional Organizations, and as it had been the initiator of the yearly meetings of the representatives of these world families. Commenting on this action of the WCC in his annual report for 1961, Dr Pradervand had this to say: 'As far as the Alliance is concerned, there is no doubt that its work is both useful and necessary. Precisely because it is aware of its ecumenical responsibilities it has never wished to create a powerful institution. It has no wish to become involved in areas where it is our belief that the World Council of Churches can speak and act in the name of all Christians. But it has tasks that no one else can fulfil. We see these tasks as first of all in the field of theology. The entry into the WCC of the great Russian Orthodox Church requires the Reformed Churches to study together more acutely the reason for their existence and the riches which they can bring to Christendom as a whole. It is for this reason that the Alliance's Department of Theology undertook in 1961 a study on Catholicity and the Reformed Tradition. It must not be forgotten that ecumenical discussions are not limited to the Churches within the ecumenical movement. On the one side, they must also be pursued with those numerous groups, often very slightly organized in an ecclesiastical sense, which have undertaken an enormous amount of missionary work and which are generally extremely powerful in the countries where our Younger Churches are established. Our Churches must also undertake, or develop, discussions with the Roman Catholic Church. The calling of the Second Vatican Council in 1962 is an event which the Reformed Churches cannot ignore. Sympathetic and discerning theological study of the meaning of all these developments for Reformed Churches and for the ecumenical movement as a whole is a responsibility which the Reformed Churches must take seriously. It is my belief that the Alliance can help them to pursue it together more completely than any of them could do it in isolation.'[11]

*   *   *

The World Confessional Organizations met in Geneva on 3 and 4 April 1962. The meeting was chaired by the General Secretary of the Alliance. The officers of the Confessional groups had to decide what attitude they should take towards the Second Vatican Council. Msgr Willebrands was in Geneva as a personal representative of the Pope and was received by the Confessional groups. After hearing him, the officers present decided that they would be glad to receive an invitation from the Vatican to send 'delegated observers'. This was an important decision; it marked the turning point in the relations between the Roman Catholic Church and several of the Protestant families of Churches.

For the Alliance, however, the year 1962 was memorable especially for the fact that it was able to organize a 'Consultation of Reformed and Presbyterian Churches', which took place at University College, Ibadan, Nigeria, from 18 to 26 August. This Conference, in which delegates from fifteen Churches and five Christian Councils along with representatives of various Ecumenical bodies and Mission Boards took part, dealt with 'The Mission of the Church in West Africa Today'. The findings of the five Study Groups were passed on to the participant Churches and were studied closely by many of them. Moreover, it helped the development of fruitful relations between some of the Churches present at Ibadan. Strangely enough, these Churches had had direct contacts with their 'mother Churches' in Europe or America, but knew very little of sister Churches living in the same area of Africa!

Many of the members of the Executive Committee were able to attend this Consultation, as the annual meeting of the Executive took place immediately afterwards at the same place. This was the first meeting of the Executive on African soil, and it enabled its members to understand more fully the many problems facing the Younger Churches.

The Executive Committee chose three delegated observers of the Alliance to attend the Second Vatican Council. The Executive made it clear that the mission entrusted to these men was limited:

'1. The primary purpose of the Alliance in sending observers is to have direct information about the work of the Second Vatican Council.

'2. The observers appointed by the Alliance will have no authority to speak for the Alliance or its member Churches or to engage in any negotiation on behalf of the Alliance or its member Churches but may informally give explanations of Reformed doctrine and practice as it may bear upon the questions being discussed in the Council.'[12]

This may seem very restrictive, but it has to be remembered that some of the member Churches of the Alliance, especially minority Churches in Roman Catholic countries, were not yet fully open to this new development of R.C.–Reformed relations.

However, the Alliance observers made full use of the possibilities
offered to them to explain the Reformed position on a number of
points, and it is certain that, together with observers from the
World Council of Churches and other World Confessional
Families, they played a positive role in the life of Vatican II.

In his report for the year 1960 the General Secretary had
expressed his hope of seeing closer relations established between
Lutheran and Reformed Churches. 1962 saw the beginning of
serious conversations between Lutheran and Reformed Churches
in North America; these conversations, which were started at the
initiative of the North American Area of the Alliance, involved
not only member Churches of the Alliance and of the Lutheran
World Federation, but also, on the Reformed side, the Christian
Reformed Church and the Orthodox Presbyterian Church and, on
the Lutheran side, the Missouri Synod.

In Europe it was decided that the conversations held under the
auspices of Faith and Order, with the collaboration of the
Lutheran World Federation and of the Alliance, should be
resumed in March 1963. This was to be the beginning of a new
and fruitful era in the sphere of Lutheran–Reformed relations.

With the atmosphere then prevailing, it seemed that the problem of religious freedom had been solved everywhere. This was
unfortunately not the case, and the Alliance remained as vigilant
as in the past in the defence of the rights of religious minorities.
The 1962 meeting of the Executive Committee felt compelled to
pass a resolution from which we quote the following passages:

'We must register once again our hope that the great Orthodox
and Roman segments of the Body of Christ will, in countries
where they respectively hold a favoured position, strengthen the
cause of that religious freedom which they claim for themselves,
by safeguarding its implementation with respect to minority
evangelical Churches which, also in accord with their distinctive
understanding of God, seek to bear faithful witness to Him and
to His Son, Jesus Christ.

'We recall that many of our member Churches have at one time
or other felt the impact of new groups which have arisen in
free response to the Gospel. At first these new groups served
only to irritate us or our fathers, evoking a stiffened reaction
to these groups. But as the years have passed we have seen that

these new groups thus arising have been instruments of God
compelling us to reexamine our own doctrine and practice and
often, as a result, to modify or rectify them in ways we now
believe to be more in keeping with God's will for His Church.
We believe that such reciprocal respect for one another, and the
mutual defence of freedom for each and all, is a major guarantee
of the health and renewal of every ecclesiastical family within the
household of God.'[13]

The Executive Committee, at its 1962 meeting, also adopted
the theme for the 19th General Council to be held in Frankfurt/M.
in 1964. It was a prayer 'Come, Creator Spirit!'. We shall see later
the significance of this theme, not only for the Alliance, but for all
the Churches of the world.

Naturally, the Geneva Staff, and especially the General Secretary, undertook numerous visits to member Churches and to
prospective members. In 1961, after having received a D.D. from
Presbyterian College, Montreal, one of the Theological Seminaries
of the Presbyterian Church in Canada, the General Secretary paid
an extensive visit to Churches of the Reformed family in the
Caribbean. At the end of the year, before and after the New Delhi
Assembly, he was able to visit several Churches of Asia, especially
the fast growing Presbyterian Church of Formosa, which was in
many ways isolated. In 1962, Dr Pradervand was in West Africa
and later in Mexico; he tried to visit the Presbytery of Cuba, but
as he was on his way the blockade of October 1962 was enforced
and he had to wait until 1963 to visit our Presbyterian brethren
there. Numerous visits were also paid to European and North
American Churches; furthermore, visits to Churches in Eastern
Europe played an important part in the travels of the General
Secretary.

The work of the Alliance was increasing, but the staff still
remained very modest. The Jubilee Secretary, Rev. James E.
Andrews, left the Alliance Office in 1960 to return to the U.S.A.,
first to Princeton, and then to Atlanta, where he later became, and
still is, the Stated Clerk of the Presbyterian Church in the U.S.
His interest for the Alliance has not diminished, and he is presently
the Treasurer of the North American Area of the Alliance.

It was not until 1962 that Mr Andrews was replaced in Geneva
by Rev. A. David Lewis, a minister of the Presbyterian Church of

England, who became the first Secretary for Information of the Alliance. As such, he undertook the responsibilities formerly held by Rev. Niall D. Watson as Associate Editor of the Alliance quarterly, *The Reformed and Presbyterian World*, in addition to editing the newly created *Reformed and Presbyterian Press Service*, which is published monthly in English, French and German, and, since 1970, in Spanish.

In the Department of Theology, Dr Lewis S. Mudge, Jr, left his post as Secretary in 1962 to become Professor at Amherst College, U.S.A. He is now playing an important role in the life of the United Presbyterian Church in the U.S.A. He was replaced by another American Presbyterian, Dr Terrence N. Tice, a Princeton graduate, who was to remain in Geneva until 1965 before returning to the U.S.A. to undertake further studies.

The 'world' character of the Alliance was now clearly apparent. In 1962 the two member Churches added to the Alliance came from Africa. At the end of the year, the Younger Churches were more numerous than the Older Churches; of the 90 Churches constituting the Alliance, 47 were Younger Churches and only 43 Older Churches. This trend was to continue, and today the Churches of Asia, Africa and Latin America form a very important part of our organization.

1963 was the year before the 19th General Council, and the meeting of the Executive Committee, at Princeton, N.J., from 29 July to 3 August, naturally devoted a great deal of time to the many problems connected with it. The members of the Committee heard with joy that a great deal of work had already been done; a preparatory leaflet prepared by the Theological Secretary had been widely distributed, over 80,000 copies of the English edition having been bought by member Churches. A German Committee was hard at work, and the financial help given by our German brethren was to be decisive in bringing to Frankfurt a record number of delegates from the Younger Churches.

Although Pope John XXIII had died and had been replaced by Pope Paul VI, the Executive Committee decided that the Alliance should continue to send delegated observers to the Second Vatican Council.

At the same time, the Executive was glad to know that an Information Service on the Vatican Council had been started by the Evangelical Confederation of Italy and that the Alliance had been instrumental in starting it. This bulletin was sent in five languages all over the world, and would not have been possible without the financial help which the Alliance was able to secure from some of its member Churches. This Information Service was important for, as the Alliance General Secretary wrote in his report to the Executive, 'In the present mood, many people seem to forget that the main issues between Rome and the Churches of the Reformation have not yet been solved. We have to guard ourselves against a vague sentimentalism which refuses to see and face the real issues. In the interest of the whole Christian Church we have to emphasize why we stand today as Reformed Christians.'[14]

The Alliance stood for unity, but not unity at any price. This was made clear early in 1964; Pope Paul VI had flown to the Holy Land, and, on 6 January, he sent a telegram from Jerusalem to the General Secretaries of the World Council of Churches and of World Confessional Organizations. In this telegram, he said: 'The door of the fold is open.' In his annual report for the year 1963, written a few days later, the General Secretary wrote: 'In our view this concept of unity is completely contrary to the one we have learned to seek at the heart of the ecumenical movement. In no sense do we wish to return to Rome. We are ready, in a spirit of obedience, to let ourselves be led by Christ to a unity which we do not yet see clearly but which He can give to His Church in the measure that it proves more obedient and faithful.'[15]

We have seen earlier that the World Confessional Organizations had come in for considerable criticism at the Third Assembly of the WCC at New Delhi, in 1961. Criticism came chiefly from the Younger Churches, as they felt that the activities of some of the Confessional organizations were delaying, if not preventing, the unity which they sought.

Therefore, the problem of 'The Alliance and Confessionalism' was again fully discussed at the 1963 meeting of the Executive Committee. Distinguished guests from several Younger Churches attended the meeting, and their voice was fully heard in the course of the deliberations of the Executive. The following resolution was unanimously adopted:

'In our discussion of Confessionalism it became clear to the Executive that one of the points troubling Churches in Asia, Africa, and Latin America, in connection with the Confessionalism problem is the tendency for these Churches to be divided by the unco-ordinated actions of the Missionary Boards and Societies including those of our own Reformed and Presbyterian Churches. While the problem of Confessionalism will ultimately only be solved by new unities and renewal achieved by the power of the Holy Spirit on a world scale, to which we pledge our efforts, it is clear that we have the responsibility now to achieve a greater unity in our own missionary activities. Therefore, the Executive Committee addresses our member Churches, asking them to join in taking responsibility for calling and arranging such consultations of Missionary Boards and Societies together with representatives of the Churches with whom they work in mission as will help develop plans of co-ordination whereby the cultural, financial and theological differences reflected in our missionary programmes and policies may be as far as possible minimised.'[16]

The subject of Confessionalism was further discussed at a Consultation held in Geneva from 3 to 5 October, 1963, under the auspices of the World Council of Churches and with the participation of representatives of the World Confessional Organizations. The Alliance was the only Confessional family to have included in its delegation two representatives of the Younger Churches, Principal C. H. Hwang, of Tainan, Formosa, and Moderator E. M. L. Odjidja, of the Presbyterian Church of Ghana. We knew that we had no right to discuss such a problem without hearing the voice of the representatives of the Younger Churches of the Reformed family.

Though little mention has been made in recent pages of the work of the Department of Women's Work, it does not mean that it had no activity. At the São Paulo Council, Mrs A. Walton Litz, of the Presbyterian Church in the U.S., had succeeded Lady MacDermott as Chairman of the Department. She greatly developed the contacts of the Department with Women's organizations of the Younger Churches, and real fellowship followed. The Department also worked incessantly for the full integration of women in the different spheres of the Church's life. It is certain that it helped a growing number of member Churches to accept women elders and, in a smaller number of cases, the ordination of women to the Ministry of Word and Sacraments.

The Alliance had decided against the creation of a Youth Department, as it believed that youth work should be conducted as much as possible on an ecumenical basis. This did not mean however that the Alliance had no interest in youth: on the contrary. The São Paulo Council had had a fair number of youth delegates. In 1963, a great 'North American Presbyterian and Reformed Youth Assembly' took place in July at Purdue University, Lafayette, Indiana. More than 2,000 young people took part in it. The theme of the Conference was the Frankfurt theme 'Come, Creator Spirit!'.

1963 marked the 400th anniversary of the Heidelberg Catechism, which is still used extensively in German- and Hungarian-speaking Reformed Churches, after having been used for centuries in many other Churches of the Reformed family on the Continent of Europe and in the U.S.A. Naturally, celebrations marked this important anniversary. The North American Area Council took place at Lancaster, Pa., theological centre of the Evangelical and Reformed Church, one of the Churches still retaining the Heidelberg Catechism, and most of the meeting was devoted to this important anniversary. A new English Edition of the Catechism was published under the auspices of the Alliance.

In the European Area the Administrative Committee held its annual meeting in Debrecen, Hungary, from 3 to 6 May, and a full day was devoted to the commemoration of the fourth centenary of the Catechism, which has played and still plays such an important part in the religious education of Hungarian Reformed children. Later, in July, celebrations were held in Heidelberg under the auspices of the Evangelical Church of Germany and of the 'Reformierter Bund'. The Alliance was fully associated to this commemoration.

* * *

In 1963, the Alliance President, Dr R. W. Lloyd, was able to continue his 'Presidential Visitation'. After attending the WCC consultation held in Geneva in October on the problem of Confessionalism, Dr Lloyd visited Churches in Latin America and was able to represent the Alliance at the Conference organized by the 'Commission for Presbyterian Cooperation in Latin America'. The theme of the Conference was 'The Nature and Mission of the Church in Latin America Today'. Once more, Dr Lloyd was able to undertake his journey without expenses to the Alliance, thanks to the generosity of an American Foundation closely connected with his family.

And so we move into 1964, the year of the 19th General Council at Frankfurt, with its prayer 'Come, Creator Spirit!' as the centre of the deliberations. In the December 1963 issue of *The Reformed and Presbyterian World*, the General Secretary wrote an Editorial on the coming Council. Here are some of his reflections: 'In what sense can the Frankfurt Council be described as important? As I see it, its importance lies in the theme chosen for this Conference, the prayer *'Come, Creator Spirit!'*. For in fact this prayer confronts us inescapably with the most important problem for the Christian, for the Church, and for the whole world, namely, the problem of *renewal*.

'To pray for this renewal is to recognize that the present situation is not what it should be . . .

'The theme of the Frankfurt Council should, therefore, in the first place, fill us with humility. But it should also fill us with hope. For we cannot utter this prayer without knowing that the Holy Spirit is at work every day, both in the Church and in the world. Above all, this prayer reminds us of the wonderful possibility of renewal for our Churches, if they really allow themselves to be imbued with the Holy Spirit, if they allow Him to re-form their structures and their witness, and if the individual members of our Churches do not shrink from being renewed by His power.'[17]

Recent events in the Church of Jesus Christ show us that this is becoming a reality for Churches and Christians alike, all over the world.

REFERENCES

1. *Proceedings 18th General Council*, p. 12.
2. Idem, p. 67.
3. Idem, p. 85.
4. Idem, pp. 103–107.
5. Idem, pp. 120–122.
6. Idem, p. 221.
7. *The Reformed and Presbyterian World*, vol. XXV, no. 6, p. 245.
8. Report of the General Secretary for 1960, p. 1.
9 Minutes of the 1960 Executive Committee, p. 106.

10. Report of the General Secretary for 1960, p. 2.
11. Report of the General Secretary for 1961, p. 3.
12. Minutes of the 1962 Executive Committee, p. 6.
13. Idem, p. 13.
14. Minutes of the 1963 Executive Committee, p. 21.
15. Report of the General Secretary for 1963, p. 1.
16. Minutes of the 1963 Executive Committee, p. 7.
17. *The Reformed and Presbyterian World*, vol. XXVII, no. 8, pp. 337–338.

CHAPTER FOURTEEN

The Theological Work of the Alliance

Theology has always been a concern of the World Alliance of Reformed Churches. But only after 1957 did this work really become an important part of the Alliance's activities. The 1954 General Council at Princeton had recommended the appointment by the Executive Committee of a Theological Commission. The Executive, at its 1955 meeting, decided 'That the Executive Committee serve in lieu of a commission on theology until the next General Council, appointing and co-opting various scholars and churchmen as members of *ad hoc* committees set up to deal with specific problems referred to the Alliance.'[1] The North American Area had just appointed a Theological Committee so the Executive recommended that the European Area do the same. A European Theological Commission was therefore formed under the chairmanship of Professor Laszlo Pap, of Budapest, a member of the Executive Committee.

In 1956, the Executive Committee took another step and decided that the Alliance should appoint a Theological Secretary who would be a member of the Alliance staff in Geneva. Following this decision Rev. (later Dr) Lewis S. Mudge, Jr, an ordained minister of the United Presbyterian Church in the U.S.A., came to Geneva late in 1957. He immediately set to work, and in 1958 began a new Alliance publication, *The Bulletin of the Department of Theology*, which appeared four times a year in English (in printed form) and in French and German (mimeographed editions). Since 1971 the English edition of the Bulletin has been incorporated into *The Reformed World* but the mimeographed editions continue to appear and make it possible for theologians who do not read English to keep in touch with the theological work of the Alliance.

The 1959 General Council of the Alliance in São Paulo expressed their appreciation of the work done in this field and decided to establish a 'Department of Theology', the members of the Department being chosen amongst the members of the Executive Committee. The new President of Princeton Theological Seminary, Rev. Dr James I. McCord, who had devoted so much time to the theological work of the Alliance and was chairman of the 'Committee for the publication of Calvin's unpublished Sermons' became the Chairman of the new Department; the Alliance's Theological Secretary, Mr Mudge, became the Secretary of the Department.

As Theological Secretary, Mr Mudge had been responsible for writing the Study Booklet for the General Council, on 'The Servant Lord and His Servant People'. At the same time, he had published a book on the subject: *In His Service—The Servant Lord* (Westminster Press, Philadelphia, 1959).

The São Paulo Council gave clear instructions about the theological work the Alliance should undertake. We give here the most important of these instructions: 'The Alliance should undertake a long range study of how to make its heritage fruitful in this ecumenical age. One of the distinguishing marks of our Reformed heritage is concisely expressed in the well known Latin statement: *Ecclesia Reformata semper est Reformanda* (The Church which is Reformed is always being Reformed). This genuine principle, if it is again and again rightly interpreted and unreservedly practised, may well serve as a mobilizing and cristallizing factor in the whole ecumenical movement. And it will prompt primarily the Reformed family of Churches to self-study with special reference to the goals of ecumenism and their proper contribution to the realization of these goals.'[2]

Mr Mudge immediately set to work. In his report to the 1960 meeting of the Executive Committee, he wrote: 'In our thinking and correspondence, the title "Catholicity of the Reformed Tradition" has emerged as an umbrella which could draw these concerns into an articulate study.'[3]

This study on 'Catholicity' quickly developed, and in 1963, after having returned to the U.S.A., Dr Mudge published a book entitled *One Church: Catholic and Reformed* (Lutterworth Press, London) which summarized the results of this study.

Early in the 1950s the Alliance General Secretary had started a modest programme of scholarships for theological students. The programme became the responsibility of the Department of

Theology and thanks to the generous co-operation of several Theological Seminaries many more students from all continents have been able to pursue their studies in other lands. The programme is still in operation.

Relations with 'Faith and Order' and with the Theological Departments of other World Confessional Organizations were also developed. Articles by the Alliance Theological Secretary appeared n 1961 in *The Lutheran World* and in *The Ecumenical Review*.

In August 1962 Dr Mudge left Geneva to become Assistant Professor of Religion and Chaplain at Amherst College, U.S.A. He was replaced by Dr Terrence N. Tice, a theologian from Princeton, N.J.

Dr Tice continued working on the many subjects which were already the responsibility of the Department of Theology. At this time it was decided that the study on 'Ordination and the Ministry' would become part of the larger study on 'Catholicity'.

On the advice of the Department of Theology the Executive Committee adopted as theme for the 19th General Council at Frankfurt/M., 1964, the prayer 'Come, Creator Spirit!' and Dr Tice was asked to write the Study Guide which was to be used in the Churches during the year preceding the Council.

The Department played an important part in the conversations which were developing between the World Alliance of Reformed Churches and the International Congregational Council. As we have already devoted a whole chapter (Chapter 12) to this problem, there is no need to say any more now.

At the suggestion of Dr McCord, Chairman of the Department of Theology, the Executive Committee decided that a Consultation of Systematic Theologians would be held prior to the 1964 General Council at Frankfurt. Dr Tice was responsible for arranging this meeting, which took place from 29 to 31 July at Hoechst, Germany; it brought together about 25 theologians of the Reformed family.

Meanwhile theological conversations between representatives of Lutheran and Reformed Churches were going on in North America and in Europe. And though the European conversations were sponsored by 'Faith and Order', the Department of Theology of the Alliance was deeply involved in these conversations, the importance of which need not be emphasized.

The 1964 General Council had decided, on the recommendation

of its Standing Committee on Theology, 'The establishment of a category of Research Associate, that would enable the Department of Theology to appoint, from time to time, persons with this designation whose task it will be to carry out or to supervise specific projects of theological research . . . Work will be done under the direction of the Department of Theology. Research Associates may work in or away from Geneva.'[4]

Having reached the end of his appointment, Dr Tice returned to the U.S.A. in 1965 to undertake further studies and teaching.

The 1964 General Council had accepted a recommendation of its Section III suggesting that the question of *episkope* (oversight) be considered by the Department of Theology. The 1965 Executive asked the Theological Secretary to start work on this important issue and to request Professor Eduard Schweizer, of Zurich, to prepare a working paper on this topic.

In view of the increasing number of member Churches involved in Church union negotiations, the Executive Committee at Baguio, Philippines, following a recommendation of the Frankfurt Council, established a 'Panel on Church Unions'; its members came from five continents. In the course of the next few years this Panel was able to give valuable counsel to several Churches of the Reformed family.

However, the most important event for the Department of Theology during 1965 was the arrival of its new Secretary, Rev. Richmond Smith, a minister of the Church of Scotland who had already held two pastorates in his native land before coming to Geneva. Mr Smith immediately felt at home in his new work, to which he gave himself with complete devotion. During the last nine years Mr Smith has expanded the work of the Department in many directions, especially in the field of bilateral conversations with several families of Churches, as we shall see in the coming pages. The Alliance owes him a great debt of gratitude.

The first report of the new Theological Secretary to the Department of Theology, on the occasion of the 1966 meeting of the Executive Committee, gives an idea of the very wide scope of interests of the Department.

The first Research Associate of the Department, elected at the 1965 meeting of the Executive, was unable to accept the position, due to changes in his schedule. But in 1966 the Department of Theology discussed the possibility of having a Research Associate on the question of the 'Eldership' with particular reference to Church Unions. This was soon to become a reality.

The Department was responsible for supervising two studies, one on 'The Holy Spirit in Church and World', as recommended by the 1964 General Council, and one on 'Episkope'. Professor Schweizer, of Zurich, was unable to provide a working paper, owing to pressure of work, but he gave considerable help to the Department of Theology, while Reformed theologians in Australia, the U.S.A., India, the Netherlands and Scotland were able to contribute working papers which helped in developing this study.

During Vatican II, the Alliance observers had sent regular reports to the Alliance headquarters. These reports were very substantial and Rev. Richmond Smith undertook to prepare a synopsis of these reports and to have them sent to member Churches in English, French, German, and, in one case, in Spanish. This helped our member Churches to be better informed about Vatican II and to know the reactions of our observers.

The 1967 meeting of the Executive Committee, in Toronto, decided, on the recommendation of the Department of Theology, to appoint Rev. Dr Robert W. Henderson, of the University of Tulsa, U.S.A., as Research Associate for the study of the eldership.

Lutheran-Reformed relations were developing in Europe as well as in North America and the Theological Secretary kept in close touch with the Reformed representatives holding these conversations. He himself took a prominent part in the European discussions; though 'Faith and Order' was the sponsor of these conversations, the Alliance's Department of Theology as well as the Department of Studies of the Lutheran World Federation were fully involved in them. The first series of talks held in North America were published in 1966 under the title *Marburg Revisited*. In April 1967 the documentation of the European conversations was published under the title *Lutheran and Reformed Churches in Europe on the Way to One Another*. This report, together with other documents, was submitted to European member Churches for their comments.

In his report to the Department of Theology, Toronto 1967, the Theological Secretary noted that the Working Committee of 'Faith and Order', meeting in Zagorsk (U.S.S.R.) in 1966, had received a memorandum from Dr Lukas Vischer on 'The Place and Task of Confessional Bodies in the Ecumenical Movement'; at the centre of the memorandum was the proposal to co-ordinate studies among the World Confessional Bodies and the World Council of Churches in such a way that there should be a real division of labour. This was welcomed by Mr Smith.

At the 1967 meeting of the Executive Committee the Theological Secretary recommended that steps be taken to express 'The significance of the Reformed position in an Ecumenical Age' as part of the preparations for the Uniting General Council in 1970. This was done, as we have seen in Chapter 12, when ICC and WARC theologians met in Stockholm in July 1968.

The Department of Theology was also responsible for proposing the theme for the Uniting General Council. After a great deal of work and correspondence the theme 'God reconciles and makes free' was finally adopted.

In January 1968, an *ad hoc* Lutheran-Reformed Study Committee met in Geneva. Following the recommendations of this group the 1968 meeting of the Executive Committee agreed to appoint a 'Joint Committee' with the Lutheran World Federation, which first met in January 1970 and which has since then done excellent work.

The North American Area of the Alliance began conversations with representatives of Orthodox Churches in North America in May 1968; the Department of Theology was gratified to hear of this development, and the Executive Committee expressed the hope that conversations going on in other parts of the world, especially in Romania, would lead to greater mutual understanding and co-operation between the Churches of the two families.

The Department of Theology was also concerned with the problem of mixed marriages, which had been a stumbling block in relations with the Roman Catholic Church for a very long time. At its request, Rev. Dr Rudolph Ehrlich of Edinburgh prepared a statement expressing the Reformed position. The Department of Theology was instructed by the Executive Committee to make this statement available to all member Churches.

The Alliance General Secretary, in his report to the 1968 meeting of the Executive Committee, had suggested the possibility of starting conversations between the World Baptist Alliance and the World Alliance of Reformed Churches. While agreeing in principle, the Department of Theology and the Executive Committee thought that it would be better to wait until after the 1970 merger of the WARC and ICC. Therefore the conversations were postponed; they started in 1974.

The 1969 meeting of the Executive Committee was a Joint WARC-ICC meeting. The Department of Theology of the Alliance, meeting with ICC representatives, became a 'Committee on Theology'. It made several recommendations to the Joint Executive, and these were accepted. It was decided that a Consultation should be held in Nairobi, from 17 to 19 August 1970, prior to the Uniting Council, the theme to be 'Theological Education in the Life of the Church'.

The Committee on Theology was able to report that studies on 'The Holy Spirit in Church and World' and 'Episkope, with special reference to Church Union Negotiations' had now been completed. The final report on the first study had been prepared by Professor Thomas D. Parker, of McCormick Theological Seminary, Chicago, while the final report on *Episkope* had been prepared by Professor J. K. S. Reid, of Aberdeen University, chairman of the European Theological Commission of the Alliance.

We have already noted the Alliance's interest in the problem of mixed marriages. In April 1969, Dr André Appel, General Secretary of the Lutheran World Federation, sent a letter to Dr Pradervand, suggesting that the Alliance be associated with the LWF in a 'Joint consultation between Reformed and Lutherans to study preparations for a possible joint dialogue with the Roman Catholic Church on the Theology of Marriage and the problem of mixed marriages.'[5]

On the recommendation of the Committee on Theology, this invitation was warmly accepted by the Joint Executive Committee; this was to be the beginning of a very happy and fruitful collaboration at world level in this important field.

The same Committee voted to approve the recommendations of the Joint Roman Catholic-Reformed consultation at Vogelenzang, Netherlands (April 1969) and to start an official dialogue with the Roman Catholic Church. These conversations, which are still going on, have added a heavy burden to the work of the Department of Theology, but they have been fully worthwhile, as we shall see later.

At Nairobi, the Committee on Theology, chaired by President James I. McCord, submitted to the Council a substantial report, which was approved by the delegates. The Council was particularly happy to hear about both the development of Lutheran-Reformed relations as well as the coming dialogue with the Roman Catholic Church.

With regard to the specific work of the Department of Theology, the Council, on the recommendation of the Committee on Theology, suggested three subjects for future study:

I. How to do Theology.
II. The Theological Basis of Human Rights and a Theology of Liberation.
III. The Participation of the Laity in Church, Society and Politics.

At Nairobi, Dr James I. McCord, who had chaired the Department of Theology, since its inception in 1959, announced that he would not stand for re-election. This was deeply regretted by the delegates of the Council, although they could not do otherwise but accept Dr McCord's decision. Consequently a new Chairman was elected, Professor Dr J. M. Lochmann, of the Evangelical Church of Czech Brethren, presently teaching at the University of Basle, Switzerland. Happily Dr McCord accepted to remain North American Secretary of the Alliance; as such, he still continues to give real leadership to our organization.

From now on one of the major tasks of the Department of Theology was to be the participation in bilateral or multilateral dialogues with other Church families, but this did not prevent the Department from giving attention to problems which were its specific responsibility.

In his report to the Department of Theology on the occasion of the 1971 meeting of the Executive Committee, in Cartigny near Geneva, Rev. Richmond Smith was able to indicate that the three studies entrusted by the Nairobi Council to the Department of Theology were already under way and that discussion papers on the three subjects had already been prepared by Professor David Willis, U.S.A. (How to do Theology), Professor Jürgen Moltmann, Germany (The Theological Basis of Human Rights and a Theology of Liberation) and Professor Daniel Jenkins, England (The Involvement of the whole People (Laos) of God in Society and Politics). Early in 1971 these papers were mailed to more than 70 Reformed theologians all over the world and their comments soon began coming into the hands of the Theological Secretary.

As for the dialogues, they were developing very fast. In March 1970 the second Leuenberg Consultation was held at Leuenberg, near Basle; it brought together European Lutheran and Reformed theologians to discuss 'Church fellowship and Church division'.

In April a small drafting Committee met at Cartigny, near Geneva, to prepare a 'Concord' or 'Agreement'. This document was submitted to the third meeting of Lutheran and Reformed representatives at Leuenberg in September 1971. It became the 'Leuenberg Concord' and was sent to all the Lutheran and Reformed Churches of Europe. The document is now being studied by all these Churches; their final decision must be sent in by September 1974. If accepted, the 'Agreement' will establish full table and pulpit fellowship and the closest possible relations. This is made clear in 'Confessions in Dialogue': 'Full church fellowship will be established if the churches accept the "concord" and fulfil these conditions: (1) The churches who sign the "concord" agree in the understanding of the Gospel as expounded in part 2 of the "concord". (2) The condemnations expressed in the confessions no longer apply to the present doctrinal position of the churches signing the "concord". Present differences in doctrine, order and life-style are not important enough to justify church division. (3) The churches who sign the "concord" acknowledge one another as part of the Church of Jesus Christ by granting to one another altar and pulpit fellowship. This includes mutual recognition of ordinations and the possibility of intercelebration.

'Organisational consequences of the declaration of church fellowship, like organic union, are left to the decision of the participating churches.'[6]

At the time of writing (July 1974) a very clear majority of both Lutheran and Reformed Churches have already accepted the 'Concord'. A continuation committee is due to meet in October 1974 to prepare future plans for closer co-operation between Lutheran and Reformed Churches in Europe. It is hoped that a first meeting of representatives of these Churches will take place in Strasbourg at Whitsun 1975; but at present these are only tentative plans.

Whatever happens, it is certain that the Leuenberg Agreement will have very positive effects in the life of the Churches of both families, not only in Europe, but also on other continents. 'Faith and Order', the Department of Studies of the Lutheran World Federation and the Department of Theology of the World Alliance of Reformed Churches can be thanked for the part they have played in making possible this 'Concord', which should only be a first step.

Proof of the importance of the Leuenberg 'Concord' is given in the fact that the Lutheran-Reformed Joint Committee will start a new phase of activity in 1975 on the world level. Both the Executive Committees of the Lutheran World Federation and of the World Alliance of Reformed Churches have given the Joint Committee the mandate to study 'The theological, ecclesiastical and ecumenical implications of the Leuenberg agreement'.

The first meeting of the Roman Catholic-Reformed Study Commission on 'The Presence of Christ in Church and World' had already taken place before the Nairobi Uniting Council, in Rome, in April 1970, to study the theme 'Christ's relation to the Church'; the ICC and WARC representatives formed the 'Reformed' group. However, the most important part of the work of this Commission has been done since the new Alliance came into being. The second round of these conversations took place at Cartigny, near Geneva, in March 1971, when the subject for discussion was 'The Teaching Authority of the Church'. In 1972 (from 31 January to 3 February) Roman Catholic and Reformed representatives of the Commission met again in Bièvres, near Paris, to discuss 'The Presence of Christ in the World'. The fourth session took place in Holland in February 1974, when the problem under discussion was 'The Eucharist'. A fifth session is planned for March 1975 in Rome, when 'The Ministry' will be studied; this is a subject which for centuries has been a cause of deep misunderstanding between the Churches of the two families. Hopefully, a sixth meeting will be held in 1976 to prepare a final report. But this is not yet history! It is enough to say that though discussions have at times been difficult, an excellent spirit has prevailed and the contacts established between the representatives of our respective Church families have real value.

We have already noted that in 1969 the Executive Committee had accepted an invitation from the General Secretary of the

Lutheran World Federation that the Alliance join with them in a study prior to a dialogue with the Roman Catholic Church on 'The Theology of Marriage and Mixed Marriages'. The Nairobi Council authorized the implementation of this Joint dialogue with the Roman Catholic Church. The first meeting of the Joint Study group was held in Strasbourg in November 1971, when 'The Theological Understanding of the Man-Woman Relationship' was discussed. A second meeting took place in December 1972; the theme of the session was 'Marriage as a Sacramental Reality?'. The third meeting, in December 1973, discussed the problem of 'Indissolubility'; as this is a central problem and a point of division between the Roman Catholic Church and the Churches of the Reformation, this subject will be the theme of the fourth session, which is due to take place in December 1974.

We have already mentioned that the Executive Committee of the Alliance, at its 1968 meeting, had in principle approved the proposal of its General Secretary that the Alliance should try and start a dialogue with the World Baptist Alliance, but decided that it would be better to wait until after Nairobi. A preliminary meeting between Baptist and Reformed representatives took place at the Baptist Seminary, Rüschlikon, near Zurich, in February 1973. It recommended that a Dialogue be started. This was approved the same year by the Executive Committee of the World Baptist Alliance. The Executive Committee of the WARC acted similarly at its meeting at Stony Point, U.S.A., in January 1974. Since then a planning meeting was held at Rüschlikon. Though these conversations, for the time being, will be located in Europe, the dialogue is a world dialogue involving the two World Alliances. The subjects to be studied at the first meeting are:

(1) Distinctive elements of the Baptist and Reformed heritage today.

(2) The Baptist and Reformed perspectives in understanding the Gospel.

As already indicated the North American Area had held a series of conversations with the Orthodox Church in America, and a volume containing the papers given to the annual meetings was published in 1973 under the title *The New Man* (Standard Press, New Brunswick, N.J., 1973).

A new round of conversations started in November 1973. Lutheran representatives took part in them and representatives of the Disciples of Christ became part of the Reformed delegation to these talks, the subject of which is 'The Christian Gospel and Social Responsibility'.

In Europe, at Debrecen, on 18 September 1972, 'the Reformed Theological Academy sponsored important new conversations with the Orthodox, which hopefully should lead to further discussions. The aim of the one day colloquium was to probe the theological boundaries of traditional and contemporary Orthodox/ Reformed thinking.'[7]

At the time of writing further developments are expected following a resolution which requested 'President Dr James I. McCord to continue to represent the World Alliance of Reformed Churches in planning and implementing dialogue between the Orthodox and the Reformed Churches of Eastern Europe taking into account the full representation of all Orthodox and Reformed churches in so far as is possible and that he be asked to report periodically through the Department of Theology to the Executive Committee.'[8]

In Romania, the Institute of Protestant Theology at Cluj is the centre of a constant dialogue between Reformed and Orthodox theologians. The Theological Secretary of the Alliance keeps in close touch with these developments.

*   *   *

We have written at length about the bilateral and multilateral dialogues in which the Alliance is involved, as they are important and form a major part of the present responsibility of the Department of Theology. But the Theological Secretary of the Alliance has many other responsibilities. *The Reformed World* carries many articles which were formerly published in *The Bulletin of the Department of Theology*, and these articles are translated and published in the mimeographed French and German editions of *The Bulletin*, which continue to appear. The scholarship programme of the Alliance has expanded, and this demands a great deal of correspondence between the Department of Theology, candidates and Theological Seminaries.

The studies undertaken by the Department of Theology at the request of the Nairobi Uniting Council continue. But Study III

(The Participation of the Laity in Church, Society and Politics) has now become part of Study II (The Theological Basis of Human Rights and a Theology of Liberation), as it was discovered that the two studies touched the same ground.

As for the important study on Eldership, undertaken by Professor Robert W. Henderson, of the University of Tulsa, U.S.A., it is nearing its end at the time of writing these lines. Professor Henderson is in Geneva on a Sabbatical leave from May 1974 to January 1975, and he then hopes to submit his final report to the Department of Theology.

Since Nairobi the Department has continued to emphasize the theological contributions available from all parts of the Reformed family on six continents. Immediately after the 1972 meeting of the Executive Committee, a consultation with Indonesian member Churches was organized in Sukabumi, West Java, from 26 to 29 July. The theme of the meeting was the same as the theme of the coming Bangkok Conference of the Division of World Mission and Evangelism of the World Council of Churches —'Salvation Today'.

An effort has also been made to involve more theologians from the Third World in the dialogues in which the Alliance takes part, but budget limitations have imposed a limit which is regrettable.

In addition to the Department of Theology, theological work is also carried out by the two organized Areas of the Alliance. Whilst the Theological Committee of the North American Area continues to function, the Theological Commission of the European Area has become merged with the European Committee, whose membership has been considerably enlarged. The Theological Secretary is deeply involved in the work of these theological groups.

In 1971, the Theological Secretary, Rev. Richmond Smith, wrote:

'Underlying much of the theological work in the member Churches of the WARC is a growing uncertainty as to how to define the direction and the nature of the theological commitment. The inescapable question behind that is the old but contemporary question of our understanding of the church and of the Gospel which creates the church. What of our strategy of planning? Have we a vision of the present and the morrow which provides an answer as to how best the WARC can fulfil its servant role in stimulating the right sort of theological awareness in the life of the church?

'The proliferation of studies and consultations and dialogues is not necessarily the answer to the need of the moment. While committed to the remit of the Nairobi Uniting General Council recommendations, we must also be alert to the emergent issue. Constantly we must ask ourselves, What are our immediate priorities? One could cite, e.g., the concern of the Faith and Order Commission at Louvain last year to explore the nature of things held in common, to try and give together the reason for the hope that is in us.

'Perhaps we in the Reformed family assume too readily that we already understand the theological nature of the unity that holds us together. What is it? Have we not a responsibility to articulate this reality and to make it available to others? Can it be defined at all—and in terms which are relevant to the 60% of our member churches located in the developing world?'[9]

This clearly indicates the direction in which the Alliance's Department of Theology is carrying on its work.

The Alliance does not do its work in isolation. This is particularly true of its Theological work. In 1973, writing in *The Reformed World* on 'The Theological work of the WARC and the Ecumenical context', Rev. Richmond Smith says:

'It would be tempting to say the Reformed family has been able to influence the ecumenical scene at this and that and the other point . . . And before long we might find ourselves basking in a self-generated and very doubtful euphoria.

'I suggest it may be much healthier for us to ask ourselves: Where has the ecumenical movement of our time made its influence felt on the Alliance as a world confessional family? Can we isolate and identify a few of the issues that arise from the mutual involvement and can we detect in what direction we shall have to travel?

'(1) As a world family of Reformed Churches have we the vision of our given responsibility to articulate on the world dimension a universal understanding of the insights we believe God has given us? Bilateral conversations present us with the possibility of lifting our various historically conditioned appre-

hensions of the Christian Faith out of the localism and the
provincialism within which the life of our member churches is
necessarily and properly set and placing the theological clash
between confessional positions in a *universal perspective*? Do we
see this task as a legitimate way forward into a fuller realization
of what fellowship in the *una sancta* may yet mean?

'It is a presupposition of ecumenical theology that conciliar
fellowship involves eucharistic fellowship. Have we worked
out the implications of that eucharistic fellowship which is
already universalised within our own world family of Reformed
Churches? As Reformed we possess a weighty and articulate
theology of intercommunion. What we say ourselves is equally
true of other world families within their own confessional
positions. Unfortunately the WCC has not yet been able to
realize a universal eucharistic fellowship. That some of the
confessional families have already reached that point individually
poses some searching questions as to the future positive role of
the world confessional families and of the WCC and their mutual
relationships in the common quest.

'(2) The interconfessional bilateral dialogue raises in an acute
form the question of our theological identity. Who are we? In
the contemporary theological pluralism of our century a statement
of faith can no longer serve as a recognizable theological identity
card. The profile is blurred round the edges. And that applies
right across the whole ecclesiastical spectrum. We must also resist
the temptation of trying to find an answer by resurrecting certain
traditional Reformed positions which we have already consciously
or unconsciously left behind.

'Is the situation not this? The question of our identity has to
be translated into the functional idiom of role and purpose, at
the growing edge of the ecumenical movement.

'Here we have a continuing element in our Reformed tradition
in the best possible sense; semper reformanda, the inevitable
restlessness of a pilgrim people. The Executive Committee of the
Alliance appointed in 1971 a committee with the specific mandate
to probe the role and purpose of the Alliance. The first interim
report has this to say, inter alia: "There is a new era of maturity
in the history of world families of churches and their relationship
to the ecumenical movement in general and to the World Council
of Churches in particular . . . Any feeling of competition has

been diminished ... There is an urgent need to examine the role and purpose of the Alliance in the present situation. This is an issue to which the Alliance has often spoken, but it is compelled to speak again out of the new situation. It seems wise now, however, that the task should not be undertaken by the Alliance alone, but we should seek the cooperation of other world families and the Department of Faith and Order of the World Council of Churches in an effort to make a common response in this new era of growing self-understanding, better mutual understanding, and increasing cooperation.'[10]

'Who knows what will come of this? The role of the Alliance both in relation to its member churches and in the wider context of our sister communions on a world basis and all within our commitment to the Gospel? There may well be questions of structure involved. These we need not fear, if the theological presuppositions of proposed change are thoroughly worked out and grounded in the obedience of faith in Him who is the Head of the one Church.'[11]

It is in this ecumenical context that the theological work of the Alliance is carried out. This is good for the Reformed Churches; we believe that it is also good for the Ecumenical movement.

REFERENCES

1. Minutes of 1955 Executive Committee, p. 11.
2. *Proceedings 18th General Council*, p. 71.
3. Minutes of 1960 Executive Committee, p. 73.
4. *Proceedings 19th General Council*, p. 270.
5. Minutes of 1969 Joint Executive Committee, p. 10.
6. *Confessions in Dialogue*, by Nils Ehrenström & Günther Gassmann, WCC, Geneva, 1972, p. 44.
7. Minutes of 1974 Executive Committee, p. 32 (Report to Dept. of Theology).
8. Idem, p. 73.
9. Report to the Department of Theology, Jakarta, July 1972, p. 1.
10. Minutes of 1971 Executive Committee, p. 10.
11. *Reformed World*, vol. XXXII, no. 7, pp. 310 and 313.

CHAPTER FIFTEEN

From Frankfurt to Nairobi

The Nineteenth General Council which convened in Frankfurt-Main, Germany, was indeed a world assembly and clearly showed that the work of the Alliance was worldwide. Of the more than 420 official delegates gathered at Frankfurt, over one-third represented the Younger Churches of the Alliance; this was not surprising for of the 95 member Churches over 50 were Younger Churches, and they were almost all represented at Frankfurt.

The universal character of the Alliance had become much more pronounced since the São Paulo Council; the General Secretary informed the Council that the 21 Churches admitted into the Alliance fellowship since the last Council in 1959, were all Younger Churches.

Apart from the delegates there were numerous corresponding members, fraternal delegates and observers from World Confessional Organizations, including, for the first time, representatives of the Roman Catholic Church. The Evangelical Churches of Germany, United and Lutheran, were also largely represented by fraternal delegates. In his report to the Council, the General Secretary emphasized the importance of their presence: 'For the first time in its history the World Alliance of Reformed Churches is holding its General Council in Germany, the land of the Reformation . . . our presence here demonstrates the fundamental unity of the great Churches of the Reformation . . . We would like to make it clear that if the World Alliance of Reformed Churches is meeting in Frankfurt, it is not with any idea of emphasizing over against our Lutheran brethren the Reformed elements of our faith. As representatives of the Reformed and Presbyterian Churches we rejoice that we are part of the great Reformation family along with our Lutheran brothers and sisters. We cannot meet here in Frankfurt without desiring to do everything possible to increase still further the unity of the Lutheran and Reformed Churches. The fact that fraternal delegates from most of the Evangelical Churches of Germany are present is surely the best evidence of the harmony which already prevails and which greatly rejoices us.'[1]

The desire for closer relations with the Lutherans was not the only ecumencial aspect of the Frankfurt Council. In Chapter 12 we have already noted the actions taken with regard to the International Congregational Council. Relations with the Roman Catholic Church were also taking a new and positive turn. In his report to the Council the General Secretary mentioned: 'We cannot forget that it was never the purpose of the Reformers to create separate Christian Churches. They sought the reformation of the whole Christian Church, which they wished to see faithful to Scripture and guided by the Holy Spirit. Can our purpose be different from theirs? We regard Christian unity as something desirable and indeed essential. We know this is the will of our Lord . . .'[2] Dr Pradervand justified the decision taken by the Executive Committee in 1962 in deciding to send Delegated Observers to the Second Vatican Council. This was endorsed by the delegates of the Churches gathered at Frankfurt.

The theme of the General Council was the prayer 'Come, Creator Spirit!'. It clearly indicated that the Reformed Churches were conscious of their shortcomings and certain that renewal could only be the work of the Holy Spirit. This was emphasized by Professor Otto Weber, of Göttingen, who spoke to the Council on 'The Renewal of the Church's common ministry'. He said: 'To say that our ministry needs renewal is to say, in the first instance, that it needs to turn back again to its source. There can be no renewal "at any price". The Spirit who brings about renewal is in fact the Spirit of God, the Holy Spirit, the Spirit of Christ. What the Church in our time needs most of all is conversion, return to its source. Besides this, everything else is secondary.'[3]

The members of the Council divided into four sections and spent a great deal of time deliberating eagerly on the given subjects which were as follows:

Section I. Come, Creator Spirit, for the re-making of man.

Section II. Come, Creator Spirit, for the renewal of worship and witness.

Section III. Come, Creator Spirit, for the calling of the Churches together.

Section IV. Come Creator Spirit, for the redemption of the world.

Apart from the plenary sessions and the time devoted to the Sections, there were also several standing Committees which made it possible for the members of the Council to be directly involved in the internal affairs of the Alliance.

The Council, which was chaired by the President of the Alliance, Rev. Dr Ralph W. Lloyd, opened and ended with services in the 'Paulus Kirche', one of the famous historic Churches of Frankfurt. The social side was not forgotten either, and the Council were entertained to a Bach concert, a reception by the civic authorities . and a memorable trip on the Rhine.

The reports of the Sections, after having been discussed in plenary sessions, were 'received and approved for transmission to the Churches' and the recommendations were adopted by the Council. Here are some extracts of these reports.

On 'The signs of the "new man" ', Section I said:

'The "signs of the Spirit" are present and real . . . not only as "gifts of the Spirit", but also as "fruits of the Spirit" . . . Among these fruits of the Spirit those which particularly exhibit the activity of the Spirit in the re-making of man are:

'1. Reconciliation between God and man, and of man with man . . .

'2. Recognition of creative possibilities for the renewal of man; for example, in the structures of justice, in contributions to new relationships in every area of human endeavour, and in the rediscovery of the sense of the ultimate value of man's own work . . . as instrumental to the purpose of God.

'3. Acceptance of responsibility for one's neighbour; the simple reality of love is the purest sign of the work of the Spirit in a world full of hatred, mistrust, fear and enmity . . .

'4. Openness to change . . .'[4]

On 'The gifts of the Spirit', Section II spoke as follows:

'Our Churches have hardly been aware of the blessing which the Holy Spirit wants to give us in the *charismata*, the gifts which He bestows upon the individuals, not in order that they might show off privately, but in order to equip them for their participation in the ongoing work of the Spirit in the Church and in the world. According to Saint Paul, no faithful Christian is without such an individual gift . . .

'Our Reformed Churches have always been afraid of disorder. This fear can go so far that we quench the Spirit and deprive the body of Christ of the variety-in-unity in which it has to exist in the world. This is one reason why the people of God has often become so passive and ineffective in its worship and witness. We have hardly thought about what the Spirit wants to give us in this field for the present time. We summon our Churches and our congregations to find the biblical corrective to the sectarian view of the gifts of the Spirit, to search out the gifts within our membership, and to make room for them in the upbuilding of the Church and the witness to the world.'[5]

On the problem of Unity, Section III spoke very clearly:

'It is necessary to emphasize that the unity of the Church of Jesus Christ must be expressed in each place in which Christians live and work. The separate existence of divided denominations in one city, town, or village
'a. hinders mission in the locality . . .; and
'b. impairs our own understanding of the Gospel and of the Church. Whatever may be the dangers from certain kinds of institutional union, institutional *disunity* certainly weakens and confuses the presentation of the Gospel. To be complacent in face of this situation is a sin.'[6]

The report of Section IV dealt at length with the racial problem. Here are some of the findings of the Section on this subject:

'We believe that:
'1. Jesus Christ was born, died and rose again for the salvation of all men . . .
'2. God has made all nations of one blood (Acts 17: 26); this implies, beyond any consideration of race, colour or nationality, the fundamental dignity, unity and solidarity of mankind.
'6. We therefore consider that the responsibility of the Church in the field of race relations involves:
'a. through preaching and teaching it must enlighten its members as to the demands of the Gospel about race relations.
C.S.—10

'b. . . . the exclusion of any person, on grounds of race, colour or nationality, from any congregation or part of the life of the Church contradicts the very nature of the Church . . .

'c. the members of the Church are also called to witness in society to justice and equality by identifying with, and accepting responsibility alongside, those who suffer. Now as violence and revolutionary action are spreading, it is of primary importance for the Church to be prepared through serious study of the Holy Scripture, and of the political situation to help its members face responsibly under the guidance of Jesus Christ such hard problems as civil disobedience and violent action.'[7]

We have already mentioned that the General Secretary, in his report to the Council, was able to speak of the new climate existing in our relations with the Roman Catholic Church. The report of the Standing Committee on Roman Catholicism made it clear that the Council was in favour of better relations with the great Roman Church. We quote two examples:

'5. . . . if we ask searching questions of the Roman Catholic Church, and hope for reforms within the life of that Church, we must expect equally searching questions to be asked concerning the Reformed Church. We must not fear the dialogue, and must be true successors of the Reformation by making it a continuing process within our own Churches.

'8. Finally, we must always bear in mind that our primary task as Christians, both Protestant and Roman Catholic, is the proclamation of the Gospel of Jesus Christ for the redemption of the world . . .'[8]

This did not mean that the Alliance was no longer concerned with the problem of religious liberty. In its report to the Council the Standing Committee on Minority Churches, Religious Liberty and Inter-Church Aid made the following recommendation: 'That we urge that the struggle for religious liberty continues unremittingly, in watchfulness and in prayer, recognizing that what is at stake is not only the furtherance of the Gospel, but the health of majority as well as of minority Churches, and, indeed, that of the entire nation in which a Church lives and serves.'[9]

A new Executive Committee was elected, and Rev. Dr Wilhelm

Niesel, Moderator of the German 'Reformierter Bund', was chosen as the new President of the World Alliance of Reformed Churches.

* * *

In April 1964, the World Council of Churches had moved its headquarters from 17 Route de Malagnou, to 150 Route de Ferney, in the new Ecumenical Centre which had been built there. The World Alliance of Reformed Churches, as well as the Lutheran World Federation moved there at the same time. The accommodation was more spacious than in the barracks at Malagnou but the Alliance Staff remained the same: seven persons in all, three in the General Secretariat and two each in the Department of Theology and in the Information Secretariat.

* * *

The year 1965 was significant for the Alliance in more than one respect. Four new Churches were admitted into its membership and by the end of the year the number of member Churches had passed the 100 mark.

A great number of our member Churches were located in Asia so it was very natural to organize the next meeting of the Executive Committee on that great continent. Therefore the 1965 meeting of the Alliance Executive took place at Baguio in the Philippines from 24 to 29 June. Several Church leaders from Asia had been invited and they were able to make the Alliance aware of their problems and opportunities. Previous to that meeting several members of the Executive, including the President and the General Secretary, had been in Formosa (Taiwan) for the celebration of the centenary of the Presbyterian Church of Taiwan, from 16 to 22 June. This was a very great occasion and those who attended the celebrations were deeply impressed by the enthusiasm and devotion of the Formosan Presbyterians.

The Executive Committee took an important decision at Baguio: a Department of Co-operation and Witness was created. Dr Margaret Shannon, who had been a faithful and active member of the Alliance Executive from 1954 to 1964 was elected as its first Chairman.

The Executive Committee also established a 'Panel on Church Unions' in order to help the numerous Alliance member Churches

involved in Church Union negotiations. This Panel immediately
set to work and there is no doubt that it gave valuable service to
several Churches.

In 1965 there were several changes in the Alliance Staff. As
mentioned in the preceding chapter the Secretary of the Department of Theology, Dr Terrence N. Tice, returned to the U.S.A.;
he was replaced by Rev. Richmond Smith, a minister of the
Church of Scotland. In the Information Secretariat, Rev.
A. David Lewis left the Alliance to return to a parish ministry
in England; he was replaced by Rev. Lewis L. Wilkins, Jr, a
minister of the Presbyterian Church in the U.S., who was to work
with the Alliance for the next three years.

*   *   *

The problem of 'confessionalism and the Younger Churches' was
abundantly discussed at this time, as the Younger Churches felt
that some confessional organizations had an activity which was
detrimental to the cause of unity. The Alliance, which had always
rejected a narrow confessionalism, was anxious to know what the
Younger Churches of the Reformed family thought and felt on
this important subject. The question had been discussed at the
1965 meeting of the Executive Committee at Baguio and it was
then decided to devote much time to this problem at the 1966
Executive. Before the meeting Dr Pradervand attended a consultation in Kandy (Ceylon, now Sri Lanka) from 6 to 9 December
1965; this meeting was organized by the East Asia Christian
Conference and was devoted to 'Confessional Movements and
Mission and Unity'. The General Secretary of the Alliance was
able to re-affirm that our organization was in favour of the
growing unity which the Younger Churches desired.

The 1966 meeting of the Executive Committee, which took
place in Strasbourg, France, from 28 July to 2 August, gave a
large place to the problem of 'The Alliance and the Younger
Churches'. Papers were presented by members of the Executive
from Asia and Latin America. In a Minute adopted after a discussion the Executive said: 'We are reminded in the World
Alliance of Reformed Churches that within our Alliance, although
some Churches are "older" and some "younger", all alike share
the same responsibilities and privileges as full member Churches...
  '... we find ourselves today in a fellowship of Churches with

diverse histories, but together seeking continual reformation in obedience to the Word of God and under the promised guidance of the Holy Spirit.

'Our confessional association in the World Alliance of Reformed Churches has the purpose of providing the member Churches with opportunities for mutual help and encouragement in confessing Christ faithfully in the contemporary situation which varies so greatly in ethnic, sociological, economic and political conditions in different parts of the world.

'Many of our member Churches have entered into unions or are discussing union with Churches of other traditions.

'As we said at Frankfurt: "The Alliance should continue to encourage its constituent Churches to enter upon co-operative enterprise with other Churches and to seek or continue union negotiations with a sense of urgency . . . We cannot treat as absolute any of the structures and confessions which we inherit; in our very loyalty, we must be ready to go wherever the Spirit leads, even if it be through that death which leads to new life".'[10]

We do not apologize for this long quotation; it shows the spirit in which the Alliance has constantly worked; this is certainly the reason why the 'Younger' Churches have felt at home in the Alliance and do not feel that they have to choose between their ecumenical work in their own land and the world family to which they belong.

The Executive Committee were happy to receive the reports of the conversations between Lutheran and Reformed representatives in North America and in Europe and expressed particular satisfaction at the successful conclusion of the first round of conversations in North America.

With regard to the Roman Catholic Church the Executive Committee reaffirmed the decision taken in 1965 at Baguio 'that the World Alliance of Reformed Churches initiate no separate theological dialogue or theological discussions with the Vatican at this time, but that we support the discussions between the World Council of Churches and the Vatican'. An *ad hoc* Committee was appointed to discuss with the WCC representatives on how best this could be done. At the same time it was made clear that the Alliance should be ready to undertake a dialogue with the R.C. Church if urgent questions should make such action necessary in the future. The necessity arose earlier than was expected and R.C.-Reformed conversations have now proved their value.

The chairman of the Department of Co-operation and Witness, Dr Margaret Shannon, who had become Director of United Church Women (U.S.A.) had, much to our regret, to resign but the Alliance was fortunate that Dr William P. Thompson, Stated Clerk of the United Presbyterian Church in the U.S.A., accepted the invitation to become the new chairman of the Department.

The Department of Women's work continued doing excellent work. Dr Wilhelma Timmermans, of the Netherlands Reformed Church, the new Chairman of the Department since Frankfurt, visited a number of Asian Women's Organizations of our member Churches in 1965, at the time of the Baguio meeting of the Executive Committee. In 1966 Dr Timmermans visited several Women's Organizations of member Churches in Europe. The Women's Organizations of our member Churches in the U.S.A. publish a yearly *Advent Tryst*, a small pamphlet of pre-Christmas meditations and this is distributed all over the world by the Geneva office of the Alliance on behalf of the Department of Women's Work (now part of the Department of Co-operation and Witness).

In 1966 the President of the Alliance, Dr Wilhelm Niesel, undertook an extensive visit of Alliance member Churches in Africa; this was made possible by the generosity of the German 'Reformierter Bund'.

The renewal of the Churches was a constant preoccupation of the Alliance. The 19th General Council at Frankfurt had requested the member Churches to report to the Executive Committee of the Alliance what, *in their practical experience*, the Holy Spirit is doing in the remaking of men and women today. To this end the member Churches in North America set up a number of task forces who worked on the question 'What does the Holy Spirit mean in my profession or job?'. Several hundred persons were involved in the work of these task forces during 1965. Their reports were presented to the North American Area Council on 12 January 1966 and were later published in brochure form under the title: *The Creator Spirit in Secular Society*. It was Dr Margaret Shannon, then chairman of the Department of Co-operation and Witness, who took the initiative of these task forces and interested many laymen in this work.

The 450th anniversary of the Reformation was celebrated in 1967 and the Alliance participated officially in the Wittenberg commemorations. The General Secretary was present, but unfortunately the Alliance President did not receive the necessary visa from the authorities of the German Democratic Republic and was consequently prevented from attending.

Fortunately relations with the Lutheran Churches were not restricted to participation in the commemoration of the Lutheran Reformation. Four years of discussions between Lutheran and Reformed theologians, under the auspices of 'Faith and Order' and of the Lutheran World Federation and World Alliance of Reformed Churches came to an end in 1967. The result of these European conversations was published under the title *Lutheran and Reformed Churches in Europe on the way to one another.*

On the occasion of the Wittenberg celebrations *The Lutheran World* and *The Reformed and Presbyterian World* published a joint issue in 1967 and the Editorial was signed by the General Secretaries of both organizations. For the first time also, the Executive Committees of both organizations exchanged fraternal delegates, a habit which has since then been continued.

The European Area Council, which met at Torre Pellice, Italy, from 9 to 12 September, sent a letter to the Lutheran Churches of Europe. It expressed gratitude for Martin Luther's Reformation and expressed the hope that an ever deepening unity between Lutheran and Reformed Churches would emerge in Europe. The letter was well received by the European Lutheran Churches and warm response was received from the presiding bishop of the United Evangelical Lutheran Church of Germany (VELKD).

While on the chapter of interconfessional relations let us mention that in 1966 the North American Area started conversations with the Roman Catholic Church in the U.S.A. At the end of 1967 a volume entitled *Reconsiderations—Roman Catholic/ Presbyterian and Reformed Theological Conversations 1966–67* was published. It touched the three essential topics discussed in these conversations: 'Revelation, Scripture and Tradition', 'The Development of Doctrine', 'Ministry and Order of the Church'.

The North American Area was to start conversations with the Orthodox Churches of North America in May 1968.

Relations with Conservative Evangelical Churches were not forgotten. The General Secretary of the Reformed Ecumenical

Synod was present as a fraternal delegate at the 1967 meeting of the Executive Committee of the Alliance, which took place in Toronto from 27 July to 1 August.

In his report for the year 1967 the General Secretary of the Alliance mentioned the need for developing relations with Conservative Evangelical Churches. He wrote: 'We would like to remind the member Churches of the WARC that they ought to do everything in their power to develop fraternal relations with these Churches wherever they exist. Special mention should be made of Pentecostal Churches whose extraordinary vitality I have seen both in Asia and in Latin America. We believe that our Churches can only profit from more direct contact with the Pentecostal Churches, who are not afraid to take seriously the prayer 'Come, Creator Spirit!' which was the theme of our 19th General Council. Our ecumenical work would be incomplete if it only brought us in contact with Churches of one orientation and if it let us forget the Evangelical Churches and the Pentecostal Churches which have also grown out of the Reformation.'[11]

Alliance leaders were aware that Church problems were not the essential problems facing Christianity. The Church is in the world and cannot ignore the problems facing the world today. In his report to the member Churches for the year 1966, Dr Pradervand wrote: 'In the extent that we are faithful to the Reformed conception of the Church we know that the Church is not an end in itself. It exists for the world for which Christ died. Christians dare not be indifferent to the world and its problems. It is perhaps necessary to repeat the fact that peace is at the center of the world's problems today. We cannot be satisfied with a situation where there is not only tension between peoples and races, but where a number of countries are also engaged in war. We must also be aware that no real and durable peace can be established until there is a just distribution of the world's riches. The Christian Churches themselves cannot resolve these problems, for gifts, important as they are, will not suffice to bring about real progress toward their solution. The Churches' responsibility is to make the governments of their respective countries aware that all nations must take the problem of distribution of the world's wealth seriously. We rejoice to think that a Swiss Reformed theologian, Dr André Biéler, was the first person to draw the attention of the Reformed and other Churches to this problem.

We hope that all our Churches will exercise their prophetic ministry in this area.'[12]

Readers of this book will remember that in 1959 the Reformed Church of France marked the 400th anniversary of its first National Synod and that in 1960 our Scottish brethren celebrated the fourth centenary of the Scottish Reformation. In 1967 it was the turn of the Reformed Church of Hungary to celebrate its 400th anniversary. The Church became a member of the Reformed family in 1567 by adopting the Second Helvetic Confession. On 19 May 1967, a formal celebration of this event took place in the 'Nagy Templon' (the Great Church) of Debrecen; this was a solemn occasion. Representatives of the World Alliance of Reformed Churches, as well as of many Reformed Churches were present and they were warmly received by our Hungarian brethren.

As we have already devoted a whole chapter to the development of relations between the Alliance and the International Congregational Council we do not mention them again in this chapter. But we must emphasize once more that already before the 1970 merger the two organizations worked more and more as one entity. One big step forward was made in 1968 when *The Reformed and Presbyterian World* became a joint publication and later the same year when Rev. Fred Kaan, a minister of the Congregational Church of England and Wales, became Secretary for Information of the WARC and associate editor of the quarterly, whilst acting at the same time as Minister and Secretary of the ICC.

The year 1968 also marked a step forward in our relationship with our Lutheran brethren. Early in the year a Lutheran–Reformed *ad hoc* Committee met in Geneva to evaluate the conversations already held in Europe and North America. The findings of this Committee were approved by the Executive Committees of both organizations, which also approved the setting up of a Lutheran–Reformed Joint Committee to proceed with the conversations. The Joint Committee was commissioned to supervise the continuing of the dialogue, to examine the practical implications of a consensus between Lutheran and Reformed Churches and to interpret the meaning of the phrase 'a closer working relationship'.

The 1968 meeting of the Executive Committee took place at

Cluj, Romania, from 25 to 29 June, at the kind invitation of the Reformed Church of Romania, whose membership is 800,000 strong. The close relationship between the Alliance and the Reformed Church of Romania was further shown when Dr Pradervand received a D.D. from the United Protestant Theological Institute, in Cluj, in November 1969.

The Executive naturally gave a great deal of its time to the 1970 Uniting Council. As an ICC–WARC theological consultation was due to be held in Stockholm in July, after the Fourth Assembly of the World Council of Churches, to work on the theme of the Nairobi Council, 'God reconciles and makes free', the Executive discussed the many practical problems connected with the holding of such a Council.

Another important question discussed at Cluj was the advisability of starting bilateral conversations with the Roman Catholic Church. Together with the General Secretary of the WCC, the Director of 'Faith and Order' and representatives of the R.C. Church, a small group was commissioned to explore elements in the new situation that might make the initiation of Reformed–Roman Catholic dialogue desirable at this time.

As a result of conversations held at Uppsala during the Fourth Assembly of the WCC, a first exploratory meeting of representatives of the WARC and of the Secretariat for Promoting Christian Unity of the Vatican was held in Geneva from 27 to 29 November 1968. The need for further exploratory thinking was felt by those present at Geneva, and as a result a larger group of R.C. and Reformed representatives met at Vogelenzang, in the Netherlands, in April 1969. This meeting, as we have seen in the preceding chapter, unanimously recommended the start of bilateral conversations. This was approved by both the Vatican and the Executive Committee of the Alliance (Beirut meeting, 1 to 6 August 1969). Since 1970 these conversations have proceeded regularly.

In 1969 there was a Joint meeting of the Executive Committees of the WARC and of the ICC at Beirut, Lebanon. Nairobi was finally chosen as the site of the Uniting Council, to be held from 20 to 30 August 1970, and problems relating to the merger of the two world families were discussed. Rev. Fred Kaan was entrusted with the preparation of a special liturgy for this important ceremony.

During the year 1969 several new member Churches were added to the Alliance and at the end of the year the membership stood at 113; 69 of these Churches were 'Younger Churches', a very high proportion indeed. It showed that the Alliance had truly become a world family.

In spite of the growing work of our organization the Geneva personnel had remained stable for many years; the staff were seven in number and it is obvious that without the help of the officers of the Alliance the tasks entrusted to the Geneva office could not have been accomplished. In his report to the member Churches for the year 1969 the General Secretary made special mention of the President, Dr W. Niesel, who came several times to Geneva to discuss various problems with the WARC staff and who spent seven weeks in Indonesia visiting our member Churches in that great country. Dr James I. McCord was also warmly thanked for his untiring work. In addition to his post as North American Secretary Dr McCord was also chairman of the most important Department of the Alliance, the Department of Theology. He had also accepted to become the General Chairman for the organization of the Nairobi Council and he continued to chair other Alliance Committees. Few men have given the Alliance as much guidance and devotion in recent years and the Alliance owes him a great debt of gratitude.

The Department of Co-operation and Witness, under the chairmanship of Dr William P. Thompson, did not remain inactive. Although limitation of space does not allow us to go into details we can say that with very limited resources and no special secretary in Geneva (the General Secretary was also Secretary of this Department) valuable help was given to several member Churches since 1965. It appeared that this Department had a real *raison d'être* and this is the reason why it was decided that after the Uniting Council the Department should take over the Department of Women's Work and the Secretariat for Information and that the Secretary for Information should become the Secretary of the enlarged Department of Co-operation and Witness. The Executive Committee and later the Nairobi Council both endorsed the suggestion made by Dr Pradervand that funds be secured outside the normal budget of the Alliance for financing the activities of this Department; its work was therefore to develop rapidly after Nairobi.

Dr Pradervand announced that as he was due to reach his 65th birthday on 7 November 1970 he wished to leave the service of the Alliance soon after the Nairobi Council (31 October 1970). A successor had to be found and a Nomination Committee was formed. It held its first meeting at Beirut, while the Executive Committees of the WARC and ICC were in session. Further meetings took place later in 1969 and early in 1970. In April 1970 the Committee was able to announce that Rev. Edmond Perret, a minister of the National Protestant Church of Geneva, who had worked several years as a minister of the United Church of Canada in Montreal, would succeed Dr Pradervand as General Secretary of the new World Alliance of Reformed Churches (Presbyterian and Congregational). Mr Perret joined the Alliance staff on 1 September and became General Secretary on 1 November 1970.

The Uniting General Council opened in Nairobi, Kenya, on 20 August 1970. As already mentioned in Chapter 12, it was preceded by short meetings of the 11th Assembly of the ICC and of the 20th General Council of the WARC. Two new Churches were received into the WARC and Dr Pradervand was able to announce that 116 WARC Churches would go into the Union with the ICC.

After the solemn service in St. Andrew's Church, reported in Chapter 12, the new Alliance started its work in earnest. The theme 'God reconciles and makes free' was studied by four sections:

Section I: Reconciliation and Creation—The Freedom of God's World.
Section II: Reconciliation and Man—The Freedom of the New Man.
Section III: Reconciliation and Society—The Freedom of a Just Order.
Section IV: Reconciliation and the Church—The Freedom of Christian Witness.

Bible studies, led by Professor Dr Eduard Schweizer, of Zurich, took place in the middle of the morning sessions for the first week, thus showing the importance of the Word of God for the Council.

The Council had been preceded by a Theological Consultation, as reported in the preceding chapter. The Council heard a report on this consultation. The Council was also given a report on the study of *Episkope* undertaken by the Department of Theology of the WARC. The report had been prepared by Professor Dr J. K. S. Reid of Aberdeen. Let us quote two passages of this report, as they express clearly the Reformed position:

'8. On the understanding of the Reformed Churches, *episkope* is a collegial responsibility. But the effective discharge of this responsibility may properly be remitted to individuals to carry out . . .

'18. Apostolic succession is primarily succession in doctrine, and in the right discharge of Christ's *episkope*. Installation within an unbroken chain of successors can never guarantee the legitimity of the succession. But it could be a sign or expression of the catholicity of the Church and its unity in time and space.'[13]

Each Section prepared two reports: a longer one, which was adopted by the Sections, and a shorter one, which was adopted by the Assembly and became an official document of the Nairobi Council. In the following lines we shall only refer to the shorter reports, called 'Assembly Reports'.

Section I said: '. . . in the light of our report, we wish to make the following recommendations:

'1. That the WARC call Christians of its member Churches, in co-operation with other groups, to initiate and support those political, economic and social measures that will encourage reconciliation and prevent domination of any culture by another . . .

'2. That the WARC support the work done by the WCC and others in the provision of aid to developing countries . . . we call on the church and its members to recognize the need for self-sacrifice on the part of the privileged . . .'[14]

Section II had this to say: '. . . enslaving systems can and must be changed. To this end Christ commands his followers to master the techniques needed for effective social and political action and to speak boldly that prophetic word which often wounds before it can heal . . .'[15]

Section III gave a great deal of time to the racial problem and this clearly appears in the Assembly Report of the Section:

'Several matters especially concern us and call for our work and prayer . . .

'These matters are:

'8. The practice of racial segregation by the Dutch Reformed Churches in South Africa in their own church life, and the impression this gives that they support the government in its policy and practice of racial segregation and white supremacy; and the lukewarmness of many members of the other Churches in South Africa in opposing oppression and injustice.

'Meeting in Africa, we have been particularly sensitive to the pervasive idolatry of white racism in our churches and societies, and we reaffirm the position on race adopted in 1964 by the former WARC at Frankfurt . . .

'But words are not enough; the Church must participate at every level in actions and programmes which incarnate its convictions, whether they are initiated by Christians or not . . .'[16]

Section IV said: '2. The Church reads the Bible, worships, works and prays, but seldom makes strenuous and bold attempts to bring Christ's reconciling power to bear on social and racial differences . . . We are particularly impressed by the scarcity of structures enabling groups of dedicated Christians to act in the world boldly and freely as small fellowships of reconciliation . . .

'Meeting in Nairobi, in Africa, our hearts and minds are particularly troubled by the mounting conflict between whites and blacks in Southern Africa and the United States . . . We recommend that the Church recognize the black–white conflict as decisive for all of us at this time . . .'[17]

The Steering Committee presented a motion which was adopted by the Council, calling for a consultation of all Alliance member Churches in South Africa, together with representatives of the Alliance, to discuss the racial problem as well as ways and means to help in this situation. Unfortunately this consultation could not take place, in spite of all the efforts of the Alliance.

The work of the Council did not prevent the delegates from having contacts with the host Church, the Presbyterian Church of East Africa. A great service was held on Sunday, 23 August, at the historic Church of the Torch, in Kikuyu, when the preacher was the Rt. Rev. Crispus Kiongo, Moderator of the Presbyterian Church of East Africa, and the interpreter Rev. John Gatu, of

Nairobi, a member of the WARC Executive Committee. Greetings from the President of Kenya, Mzee Jomo Kenyatta, were conveyed by the Minister for Information and Broadcasting of the Republic of Kenya. After the service the delegates were the guests of the people of Kikuyu for an open-air lunch. It was a great and moving occasion.

At Nairobi, the Permanent Committee on Information, which Rev. Jacques Marchand, of Marseille, had chaired for many years, became part of the Department of Co-operation and Witness. As for the Department of Finance it was replaced by a Permanent Committee on Finance, as the Alliance's Finances did not seem to justify the existence of a Department, which had been created at São Paulo in 1959.

A new Executive Committee was elected; it was smaller than the Committee elected in 1964, as the number of vice-presidents was changed from nine to two. Dr William P. Thompson, Stated Clerk of the United Presbyterian Church in the U.S.A. and, since 1956, chairman of the Department of Co-operation and Witness, succeeded Rev. Dr W. Niesel, who had served the Alliance faithfully and actively since 1964, as President of the Alliance.

People who had come to Nairobi as representatives of 'The Alliance of Reformed Churches throughout the World holding the Presbyterian Order' or of the 'International Congregational Council' left Nairobi as representatives of the 'World Alliance of Reformed Churches (Presbyterian and Congregational)'. A new day had indeed begun for the Alliance. By coming together the former WARC and the ICC had shown that they served no narrow confessional interests but were anxious to be of service to the whole Church of Christ. This spirit was expressed in the message adopted by the Council. Here are some extracts:

'This message is addressed to the local congregations whose representatives we have had the privilege of being in this uniting Assembly of the World Alliance of Reformed Churches and the International Congregational Council . . .

'Our message to you is that "God was in Christ, reconciling the world to himself, not counting against men their transgressions, and has given us the message of reconciliation" (2 Cor. 5:19) . . . It is in this context that we give thanks to God for uniting us, Presbyterians and Congregationalists, in this new strengthening of the Reformed heritage. We pray that God will not let us rest at ease with our common identity but will use us, as we hope he will use other world confessional bodies, not to retard but to hasten the wider unity which he wills among all Christians.

'The reconciliation which is of God is not human togetherness based on appeasement, sentimentality, or clever manipulation of other people until they conform to our favourite programme. Reconciliation is the renewal of life based on God's word of judgment and forgiveness. It is the costly and joyous process of change, of personal and social conversion, in which God liberates us and enables us to move forward as hopeful people confident in his promises to make us fit instruments of his will . . .

'Relying on God's promises, we trust that he will not leave us to our own devices, but will stir us up, will direct us in ways we do not yet discern, and will equip us for the service of reconciliation and liberation in his world.'[18]

REFERENCES
1. *Proceedings 19th General Council*, p. 59.
2. Idem, p. 65.
3. Idem, p. 123.
4. Idem, p. 207.
5. Idem, p. 217.
6. Idem, p. 223.
7. Idem, p. 231.
8. Idem, p. 245.
9. Idem, p. 241.
10. Minutes of the 1966 Executive Committee, p. 14.
11. Report of the General Secretary for 1967, p. 3.
12. Report of the General Secretary for 1966, p. 4.
13. *Proceedings of the Uniting General Council*, pp. 187 and 189.
14. Idem, p. 216.
15. Idem, p. 222.
16. Idem, p. 232.
17. Idem, p. 243.
18. Idem, p. 248.

CHAPTER SIXTEEN

The Last Years of the First Century

The Nairobi Council was now over. A new 'World Alliance of Reformed Churches (Presbyterian and Congregational)' was now in existence.

On 1 September 1970, the new General Secretary Designate, Rev. Edmond Perret, joined the Alliance staff. On 31 October Rev. Dr Marcel Pradervand retired after 22 years' service as Executive and then as General Secretary of the Alliance and on 1 November Rev. Edmond Perret became General Secretary of the WARC.

He was fortunate in having at his side an excellent team of colleagues: Miss Paulette Piguet, the efficient Associate Secretary who had been with the Alliance since 1950, Rev. Richmond Smith who was secretary of the Department of Theology since 1965 and Rev. Fred H. Kaan who had been Information Secretary of the Alliance since 1968, acting at the same time as 'Minister and Secretary' of the International Congregational Council. He was now secretary of the expanded 'Department of Co-operation and Witness'.

Mr Perret immediately set to work with intelligence and devotion. In his first annual report (for the year 1970) written in January 1971, he commented on the merger which had taken place at Nairobi:

'The merger of the two international organizations, the International Congregational Council and the former World Alliance of Reformed Churches, is not merely to be regarded as the administrative amalgamation of two confessional groups which had reached the conclusion that it was wiser to join forces in order to be able to make a greater contribution.Far from being a defensive action, the merger was, in fact, an act of faith. In this modern world and within the ecumenical movement, these two groups have taken on the task of completely overhauling their traditional structures, with the long job of restructure culminating in one organic unit. But this act of faith, mobilized by the assembly at Nairobi, means, above all, that the member churches of the Alliance truly want to bear a living, faithful witness, at the same time keeping their eyes turned towards the future. It is not for the churches themselves that the two organizations have merged, but rather because of their own mission.'[1]

In his report the new General Secretary mentioned that since the autumn of 1970 the World Alliance of Reformed Churches had been one of the sponsor organizations of 'Intervox', a co-operative tape news service, along with the World Council of Churches, the Lutheran World Federation and the World Association of Christian Communication, the founder organizations. The aim of Intervox was to issue news of church life in the world and of christian involvement in the major problems of today's society.

The 1971 meeting of the new Executive Committee took place at Cartigny near Geneva from 25 to 31 August. The General Secretary of the Lutheran World Federation, Dr André Appel, attended the meeting as a fraternal delegate, as exchanges of delegates between the two organizations had now become the rule.

In his report to the Executive the General Secretary dealt at length with 'The Role of a Confessional Body'. He wrote: 'This question is continually with me. During the few visits I have made, I have become more aware of the different attitudes which exist as regards a confessional family such as ours. We sometimes encounter opposition which, although it may not be made apparent immediately, is nevertheless definitive. "Confessional alliances are only the archaeological remains of the past which has definitely come to an end and as such must expire." We sometimes come across a deferential politeness; more often, however, we encounter a real friendship within the Reformed family, frequently from the representatives of our Asian or African churches, who underline how important the fact of belonging to a confessional family seems to them. All those who share these various attitudes—even those who are opposed—have an inkling that belonging to a confessional communion might be worthwhile. Nevertheless they find it difficult to define its value.

'At a time when a new WARC has been constituted, at a time when a new executive committee takes up its work and at a time when it is necessary to choose the emphasis for the 1977 celebrations [centennial of the first General Council, *Ed.*] is it not of the utmost importance to think about our *raison d'être*?'[2]

The Executive Committee was of the same opinion and one of its first decisions was to set up an *ad hoc* committee on the Role and Purpose of the Alliance, to meet during the meeting of the Executive and to report before adjournment.

In his interim report to the Executive the Convener of the *ad hoc* committee, Dr James I. McCord, President of Princeton Theological Seminary, said: 'There is general agreement that the Alliance exists to serve the Churches which are its members, but equally there is agreement that the Alliance has a provisional character. It must always be ready to raise the question of its role and purpose, and this question is urgently before us afresh today. The same question confronts other world families of christians and, indeed, most ecumenical organizations. In part it is occasioned by today's anti-institutionalism and, in part, by severely reduced funds for para-organizations. Moreover, the emphasis on localism tends to be at the expense of world organizations and some national organizations. This is not to say that the question of role and purpose is not raised in different ways in different situations and for different groups, but it would be unwise to under-emphasize the general climate in which the ecumenical organizations now exist.

'On the other hand there is a new era of maturity in the history of world families of churches and in their relationship to the ecumenical movement in general and to the World Council of Churches in particular. Any feeling of competition has been diminished, and there is a new atmosphere of partnership among these several bodies. Separate roles are being more clearly defined and opportunities for cooperation are being increasingly explored. Hence the question of role and purpose can be asked with much greater freedom now and the response should be devoid of old fears and defensiveness.'[3]

Dr McCord suggested that the time had come to examine afresh the role and purpose of the Alliance in the present situation. But it seemed wise to him that this task should be undertaken in co-operation with other world confessional families and with

'Faith and Order'. Dr McCord offered to discuss the problem with the General Secretary of the WCC and with the Director of 'Faith and Order'. This was approved by the Executive Committee.

The Executive Committee admitted four Churches into the Alliance membership. Two of them were really 'new' members (Lesotho Evangelical Church and Hong Kong Council of the Church of Christ in China) whilst the Church of North India was a new Union Church of which the United Church of North India, an old member of the Alliance, was part; as for the Swedish Mission Covenant Church, it had been a member of the International Congregational Council but had refrained from joining the new WARC in 1970.

South Africa occupied much of the time of the Executive Committee. This is not surprising: the Nairobi General Council had voted that the Alliance should try and organize a Consultation of its member Churches in the Republic of South Africa on the racial problem. While some Churches in that country had immediately reacted favourably to this suggestion the largest Church of the Reformed family there, the 'Nederduitse Gereformeerde Kerk' [an Afrikaans Church, *Ed.*] was strongly opposed to this proposal, whilst welcoming the idea of an official visit of the General Secretary of the Alliance.

Finally the Executive Committee decided that the Alliance General Secretary, Rev. Edmond Perret, and the Secretary of the Department of Co-operation and Witness, Rev. Fred H. Kaan, should undertake a visit to South Africa before the end of the year.

Reporting on this visit in his annual report for the year 1971 the General Secretary wrote: 'From 1st to 27th October, the Rev. Fred Kaan and I visited several member Churches in South Africa. The extent and the complexity of the problems were revealed to us as we travelled from Cape Town to Northern Transvaal, from one end of the country to the other. We gained very valuable information from numerous private and collective meetings and from representatives of all our member Churches, who expressed their diverse viewpoints.

'We are glad to report that the member Churches in the Republic of South Africa have agreed, in principle, to form a group in which they will be able to share their concerns and work together meaningfully.'[4]

As for the proposed Consultation on the race issue, no real progress could be reported after the visit of the two Alliance secretaries, the 'Nederduitse Gereformeerde Kerk' maintaining its opposition to such a consultation.

South Africa was not the only country which preoccupied the Alliance. Violence had broken out in Ireland and at the invitation of the Presbyterian Church in that country the Administrative Committee of the European Area sent two of its members, Rev. Neri Giampiccoli, chairman of the Area, and Rev. Arnold Mobbs, for a fraternal visit which took place in October 1971. They were accompanied by Rev. A. A. Fleming, sent by the Church of Scotland.

In his report the General Secretary also referred to the conflict between India and Pakistan which was affecting Alliance member Churches and to instability in the field of politics and economics everywhere. 'Today we are living in times of uncertainty' he remarked, 'we do not know under what conditions we shall be called to live tomorrow.

'There is one certainty accompanying us however, a certainty which is stronger than all uncertainty: Jesus Christ is alive and calls us in faith and hope to bear our witness. All our questions, all our problems, all our worries, must be marked and inspired by that great certainty.'[5]

We have not spoken here of the theological work of the Alliance; it was important and growing constantly. But as we have devoted a whole chapter to this work (Chapter 14) we refer our readers to these pages.

*   *   *

The 1972 meeting of the Executive Committee took place at Jakarta, Indonesia, from 20 to 25 July. It is not surprising that the Alliance's Executive met there as there were more member Churches in that great country than in any other country of the world.

On this occasion there were two special meetings: a meeting of the Executive Committees of the Lutheran World Federation and of the World Alliance of Reformed Churches as well as a meeting of the two above mentioned with representatives of the Indonesian Council of Churches. The meeting of the Alliance

Executive was also followed by a consultation with representatives of Indonesian member Churches. This meeting took place at Sukabumi, West Java, from 26 to 29 July; the theme of the meeting was the same as the theme of the Bangkok Conference of the Division of World Mission and Evangelism of the World Council of Churches, 'Salvation Today'.

In his report to the Executive Committee the General Secretary dealt at length with the financial situation of the Alliance which was becoming more difficult: the re-evaluation of the Swiss Franc and the devaluation of the U.S. Dollar and other currencies were sufficient reason to explain these difficulties. Though the contributions of the European Churches to the Alliance had greatly increased since 1949 (when the headquarters were established at Geneva) the Churches of the North American Area still provided almost two-thirds of the income of the Alliance. As these Churches were themselves facing new financial difficulties it was not possible for them to increase their contributions to the point of compensating the devaluation of the American and Canadian Dollars.

The Alliance, like all other organizations, was also faced with a new financial problem, that of growing inflation which has now become one of the main anxieties of all nations but which was already evident in 1972. It was therefore decided to economize wherever possible in order to meet this new situation.

The Jakarta Executive again considered the 'Role and Purpose of the Alliance' which had already been on the agenda of the 1971 meeting. The Alliance President, Dr William P. Thompson, reported on behalf of the *ad hoc* committee. Among the specific functions of the Alliance the Committee mentioned the four following fields of responsibility:

'1. special responsibility for minority churches;

'2. providing the agency through which churches can participate in bilateral dialogues (LWF, R.C., Orthodox);

'3. providing a bridge into the Ecumenical movement for member Churches which, for a variety of reasons are not members of the WCC;

'4. the contribution the Alliance can make to the Ecumenical movement, particularly to the WCC which in recent years has moved from a position of antagonism to confessional organizations to a position of seeking advice and cooperation from these bodies.'[6]

On the recommendation of the *ad hoc* committee it was further decided that the General Secretary be asked to designate a member of the staff to ensure the continuity of the study process.

A sub-committee was appointed during the meeting of the Executive to examine the possibility for the Alliance of applying for observer status with the Economic and Social Council (ECOSOC) of the United Nations Organization. The sub-committee reported favourably and this was endorsed by the Executive. Action was then taken by the Alliance and the WARC now enjoys, together with other similar organizations, the observer status with ECOSOC.

With regard to the Republic of South Africa the General Secretary reported that though an official letter had been sent to all member Churches there with regard to a Consultation on the race issue, no real progress had been made owing to the opposition of the largest Church in that country. However it was encouraging to note that a group of member Churches was set up to discuss other matters.

During these years numerous journeys were undertaken by Staff members of the WARC. The General Secretary, Rev. Edmond Perret, visited some member Churches in North America and attended the North American Area Council early in 1971. During the same year the Secretary of the Department of Co-operation and Witness, Rev. Fred H. Kaan, paid a visit to several member Churches in Asia. Both of them then went to South Africa as already reported above. Other journeys were undertaken in Europe. As for the Secretary of the Department of Theology, his travels were dictated by the location of the various Dialogues in which the Alliance was engaged.

In 1972, particularly in relation to the Jakarta meeting of the Executive Committee, members of this Committee and staff members participated in a large and carefully co-ordinated visitation programme of churches. In Indonesia itself, 19 out of the (then) 20 member Churches were visited, while on the way to and from Indonesia another 15 churches received visits from Alliance representatives. Never before had so much detailed emphasis been put on relating the thought and work of the

Executive Committee to the life of the churches in the country in which it had been invited to meet. As was said in the June 1972 editorial in *The Reformed World*: 'Relating Executive Committees closely, responsibly and with adequate preparation to the life of the churches in a given region of the world, cultivating the ability to "sit where they sit" and listen attentively, and travelling according to an adaptable time-table and with a flexible agenda may well belong to the most important prerequisites to discovering a new style of life for the Alliance.'

Under the leadership of its chairman, Rev. Dr Raymond V. Kearns, of New York, and of its Secretary, Rev. Fred H. Kaan, the Department of Co-operation and Witness was developing its activities in many directions. In his report to the member Churches for 1972 the General Secretary of the Alliance spoke of the work of the Department: 'It has often been repeated that the WARC itself has no interchurch aid service of its own, and it should be underlined that its member churches contribute, and many of them substantially, to the Interchurch Aid Service of the WCC (from which—of course—others of our member churches receive help). We believe this to be the right approach and we are very grateful to the churches of the WARC who play their part in this ecumenical effort. Our cooperation with the various services of Interchurch Aid of the WCC is on the increase. The Special Services Fund which comes under the jurisdiction of the Department of Co-operation and Witness is not intended for interchurch aid in the strict sense of the word: our role is much more that of strengthening fellowship and rendering an "enabling" ministry. The annual target sum of SwFr. 100,000 for this fund has not yet been achieved. During the last 12 months, 7 projects, very specific and carefully delineated, have been undertaken in close cooperation with our member churches in Burma, Indonesia, Sudan, Cameroon, Egypt and Latin America; the total amount involved was just over SwFr. 56,000. This kind of cooperation within the Reformed family in cases where the terms of reference of ecumenical interchurch aid services made no provisions, should continue undiminished.'[7]

In 1972 Mozambique occupied a special place in the Alliance's ministry. During his visit to South Africa, in October 1971, Rev. Edmond Perret had already visited the Presbyterian Church in Mozambique and had had talks with its President, Rev. Z.

Manganhela. In 1972, this Church had to go through the worst period of its difficult history, owing to the harsh attitude of the Portuguese government. In his report for 1972, the General Secretary of the Alliance wrote: 'the fate of several hundreds of prisoners in Mozambique, arrested mid-June of this year, remains uncertain. Among them are 31 leaders and members of the Presbyterian Church in Mozambique including its president, the Rev. Z. Manganhela, news of whose tragic death while in prison reached us on December 12. An approach has already been made to the Portuguese authorities, demanding an independent enquiry into the circumstances that led to the death of Mr. Manganhela. We are in close touch with our colleagues of the World Council of Churches, and of the Mission Department of the French-speaking Churches in Switzerland (who have particularly close links with Mozambique) over this matter. We are profoundly grateful to all those in Mozambique, including the Anglican bishop of Lourenço Marques, who have been giving such assistance to those in prison as the circumstances allow.'[8]

From now on and until 1974, when the Portuguese revolution led by General Spinola put an end to the oppression of the people of Mozambique, the Alliance was constantly active on behalf of our brethren in that country and Rev. Edmond Perret, the General Secretary, multiplied appeals on behalf of Reformed brethren there.

*   *   *

In October 1972 the Presbyterian Church of England and the Congregational Church of England and Wales merged to form the United Reformed Church of England and Wales. As Mr Perret noted in his annual report: 'It was an event of great importance, first of all for Great Britain, where it constituted the first trans-confessional union since the 16th century; secondly for the WARC because it was the first union to take place since in 1970 the two world confessional families, to which these two churches belonged, united: the former WARC and the International Congregational Council.'[9]

*   *   *

It was decided at Jakarta that the Executive Committee of the WARC would hold no meeting in 1973 and that the next meeting would take place in January 1974 in connection with the North American Area Council, scheduled to take place in the Caribbean; this was later changed and the meeting took place in the U.S.A., as we shall see later.

The fact that there was no meeting of the Executive in 1973 did not mean a slackening of the activities of the Alliance.

For the European Area, 1973 was an important year as a European Area Council took place at Amsterdam from 6 to 11 September. Approximately 150 people representing 31 Congregational, Presbyterian and Reformed Churches from 22 European countries were present. The theme of the Council was 'Who do you say I am?'. Bible studies, most ably led by Rev. Dr Hans Ruedi Weber, a Reformed theologian at the World Council of Churches, formed the central point of discussion. A new European Committee was elected; its chairman was Professor Guus Meuleman, vice-rector of the Free University of Amsterdam (where the Council was held) and a member of the Reformed Churches in the Netherlands.

*   *   *

'The Role and Purpose of the Alliance' continued to be on the agenda of the WARC staff. It had been decided in 1971 that this study should be undertaken in co-operation with the World Council of Churches and other World Confessional organizations. The whole problem was therefore examined by the Conference of Secretaries of the World Families of Churches, in November 1973. The annual report for 1973 quotes a statement adopted by this meeting: 'We are in a new era of common understanding and increased mutual trust and cooperation, in which questions, which inevitably touch self-understanding and identity, can be asked with a new freedom and a new sense of responsibility towards the world.'[10] The same Conference of Secretaries of the World Families of Churches agreed on plans for a joint study involving the World Families of Churches and the World Council of Churches together in drafting a joint discussion paper on their roles in the ecumenical movement.

Relations with the Roman Catholic Church continued to develop and the Roman Catholic-Reformed Dialogue was progressing normally. It had been suggested by the Secretariat for Promoting Christian Unity that a visit to the Vatican by some of the staff members of the Alliance would be welcome. The General Secretary mentioned this in his report to the Executive Committee in 1972. The visit finally took place from 5 to 9 February 1973. Rev. Edmond Perret, General Secretary, as well as Rev. Richmond Smith, Secretary of the Department of Theology and Rev. Fred H. Kaan, Secretary of the Department of Co-operation and Witness, made the journey to Rome. In the course of the four days they spent there they not only saw the members of the Secretariat for Promoting Christian Unity, but also members of other Secretariats and Congregations and were able to explain in great detail what the Alliance stood for and how it worked. During their visit to the Vatican the WARC representatives were also received in private audience by the Pope, a sign of the changing situation.

In November 1973 Rev. Edmond Perret paid another visit to the Churches of the Reformed family in the Republic of South Africa. It had rapidly become clear that the Consultation on the race issue proposed by the Uniting Council at Nairobi could not take place as the largest South African Church maintained its opposition. But, as the General Secretary wrote in his report for the year 1973: 'Already in 1971, the member churches of the WARC in the Republic of South Africa had declared themselves in favour of setting up a common working group. In the spring of 1973, plans were drawn up which provided for the organizing of five regional conferences. The statement announcing the plan indicated: "It is not anticipated that these conferences at local level will take decisions binding the churches. Their purpose is, rather, to encourage an understanding of one another." The theme chosen is that of reconciliation. The first meeting was held in Johannesburg, November 14th. I am convinced that in the long run these regional conferences will contribute significantly to an improvement in the South African situation. In order to create a new climate, it is essential for people to meet face to face in a brotherly spirit that does not avoid difficult issues. I am happy that there is an opportunity for this within the group of Alliance member Churches in South Africa.'[11]

While in Southern Africa Rev. Edmond Perret paid another visit to the Presbyterian Church of Mozambique. In his report to the member Churches, he wrote: 'My 1972 report ended with the announcement of the release of the members of the Presbyterian

Church of Mozambique who had been imprisoned for six months at Machava, near Lourenço Marques. Throughout 1973, the whole year was characterized by events relevant to this Church: in the opinion of several observers the movement of fraternal concern expressed throughout the world has played an important role on behalf of the release of the detained: a new Synodal Council has been elected which has taken up with courage the oversight of this Church; the general secretary of the WARC and the general secretary of the Presbyterian Church of Southern Africa, Rev. Edwin Pons, took part in the Synod of this Church in November 1973 and at a service of Holy Communion which was held on that occasion in the prison of Machava with 19 other detained members of this Church. Finally we learned at the end of November that these 19 detainees had been released and that the 37 members, released in November 1972, have been informed that proceedings are filed against them. At the same time, there remains the question of how to interpret their liberation. It is clear that only a forthright statement setting aside the prosecution can be acceptable, for grave charges have been brought by the political police in Mozambique both against the Presbyterian Church in this country and with reference to the Mission Board of Reformed Churches of French-speaking Switzerland.'[12]

*   *   *

The 1974 meeting of the Executive Committee took place at Stony Point, New York, from 10 to 14 January. It followed immediately the North American Area Council, which was held at the same place from 8 to 10 January. Members of the Executive attended the North American meeting and this established closer contacts between the North American member Churches and the leaders of the Alliance.

The North American Area Council expressed its concern about the suppression of basic freedoms in the Republic of South Korea and passed two resolutions, the first of which reads as follows:

'The North American Area Council of the World Alliance of Reformed Churches, noting the courageous leadership given by Presbyterian churchmen in Korea in the search for freedom of expression in their country, and the recent instances whereby a number of Presbyterian pastors, church members and student leaders have been arrested and interrogated on the ground of their activities and pronouncements in this search for freedom:

'assures the WARC member Churches in Korea, the NCC [National Council of Churches, *Ed.*] and the KSCF [Korean Student Christian Federation, *Ed.*] of its profound concern and its solidarity with them, and commits the well-being of their whole nation to God who in Christ has reconciled all men to himself.'[13]

Two months prior to the Stony Point meeting, Rev. Fred H. Kaan had paid a week-long visit to Korea as part of an extensive journey through Asia. In Korea he met leaders of the two Alliance member Churches in that country, as well as leading personalities in university circles, the National Council of Churches and other ecumenical bodies. Mr Kaan, who was also able to establish contact with some of those who had been arrested and imprisoned under the emergency presidential decrees, was invited by the North American Area Council to give first-hand impressions of his Korean visit.

The Executive Committee devoted a great deal of its time to the next General Council, due to take place in August 1977. The Committee confirmed that the Centennial Council (to mark the hundredth anniversary of the First General Council, Edinburgh, 1877) should be held in St. Andrews, Scotland, on the campus of the University. Several committees were appointed and Rev. Dr R. Stuart Louden, of Edinburgh, was elected General Chairman. The theme adopted by the Executive Committee, following the results of an extensive study conducted by the Alliance through the member Churches, is to be 'The Glory of God and the Future of Man'.

Financial matters again occupied an important place in the deliberations of the Executive Committee. The General Treasurer, Mr Jean-François Rochette, a Geneva banker who had succeeded Mr Georges Lombard in 1971, was present and was able to give valuable information on the state of the Alliance's finances.

The Executive Committee admitted to membership a 21st Indonesian church, thus bringing Alliance membership to 138.

The General Secretary reported to the Executive that shortly before the Stony Point meeting he had discussions with the

Geneva representative of the United Presbyterian Church in the
U.S.A. about the possibility of the Alliance taking over 'John
Knox House', a student centre in Geneva created by the United
Presbyterian Church in the U.S.A. in 1953 and run by an international committee. A great deal of time was devoted to this
problem but no final decision was taken. Negotiations between
the Alliance and those responsible for 'John Knox House'
continued, and the July 1974 issue of *The Reformed Press Service*
contained the following statement issued by the Alliance General
Secretary, Dr Edmond Perret:

'The Executive Committee of the WARC by postal ballot has
in principle agreed to the take-over by the Alliance of the Geneva
property of the John Knox House Association.

'Founded in 1953 as a students' hostel, John Knox House
traces its origins to an initiative launched by a local Presbyterian
congregation in Denver, Colorado, USA. The United Presbyterian Church in the USA has given major financial support to
this project over the past 20 years of its existence.

'In 1970 a conference centre was added to the students' hostel,
the same year in which a Europe-Third World Study Centre
was also located there.

'Changing conditions pertaining to students' accommodation
in Geneva and the style of work with students at Geneva University have made it increasingly difficult to maintain the House
as a students' hostel, which will—therefore—close as such on
August 31, 1974. As to the Europe-Third World Centre, which
is pursuing its activities, its status in relation to the new institution
has still to be worked out.

'Details related to the take-over of responsibility, and to
eventual modification of the aims and objects of the House are
currently under scrutiny. It is the intention that the ecumenical
character of the House will be retained, and that, if possible, new
programmes of activities be developed that would be helpful to
the life of the member churches of the Alliance.

'Initially, however, the House, which may be known as "The
John Knox House International Reformed Centre", will mainly
be used as an Ecumenical guesthouse and conference centre.

'Contact has been made with ecumenical, world confessional
and church organizations which would be prepared to cooperate

with this new institution which legally, administratively and
financially will be run independently from the WARC.'[14]

As these lines are being written (early September 1974) the
Alliance has officially taken over the John Knox House. It was
decided that the 1975 meeting of the WARC Executive should be
held there in March, so that leaders of the Alliance can get
personally acquainted with the centre.

The General Secretary and his colleagues continued visiting
many Churches and this contributed to a strengthening of
relations between the WARC member Churches and our organization.

The cordiality of relations existing between the great Reformed
Church of Romania and the Alliance was indicated by the fact
that in May 1974 Rev. Edmond Perret was awarded a D.D. by
the United Protestant Theological Institute in Cluj. In the course
of the ceremonies marking this occasion Dr Perret spoke on
'The Fathers of the Church, especially the Eastern Fathers and
Calvin's Institutes'. This was a contribution to the Dialogue
between Orthodox and Protestants and was very well received.

In August 1974 Dr Perret attended the celebrations in Torre
Pellice marking the 800th anniversary of the Waldensian Church
of Italy, the oldest member Church of the Alliance. His presence
was a reminder of the close ties existing between the Alliance and
this courageous and active minority Church, ties which had
started in 1875 and had found a practical expression in the early
1880s, when the Alliance undertook on behalf of this Church the
first 'Inter-church Aid action' of its long history.

The Alliance is now well into its hundredth year and its
membership stands at 142 Churches. Before the founding of the
Alliance, Dr McCosh, writing to Dr Blaikie, clearly indicated the
spirit which should guide the Alliance's activities: '. . . we
endeavoured to give the whole movement an evangelistic
missionary character rather than an ecclesiastical one. I attach
great important to this . . . May the great Head watch over our
movement.'[15] Throughout the years the Alliance leaders have
remembered Dr McCosh's prayer and tried to make the Alliance
an instrument in the service of Jesus Christ. They have constantly
fought against the development of a heavy bureaucracy. The
Alliance has remained a small organization but we believe that its

work has not been without value to the whole Church of Jesus Christ.

Our prayer is that the evangelical spirit of its founders may continue to inspire the Alliance's activities.

REFERENCES

1. Report of the General Secretary for 1970, p. 2.
2. Minutes of 1971 Executive Committee, p. 23.
3. Minutes of 1971 Executive Committee, p. 9.
4. Report of the General Secretary for 1971, p. 4.
5. Idem, p. 6.
6. Minutes of 1972 Executive Committee, p. 8.
7. Report of the General Secretary for 1972, p. 3.
8. Idem, p. 5.
9. Idem, p. 6.
10. Report of the General Secretary for 1973, p. 2.
11. Idem, p. 3.
12. Idem, p. 2.
13. *Reformed Press Service*, no. 114, February 1974, p. 3.
14. *Reformed Press Service*, no. 119, July 1974, p. 3.
15. WARC Archives, Geneva, WPA/HA1.

Index